THE LETTERS OF OLIVER GOLDSMITH

This first modern scholarly edition of the letters of Oliver Goldsmith (1728–74) sets the author of *The Vicar of Wakefield*, *The Deserted Village* and *She Stoops to Conquer* into a rich context, showing how Goldsmith's Irish identity was marked and complicated by cosmopolitan ambition. He was at the very heart of Grub Street culture and the Georgian theatre, and was a founding member of Dr Johnson's Literary Club; his circle included Edmund Burke, Joshua Reynolds, David Garrick, George Colman and Hester Piozzi. Containing a detailed introduction and extensive notes, this edition is essential for those wishing to know more about Goldsmith the man and the writer, and provides a rich and suggestive nexus for understanding the cultural cross-currents of the literary Enlightenment in eighteenth-century London.

Michael Griffin is a senior lecturer in English at the University of Limerick. He is the author of *Enlightenment in Ruins: The Geographies of Oliver Goldsmith* (2013). He has also edited *The Selected Writings of Thomas Dermody* (2012) and *The Collected Poems of Laurence Whyte* (2016).

David O'Shaughnessy is an associate professor in English at Trinity College Dublin. He is the author of *William Godwin and the Theatre* (2010), editor of *The Plays of William Godwin* (2010) and co-editor of the online edition of Godwin's diary. He has also edited a special issue of *Eighteenth-Century Life* (2015) on the London Irish of the eighteenth century.

THE LETTERS OF
OLIVER GOLDSMITH

Edited by

MICHAEL GRIFFIN
University of Limerick

DAVID O'SHAUGHNESSY
Trinity College Dublin

CAMBRIDGE
UNIVERSITY PRESS

CAMBRIDGE
UNIVERSITY PRESS

University Printing House, Cambridge CB2 8BS, United Kingdom

One Liberty Plaza, 20th Floor, New York, NY 10006, USA

477 Williamstown Road, Port Melbourne, VIC 3207, Australia

314–321, 3rd Floor, Plot 3, Splendor Forum, Jasola District Centre, New Delhi – 110025, India

79 Anson Road, #06–04/06, Singapore 079906

Cambridge University Press is part of the University of Cambridge.

It furthers the University's mission by disseminating knowledge in the pursuit of education, learning, and research at the highest international levels of excellence.

www.cambridge.org
Information on this title: www.cambridge.org/9781107093539
DOI: 10.1017/9781316145203

First published 2018

Printed in the United States of America by Sheridan Books, Inc.

A catalogue record for this publication is available from the British Library.

ISBN 978-1-107-09353-9 Hardback

For Roger Lonsdale and Jon Mee,
with deep appreciation

CONTENTS

LETTERS

ILLUSTRATIONS

ACKNOWLEDGEMENTS

The editors would like to thank the staff at all of the various libraries that responded to our queries as we searched for letters. In particular, we would like to thank members of staff at the British Library; the Free Library of Philadelphia; the Rosenbach of the Free Library of Philadelphia; the Library of the Historical Society of Pennsylvania; the Beinecke Library at Yale University (in particular Alison Clemens); the Houghton Library, Harvard University (in particular John Overholt); the Huntington Library, San Marino; the Bibliotheca Bodmeriana, Switzerland; and the Library of the Royal Irish Academy. Colleagues in the libraries of the University of Limerick and Trinity College Dublin were unfailingly helpful over the course of the edition's preparation.

We would like to thank the National Portrait Gallery, London; the Houghton Library at Harvard University; and the Board of Trinity College Dublin for permission to use their images. Loren R. Rothschild graciously gave us access to the Goldsmith letters in his personal collection. Roger Lonsdale shared his notes on Goldsmith items which had emerged since Katharine Balderston's edition of 1928. Pamela Clemit kindly gave us a database of institutional addresses which was very useful as we searched for letters. Paddy Bullard was very helpful with a query on Burke's handwriting.

Research trips were facilitated by the generous support of an A.C. Elias award from the American Society for Eighteenth-Century Studies, a Huntington Library Fellowship, and a Marie Curie Career Integration Grant. Support for images was kindly provided by the 'Manuscripts, Book and Print Culture' research theme at Trinity College Dublin.

We also wish to thank Victoria Parrin and Tim Mason at Cambridge University Press for their expert assistance in the preparation of this edition. Linda Bree was a wonderfully patient and supportive champion of this edition from its inception. Leigh Mueller's copy-editing was scrupulous.

We are very grateful to Norma Clarke and Jim Watt for taking the time to comment on an advanced draft of our introduction. James Scanlon provided invaluable research assistance early on in the project. Our thanks also to James Little for his excellent work on the index.

Finally, we would like to take this opportunity to acknowledge the tremendous contribution that Roger Lonsdale and Jon Mee have made to our scholarly careers. They have been our teachers and our inspiration.

ABBREVIATIONS

The following texts are cited throughout the book; all references to them will be abbreviated as follows:

BL: Oliver Goldsmith. *The Collected Letters*, ed. Katharine C. Balderston. Cambridge University Press, 1928.

CW: Oliver Goldsmith. *The Collected Works*, ed. Arthur Friedman, 5 vols. Oxford: Clarendon Press, 1966.

P: James Prior. *Life of Oliver Goldsmith, M. B.*, 2 vols. London: John Murray, 1837.

W: Ralph Wardle. *Oliver Goldsmith*. Lawrence: University of Kansas Press, 1957.

INTRODUCTION

Though he wrote copiously across the genres in order to provide for himself, Oliver Goldsmith's corpus of letters is one of the least extensive of any major writer of his age. His 'disinclination to epistolary communication' was, according to James Prior's 1837 biography, well known. James Grainger's letter to Goldsmith's friend and first biographer Thomas Percy, of 24 March 1764, records as much: 'When I taxed little Goldsmith for not writing as he promised, his answer was, that he never wrote a letter in his life; and faith I believe him – except to a bookseller for money.'[1] Though not exactly true, it was certainly the case that, except for professional requests and courtesies, Goldsmith's correspondence, never copious to begin with, dwindled considerably once he had established himself in London. His communications became less effusive than those he sent to family and friends when he first set off on his medical studies in Edinburgh and Leiden and upon his first arriving in London. Once established, Goldsmith composed letters largely as or for favours. It is fair to say that, apart from missives to George Colman and David Garrick regarding theatre matters, and more particularly the production of *The Good Natur'd Man* in 1767,

[1] Cited in *P*, I: 487. James Prior's is the biography to which all other subsequent biographies are indebted. Building on the insights of Thomas Percy's 1801 biographical preface and assiduous in its collection of correspondence and detail on Goldsmith's early life in Ireland, Prior was a key source for John Forster, *The Life and Adventures of Oliver Goldsmith*, 2 vols. (London: Chapman and Hall, 1848), and Washington Irving, *Oliver Goldsmith: A Biography* (London: Henry G. Bohn, 1850). The second half of the twentieth century saw the publication of three biographies which have been more substantial and analytical in their treatment of the complexities and contexts of Goldsmith's dealings in the increasingly professionalized world of eighteenth-century writing. Ralph Wardle (*W*) augments the nineteenth-century biographical tradition in the light of twentieth-century scholarship to that point; A. Lytton Sells, *Oliver Goldsmith: His Life and Works* (London: George Allen & Unwin, 1974) emphasizes Goldsmith's Tory politics, as well as his command of the French language and sources; John Ginger, *The Notable Man: The Life and Times of Oliver Goldsmith* (London: Hamilton, 1977) situates Goldsmith's career amidst the increasing cultural influence of the middle class.

correspondence is sparse. Only in 1773 is there another flurry of correspondence concerning the production and positive reception of *She Stoops to Conquer*.[2]

The paucity of the corpus is evidence, perhaps, of Goldsmith's general lack of interest in biographical posterity, and it has long been the first obstacle to those who sought to reconstruct the life. Early biographers James Prior and John Mitford corresponded regarding this lack of biographical and epistolary materials. Prior wrote:

> I fear you found the pursuit of documents for the Life, laborious and unsatisfactory. It is astonishing how few there are available to the biographer. My search has been very extensive and unremitting for fourteen months; and though certainly I have gleaned a great deal, and found much new matter in his literary history and many press and political pieces not acknowledged by him, but unquestionably genuine, I find much difficulty in seeing letters of his which exist.— the illiberality of some of the collectors is surprising; I had almost said disgraceful; those I allude to are indeed men of no high character; but I could scarcely expect falsehood and meanness from men with the smallest pretension to a love of literature.[3]

Thankfully, by the time Katharine Balderston came to edit Goldsmith's letters in 1928, the original collectors' successors, or descendants, had become somewhat more liberal, and in the ninety years since, many of the letters collected by private citizens have, with a couple of mysterious exceptions, been deposited in libraries.

Yet obscurities and blind spots remain. Added to the small size of his epistolary oeuvre was Goldsmith's tendency to mislead or obfuscate where his own family background and early life and travels were concerned. Matters are only clarified (somewhat) where there are brief bursts of letter writing: during his medical education at Edinburgh and Leiden; during his initial, troubled acclimatization to London life and the world of professional writing; and around his attempt to gather Irish subscriptions for *An Enquiry into the Present State of Polite Learning in Europe*, his first major work. With a view to putting the correspondence in biographical and intellectual context, we give here an introduction which foregrounds those periods in his life around which the letters are clustered. And so, to begin, we give a brief account of Goldsmith's origins and his early life.

[2] Edmond Malone was also struck by the paucity of letters on reading Percy's *Life of Goldsmith*, commenting to Percy: 'Surely I once read two or three more letters than we have in print.' Letter from Edmond Malone to Thomas Percy, 5 June 1802, *The Correspondence of Thomas Percy & Edmond Malone*, ed. Arthur Tillotson (Baton Rouge: Louisiana State University Press, 1944), 97.

[3] James Prior to John Mitford, 26 January 1832. John Mitford Collection, Yale University Library, Osborn FC76 1/38, 39.

The Early Life

At the Duke of Northumberland's house, on 28 April 1773, Goldsmith gave to Thomas Percy details of his life which were to be collected for a biography – the first of substance – which would pass through a tortuous gestation, and through many hands, before publication in 1801.[4] Goldsmith dictated to Percy that he was descended from a Spaniard named Romeiro or Romero, who had married, and taken the surname of, a Miss Goldsmith, in the sixteenth century. In order to confirm or clarify this supposed connection and because Goldsmith had a tendency to lie about himself and his family background, Percy looked to Goldsmith's youngest brother Maurice for verification. Juan Romero, maintained Maurice, was Oliver's great-grandfather; he had come to Ireland in the seventeenth century as a private tutor to a touring Spanish nobleman.

A more clearly drawn ancestor was an early seventeenth-century John Goldsmith, who was Vicar of Burrishoole in Co. Mayo: Oliver's great-great grandfather (he may indeed have been the father or uncle of the Miss Goldsmith who married Juan Romero). John Goldsmith, apparently a convert to the Protestant faith, is noted as an owner of 20 acres of good land in 1641, the year of a violent Irish Catholic uprising. Men in his position would have had good reason to feel threatened. The middle of the seventeenth century saw the transfer of Irish property largely into Protestant hands. Some Catholics had converted to make their accommodations with the new dispensation, while many Catholic clergy travelled to the continent to study and worship more freely in Irish colleges there. John and his brother Francis fell on either side of this bifurcation. John was examined on oath by the commissioners assigned to measure the damage done to Protestants during the rebellion of that year. He relayed a warning conveyed to him in the preceding years by Francis, a Catholic priest in Antwerp, that he should take his family out of Ireland for their own protection. In his deposition, John Goldsmith indicated the mixed religious character of the Goldsmith family. The 'parson of Brashawl, or Burrishoole, 'saith he perceiues by Letters of his brother a priest at Antwerp that the papists of this land entended the rebellion 4 yeares before that when it was ready to break out, he dicouered by their making so many skeines it was & gaue notice &c.'[5] In all likelihood, Father Francis Goldsmith would have resided at the Irish College in Antwerp. A familial or

[4] See Katharine C. Balderston, *The History and Sources of Percy's Memoir of Goldsmith* (Cambridge University Press, 1926); see also Thomas Percy, 'The Life of Dr. Oliver Goldsmith', *The Miscellaneous Works of Oliver Goldsmith*, 4 vols. (London: Printed for J. Johnson et al., 1801), I: 1–118.

[5] Folio 123r of the 1641 depositions, Trinity College Dublin.

ancestral connection to a continental culture of Irish Catholicism was possibly a factor in Goldsmith's sporadic residence in Irish colleges while on his travels through Europe in the 1750s.

The relative recentness and modest social class of the Goldsmith family's Protestantism was such that it did not condescend to the Catholic culture which surrounded it in the midlands, and interfaith relations in the region seem to have been generally benign in Goldsmith's time. Nonetheless, the memory of the 1641 rebellion was still very much alive, and fear among the administrative elite that Catholics might once again assert themselves, this time in support of the exiled Stuart monarchy, was genuinely felt. Whatever the relations between Catholics and Protestants on the ground – and there were some High Church Anglicans who had a nostalgia, even a sneaking regard, for the Stuarts and for the pre-commercial society with which they were associated – there was at the level of officialdom a profound suspicion of Catholicism. Thus, Goldsmith may have had cause to embellish the soundly Protestant, even solidly English, nature of his family's history. He related to Percy that his father was a native of Durham who had moved to Ireland to study at Trinity College Dublin before gaining a small living in England, returning to Ireland to become the rector of Kilkenny West in Co. Westmeath. Maurice, however, described their father as a native of the diocese of Elphin, from Ballyoughter in Co. Roscommon, and not of Durham, as his brother had claimed. Quite apart from political concerns, Goldsmith may have felt compelled to make an Englishman of his father to mitigate some of his cultural anxiety as an Irishman in London.

Goldsmith's father Charles, an Anglican vicar, married Ann Jones, the daughter of the Reverend Oliver Jones of Smith Hill, Co. Roscommon in 1718. An uncle of Ann's, who was rector of the parish of Kilkenny West, would give the young couple the use of a house in Pallas just across the county border in Longford (Figure 1). The family lived at Pallas for twelve years. Catherine was the oldest child; Henry, the second; Oliver himself, the third. Oliver was born, either in that house or in Smith Hill near Elphin, his mother's home place, on 10 November 1728. His younger brothers were Charles and Maurice. Another younger brother, John or 'Jack', died at an early age when Oliver was in Edinburgh. Their father became the curate of Kilkenny West in 1730, when the future author was just an infant, at which point the family moved to the Lissoy parsonage, where they held considerably more land and were measurably more comfortable.

As a child Goldsmith was stricken with a dose of smallpox, a misfortune which caused the pock-marked ugliness much commented upon by uncharitable peers – and even several friends – throughout his life. It was initially thought, given his illness, that he might not achieve much academically, but the precocious wit with which he responded to condescending remarks about his

Figure 1 A number of places referenced in the letters can be found on this contemporary map of the Irish midlands. Pallas, Goldsmith's birthplace, does not appear but it is located 3 miles east of Ballymahon ('Ballimahon' as marked on the map, just below 'LONGFORD'), Co. Longford. Lissoy, Co. Westmeath, where he grew up, does not appear either but is 6 miles southwest of Ballymahon. From *A new and accurate map of the Kingdom of Ireland* by Thomas Jeffreys [1759]. Reproduced by permission of the Board of Trinity College Dublin.

appearance indicated otherwise. When asked to dance a hornpipe for visitors to the family home, one of the company ridiculed his appearance as 'the personification of Æsop', to which Goldsmith briskly replied with an improvised couplet: 'Our herald hath proclaim'd this saying, / See Æsop dancing and his monkey playing'. Yet another visiting relative mockingly asked: 'Why, Noll, you are become a fright; when do you mean to get handsome again?' Goldsmith gave a cutting response: 'I mean to get better, Sir, when you do.'[6] Goldsmith may have been ugly, but he was feisty.

In spite of such inauspicious beginnings, Goldsmith began to flourish under a series of effective teachers: Thomas Byrne at the village school at Lissoy, Michael Griffin at the diocesan school at Elphin, and Patrick Hughes in Edgeworthstown. Thomas Percy would recount that Hughes was the most important of Goldsmith's teachers and that it was under Hughes that Goldsmith acquired a substantial starting store of knowledge in the classics. Washington Irving subsequently speculated that Goldsmith may have received additional tutelage in the French language from Catholic priests around Ballymahon in Longford.[7] Irving's theory has been supported by A. Lytton Sells, one of the best scholars of Goldsmith's French sources – in addition to being one of his most recent biographers.[8] Whenever and from whomever it was acquired, his knowledge of French and his facility with translation from French sources would be the bedrock of his survival as a professional writer in London. The relative rarity of French speakers in his native scene was a matter of which Goldsmith was aware; he wrote in December 1753 to his uncle Thomas Contarine with an air of confidence and relative superiority: 'I am perfectly acquainted with that language, and Few who leave Ireland are so' (Letter 4).

When his older sister Catherine eloped with Daniel Hodson, their father Charles, though greatly aggrieved, undertook to support his daughter to the amount of £52 a year, which rather dented Oliver's financial prospects, channelling money away from funds intended for his education. Thus deprived, he entered Trinity College Dublin in June 1745 as a sizar, that lowlier class of student who would pay their way by doing menial tasks for wealthier students. He was supported partially by his uncle the Reverend Thomas Contarine, a Contarini of noble Venetian extraction who married Charles's sister Jane and was given the prebendary of Oran near Elphin. Seemingly a man of considerable means, Contarine undertook to support Goldsmith for the longer term. His largesse was reflected in the substance and deference of Goldsmith's subsequent letters to him from Scotland and Holland.

[6] *P*, I: 28–30.

[7] Irving, *Goldsmith*, 35.

[8] See Sells, *Les Sources françaises de Goldsmith* (Paris: Librairie Ancienne Edouard Champion, 1924).

No letters from Goldsmith to his family survive from his years at Trinity College. He improved his knowledge of the classics and French at university. He suffered somewhat under the poor, ill-tempered and often oppressive tutelage of one Theaker Wilder (1717–78), originally from Abbeyshrule in Co. Longford, near Goldsmith's home place. It was thought, given their shared geographical provenance, that Wilder might provide good counsel to Goldsmith; their tempers were not well matched, however, and Goldsmith was consequently the object of harsh discipline. He did, however, cement his friendship with his distant cousin Edward Mills, with whom he would correspond from farther afield at a later point. Legend – rather than any firm evidence – holds that Goldsmith began his first forays into poetry and mercenary ballad writing in these Dublin years.

Charles Goldsmith died in 1747 and in May of that year the young student took a leading and dangerous part in a riot which engaged the police over the imprisonment of two student debtors. Goldsmith received a stern reprimand for his involvement. It could have been worse – two people died in the disturbance – but the incident suggests a young man more than a little unsettled at the death of his father.[9] After this point, his behaviour and academic performance at Trinity faltered, though he eventually took a Bachelor of Arts in 1750, two years later than he should have. Contarine used his influence to acquire for his nephew a living in the church; however, Goldsmith failed to impress in his interview with Dr Edward Synge, Bishop of Elphin, due to a perceived immaturity and lack of scholarly application.[10]

Upon his return to the midlands, Goldsmith spent much time in the company of Robert Bryanton – another future correspondent. The two socialized at George Conway's tavern – a model, legend holds, for the Three Jolly Pigeons in *She Stoops to Conquer*. There Goldsmith indulged with his friends a penchant for argument, for singing ballads and playing the flute, developing talents which would stand him in good stead on his later travels. He soon found something approximating gainful employment, thanks again to Contarine's solicitations, as a tutor to the well-to-do Flinn family of Roscommon. A row over a card game led to the discontinuation of his employment, with a severance of £30 and a horse, both of which he used to make his way to Cork with a view to emigrating to America.

He never emigrated; rather too literally, he missed the boat. After much misadventure, narrated by his sister Catherine in her account of his young life, Goldsmith returned to his displeased family in the midlands.[11] He lived with

[9] According to Edmond Malone, the incident was described in a letter, now lost, from Dr Thomas Wilson (1727?–99), a classmate of Goldsmith's. Letter from Edmond Malone to Thomas Percy, 2 March 1785, *The Correspondence of Thomas Percy & Edmond Malone*, 18.

[10] See *P*, I: 110.

[11] Catherine Hodson's 1776 narrative, the manuscript of which is in the British Library (Add. MSS 42516, fols. 20–26b), was included as an appendix in *BL*, 162–77.

the Hodsons for a spell before being sent to Dublin with £50 from Contarine to study the law in the winter of 1751–2. This money too was squandered. Goldsmith may have lived around this time with Contarine and his daughter Jane (later Jane Lawder, also a correspondent). Whatever his fallings-out with his immediate family – and they were no doubt beyond exasperated by his behaviour to this point – both Contarines were perennially fond and supportive of Oliver, and it was decided as a solution to his waywardness, and at the prompting of Isaac Goldsmith, a family cousin and the Dean of Cloyne, that Goldsmith should be further educated in the medical sphere. Contarine would provide £10 a year for the three years that a medical qualification would take, and an additional £15 was to be provided by other members of the family. Goldsmith set out for Edinburgh to take up his studies at that city's medical school in October 1752. It is at this point that Goldsmith's known correspondence begins, as he reports to family and friends the sights, sounds and intellectual life of Scotland in ways that would prefigure the cosmopolitanism of his later writing.

The Apprentice Cosmopolitan: Goldsmith in Edinburgh and Leiden

The tension between local attachment, national sentiment and cosmopolitanism infuses a great deal of Goldsmith's writing, not least his epistolary classic *The Citizen of the World* (1762). Such tension is evident in his own early correspondence from Edinburgh (and farther afield) to family and friends in the Irish midlands. Alan McKillop's 1965 piece on local attachment and cosmopolitanism remains a useful guide in thinking through some of Goldsmith's epistolary motifs, his will to Enlightenment rationality running up against, but not necessarily contradicting, his familial and local affiliations. Goldsmith was interested in cultural comparison, adept and accomplished at imaginative explorations of discrepancies between ways of thinking and being, between East and West, between Irish, Scottish, Dutch, English and French; his letters give, in their own initial orbit, an interesting perspective on mid-Enlightenment issues of cultural difference. As a younger man, writing longer letters home from places of learning and literary activity abroad, his commentaries instance the predicament of a young intellectual well equipped with useful knowledge in the sciences, in the classical languages and in French, searching for, and to some extent finding, an intriguing voice, at once cosmopolitan and homesick, and all the more revealing for that seeming contradiction.[12]

[12] See Alan D. McKillop, 'Local Attachment and Cosmopolitanism: The Eighteenth-Century Pattern', *From Sensibility to Romanticism: Essays Presented to Frederick A. Pottle*, ed. Frederick W. Hilles and Harold Bloom (New York: Oxford University Press, 1965), 191–218. See also James Watt, '"The Indigent Philosopher": Oliver Goldsmith', *The Blackwell Companion to Irish Literature*, ed. Julia M. Wright, 2 vols. (Oxford: Blackwell, 2010), I: 210–25; and Watt, 'Goldsmith's Cosmopolitanism', *Eighteenth-Century Life* 30.1 (2006), 56–75.

The earliest extant Goldsmith letter – to his brother-in-law Dan Hodson – reports on his early experiences of Edinburgh. It illustrates perfectly Goldsmith's awareness of his role as correspondent, acknowledging also his inability to fulfil that role satisfactorily. Unable to muster much in the way of cultural commentary, he accounts instead for his own average day:

> This country has little or nothing [which I can] give an account of so instead of a D[escription of the] country you must be contented with [an account of the] manner in which I spend my Time, [during the] day I am obligd to attend the Publick L[ectures. At night] I am in my Lodging I have hardly an[y other s]ociety but a Folio book a skeleton my cat and my meagre landlady I pay 22£6 per am for Diet washing and Lodging being the cheapest that is to be got in Edinburgh all things here being much dearer than in Ireland

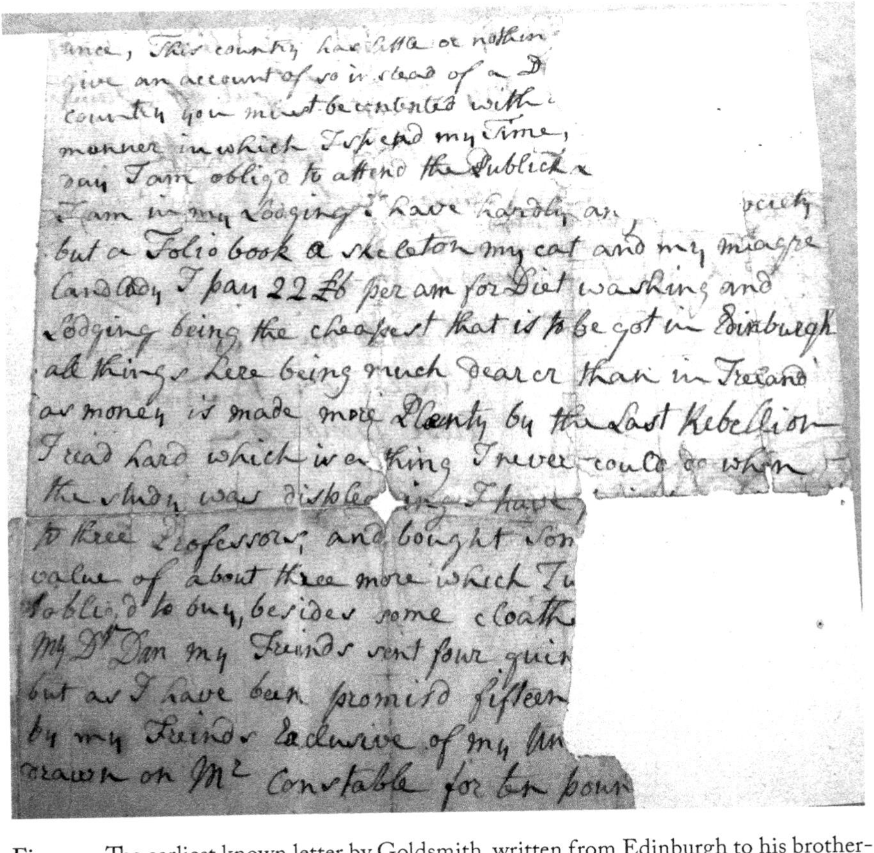
ance, This country has little or nothin
give an account of so in stead of a D
country you must be contented with
manner in which I spend my Time,
day I am obligd to attend the Publick L
I am in my Lodging I have hardly an ociety
but a Folio book a skeleton my cat and my meagre
Landlady I pay 22£6 per am for Diet washing and
Lodging being the cheapest that is to be got in Edinburgh
all things here being much dearer than in Ireland
as money is made more Plenty by the Last Rebellion
I read hard which is a thing I never could do when
the study was disple I have
to three Professors and bought som
value of about three more which I w
obligd to buy, besides some cloath
My Dr Dan my Friends sent four guin
but as I have been promisd fifteen
by my Friends Exclusive of my An
drawn on Mr Constable for ten poun

Figure 2 The earliest known letter by Goldsmith, written from Edinburgh to his brother-in-law Daniel Hodson in 1752. Reproduced by permission of the Huntington Library, San Marino.

> as money is made more Plenty by the Last Rebellion I read hard which is a thing I never could do when the study was displea[s]ing. (Letter 1, Figure 2)

The tone of this letter is informal, and it conveys with downbeat honesty the loneliness of the new emigrant. It touches only briefly on the nature of his scientific study, which the evidence of his correspondence generally indicates he found absorbing. In a more polite and deferential letter from Edinburgh to Contarine, 8 May 1753, Goldsmith worries that he may have rescinded his claim to be an aspiring philosopher by having

> le[f]t behind in Ireland Every thing I think worth posessing freinds that I love and a Society that pleasd while it instructed, who but must regret the Loss of such Enjoyments who but must regret his abscence from [Ki]lmore that Ever knew i[t] as I did, here as recluse as the Turkish Spy at Parris I am almost unknown to Every body Except some few who attend the Proffesors of Physick as I do. (Letter 2)

His reference point here is revealing: *The Turkish Spy*, a popular text in later seventeenth- and early eighteenth-century Britain and France, may have given Goldsmith the first hint of an idea for a work of epistolary Orientalism and, if so, it provides an interesting sidelight on his later work. Originally published in 1684, and composed by Giovanni Paola Marana, a Genoese political refugee in the French court of Louis XIV, *L'Espion Turc* was published several times in translation through the following decades as *The Eighte Volumes of Letters Writ by a Turkish Spy, who liv'd five and forty years, undiscover'd at Paris*. Marana's work was a key inspiration and model for Charles-Louis Secondat, Baron de Montesquieu's *Lettres Persanes* (1721) – an epistolary novel recounting the experiences and observations of two Persian noblemen who travel to France – and by extension *The Citizen of the World*.

When Goldsmith arrived at his lodgings at Trunk Close in central Edinburgh, the city was half the size of Dublin (Figure 3). Made up mainly of the old town bracketed by the castle and Holyrood with narrow streets flanked by medieval buildings, the city was quite unlike the emerging Palladian Dublin which Goldsmith had left behind. With a population not much more than 30,000, the city was still recovering from the effects of the Jacobite rebellion some seven years before, though, as Goldsmith's correspondence indicates, money was flowing freely into a Scottish economy now deemed more definitively stable, driving rents and prices upwards. The new town of Edinburgh would not be built until later in the eighteenth century; in the meantime, some of the fabric of the city was still somewhat shabby. The college buildings – clustered in the various structures that were in or near Infirmary Street, such as the Royal Infirmary of Edinburgh – were generally thought to be in a near-ruinous state.

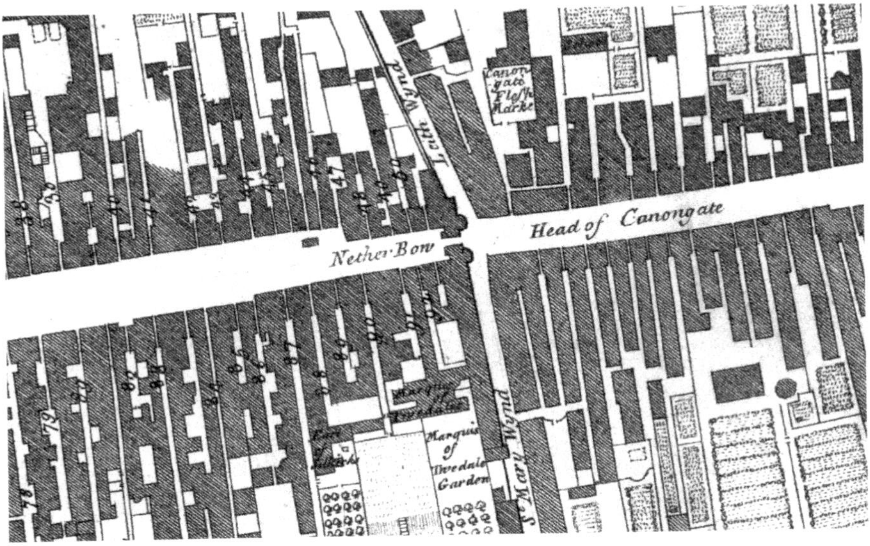

Figure 3 Goldsmith lived in Trunk Close, or Trunk's Close, a courtyard near the crossing of Nether Bow (now part of Edinburgh's Royal Mile) with Leith Wynd, which is site no. 48 on William Edgar's *Plan of the City and Castle of Edinburgh* (1742). Reproduced by permission of the Board of Trinity College Dublin.

While a student in Edinburgh, Goldsmith participated, with considerable enthusiasm, in the popular anatomy classes given by Alexander Monro (1697–1767), the founder of the Edinburgh Medical School, who had studied in Leiden under Herman Boerhaave (1669–1738), the most famous medical man of early eighteenth-century Europe. Under Boerhaave's auspices, Leiden, to which Goldsmith would eventually travel for further education, was an internationally renowned centre of scientific and medical influence. Many of Boerhaave's students went on to establish their own medical schools: in Edinburgh, but also in Vienna, Göttingen and in the American colonies. As Andrew Cunningham speculates, his influence was not due to any significant discovery of his own: his Scottish students seem instead to have been particularly excited by his teaching style; his lectures in themselves became the primary textbooks of the day. Cunningham cites the Scottish student James Houstoun to illustrate that it was Boerhaave's brilliant teaching that was crucial to the latter's reputation:

> I can no more judge of the *Genius* and Temper of the *Dutch*, than if I had never lived amongst them, for I knew no *Dutchmen*, but my Professors; but, if I am allowed to take Dr. *Boerhaave* for a Sample of the whole, I do say, that he was the most extraordinary Man of his Age perhaps in the whole

> World; a clear Understanding, sound Judgement, with Strength of Memory that nothing could exceed, and indefatigably laborious: It is true, he had not the Brightness of Invention, that some Authors may have; but with these his Talents he has done more Service to the World in the Knowledge of *Physick*, than all his Predecessors in the whole World put together; by digesting a huge Heap of Jargon and indigested Stuff into an intelligible, regular, and rational System.[13]

The whole culture of the Edinburgh school had been influenced by Boerhaave and informed by his pedagogical and experimental methods. Monro was appointed Professor of Anatomy in 1725, a year ahead of the inauguration of the school itself. Andrew Sinclair (*c.* 1698–1760) and John Rutherford (1695–1779) were appointed as joint Professors of the Theory and Practice of Medicine, while Andrew Plummer (1697–1756) and John Innes (1696–1733) were jointly Professors of Medicine and Chemistry. All five professors had been pupils of Boerhaave and taught using his texts. Monro was the brightest intellectual light at Edinburgh: the English Quaker physician John Coakley Lettsom (1744–1815) called him 'that great anatomical oracle, Monro, [who] attended to his numerous pupils with so much sedulous care, as justly denominated him the Father of the College; and no man knew better how to discriminate the genius of his pupils'.[14] Goldsmith's correspondence concurs on the issue of Monro's brilliance.

Non-conformist English students excluded from Oxford and Cambridge were welcomed in Edinburgh; so too were Irish students who for religious reasons were excluded from Trinity College. In the eighteenth century, only a fifth of Edinburgh's medical school was Scottish, another fifth was English, and a quarter, Irish. The remaining students were from the continent, from America, and beyond. As Matthew Kaufman explains:

> it was only after 1745, once the country had settled down after the Jacobite rebellion, that the cosmopolitan character of the Edinburgh medical intake became increasingly apparent. At the same time, the character of the clinical instruction available, based on the system that many of the early teachers had experienced in Leiden, proved to be extremely popular. Students came

13 James Houstoun, *Dr. James Houstoun's Memoirs of his own Life-Time* (London: Printed for Lawton Gilliver, 1747), 56–7. See also Andrew Cunningham, 'Medicine to Calm the Mind: Boerhaave's Medical System, and Why it was Adapted in Edinburgh', *The Medical Enlightenment of the Eighteenth Century*, ed. Cunningham and Roger French (Cambridge University Press, 1990), 40–66. See also John Struthers, *Historical Sketch of the Edinburgh Medical School* (Edinburgh: Maclachlan and Stewart, 1867).

14 John Coakley Lettsom, *Some Account of the late John Fothergill, M.D.* (London: Printed for C. Dilly, L. David, T. Cadell and J. Phillips, 1783), vii.

> to Edinburgh from not only the English speaking world, but from most of the non English speaking countries of Europe and from even further afield.[15]

The School's reputation for training medics was quickly consolidated, and though it educated many Americans in the later eighteenth and early nineteenth centuries before sending them back across the Atlantic to set up schools in the young republic, many students matriculated without necessarily seeing out their degrees there. Goldsmith was one such student.

Goldsmith's letter of 8 May 1753 to his uncle Contarine summarized the city's intellectual and pedagogical attractions. Apart from his studies and Monro's lectures, however, Goldsmith seemed to find little to admire in the city or the surrounding countryside. To his Longford-born friend and Trinity College classmate Robert Bryanton, Goldsmith adopts rather a different tone in his reportage: a little cruder, more laddish, and concerned primarily with social class and the relative deportments and qualities of women. As James Watt has pointed out, these early emigrant letters display 'a fascination with class distinction, or [refer] to the anxious and unstable condition of the modern writer'.[16] From Edinburgh, on 26 September 1753, Goldsmith explores some of these points of distinction in such a way as to reflect negatively on the breeding of the minor aristocracy in his home country:

> the Gentlemen here are much better bred, then among us; no such character here as our Fox hunter and they have expresed great surprize when I informed them that some men of a thousand pound a year in Ireland spend their whole lives in runing after a hare, drinking to be drunk, and geting every Girl with Child, that will let them; and truly if such a being, equiped in his hunting dress, came among a circle of scots Gentlemen, they wou'd behold him with the same astonishment that a Country man does King George on horseback. (Letter 3)

After an interlude characterized by homesickness, thus, Goldsmith appears at this point to exhibit a somewhat condescending attitude; he writes with an air of superiority which he would modify as he gradually came around to a more poetically appreciative disposition towards his origins over the course of the following decade and a half.

[15] Matthew H. Kaufman, *Medical Teaching in Edinburgh during the Eighteenth and Nineteenth Centuries* (The Royal College of Surgeons of Edinburgh, 2003), 47. See also D. Hamilton, *The Healers: A History of Medicine in Scotland* (Edinburgh: Canongate, 1981), 119; W. R. O. Goslings, 'Leiden and Edinburgh: the Seed, the Soil and the Climate', *The Early Years of the Edinburgh Medical School*, ed. R. G. W. Anderson and A. D. C. Simpson (Edinburgh: The Royal Scottish Museum, 1976), 1–24.

[16] Watt, 'Goldsmith's Cosmopolitanism', 59.

Neither did the limitations of life in Ireland cloud his assessment of life abroad. In his letter to Contarine of December 1753 Goldsmith conveys his ennui in Edinburgh. He was weary of the social scene, which had come to consist of his being something of a court jester to the Duke of Hamilton and his Irish wife, a prescient nod to Joyce's infamous comment on him.[17] He declared himself, perhaps prematurely, confident that he had absorbed 'all that this country can exhibit in the medical way', intending now to move to Paris to complete his medical education. His knowledge of French, rare among Irishmen of his time, will, he declares, be an asset to him. It would indeed be an asset, but more so in the literary than in the medical world, as the French materials that he read in these years would provide the basis for so much of his professional and journalistic writing.

Goldsmith left Edinburgh early in 1754, embarking on the *St Andrew*, a Scottish vessel bound for Bordeaux which was diverted by storms into Newcastle-upon-Tyne, where he went ashore with friends only to be arrested for debt in mysterious circumstances which he attempted to explain to his uncle (Letter 6). His boat for Bordeaux sailed without him, and, in the meantime, he was assisted by his Irish friends and fellow Edinburgh students Joseph Fenn Sleigh and Laughlin Maclane. Freed, and with his own debt paid, Goldsmith was able to travel on to Rotterdam, and then to Leiden by mid-March 1754. From Leiden on 6 May 1754, he communicated to Contarine an ambiguous account of events in Newcastle, to which he added his positive impressions of Dutch manners, customs and the tidy industry evident in the landscape. With the university, however, he was underwhelmed: he thought the quality of teaching low compared with Edinburgh, though he was impressed by the Professor of Chemistry Jerome Gaubius (1705–80).

Beyond Gaubius and his enjoyment of the French books that the Dutch book trade furnished, Goldsmith's mood in Holland was ambivalent. He expressed at this time, tellingly, his desire to see Contarine, and all of his family, upon a proposed return to Ireland the following spring. He would, however, never return to Ireland, and instead indulged a wanderlust which would propel him around Europe for much of the following two years, inspired partially, it would seem, by the example of the Danish author Baron Lewis (Ludvig) Holberg (1684–1754):

> Without money, recommendations or friends, he undertook to set out upon his travels, and make the tour of Europe on foot. A good voice, and a trifling

[17] In which Joyce places Goldsmith in the tradition of Irish comic writers, including Richard Brinsley Sheridan, George Bernard Shaw and Oscar Wilde, who could be seen as 'court jesters to the English': Joyce, 'Oscar Wilde: The Poet of "Salomé"' (1909), *The Critical Writings of James Joyce*, ed. Ellsworth Mason and Richard Ellman (New York: Viking, 1959), 202.

> skill in musick, were the only finances he had to support an undertaking so extensive; so he travelled by day, and at night sung at the doors of peasants houses, to get himself a lodging. In this manner, young Holberg passed thro' France, Germany and Holland. (*An Enquiry into the Present State of Polite Learning in Europe*, *CW*, I: 284)

James Prior claims that, when Goldsmith set off for the continent in 1755 after some time in Leiden, Holberg's 'example was in his eye, and in fact became the model of his conduct'.[18] Holberg's mode of travel was advocated in *An Enquiry into the Present State of Polite Learning in Europe* (1759): 'Countries wear very different appearances to travellers of different circumstances', wrote Goldsmith; 'A man who is whirled through Europe in a post chaise, and the pilgrim who walks the grand tour on foot, will form very different conclusions' (*CW*, I: 331). Thus, Goldsmith travelled on foot, by necessity as much as by Romantic inclination, playing music and disputing his way through France, Germany and Italy, through which he set off on his own bohemian version of the Grand Tour in 1755. Little enough is known about the specifics of his travels, apart from what we can speculatively glean from his work, and in particular from the fictional travels of George Primrose in *The Vicar of Wakefield*. Goldsmith made his way to Paris through Antwerp, Louvain, and Brussels, reaching Paris about the end of February 1755. In Paris, he may have found Irish company in the vicinity of the Irish College, and at the Communauté des Clercs in the rue de Cheval-Vert. There were many exiled Irish priests living in Paris at the time, and Goldsmith, with his vaguely Catholic family background and the influence of Jesuits on his education in the French language, would have sought out such company in which to deploy his musical and debating skills in order to acquire lodgings and food from the expatriate community.

Goldsmith had expressed to Contarine from Edinburgh his intention to attend medical lectures in Paris, but there is little evidence that he followed through with this plan, immersing himself instead in the intellectual and cultural life of the city. Goldsmith left Paris in late spring, making his way to Strasbourg and into Switzerland, a country which would later provide a metaphorical platform from which he surveyed European cultures in *The Traveller*. Moving on through the Alps, Goldsmith proceeded to spend several months in Padua in Italy, beginning in late summer of 1755. In Padua, he may have attended medical lectures, edging towards a medical qualification (though there is no evidence that a degree was earned, nor can his name be found in the medical register there). At the turn of the year, he made his way north by a more direct route, and landed at Dover on 1 February 1756; from thence, with no firm medical degree, qualification or clear prospects, he made his way to London.

[18] *P*, I: 172.

London and the Beginnings of a Literary Career

When Goldsmith arrived in London in February 1756, aged 27, he was in quite an impoverished state. By this point, he felt somewhat aggrieved at the lack of communication from his relatives. He took a number of short-term jobs upon arriving in London, working for a time as an apothecary's assistant, and as an usher in a boys' school. The sixth number of the *Bee* conveys some of his alienation in the latter post:

> It were well, however, if parents, upon fixing their children in one of these homes, would examine the abilities of the usher as well as the master; for, whatever they are told to the contrary, the usher is generally the person most employed in their education. If then, a gentleman, upon putting out his son to one of these houses, sees the usher disregarded by the master, he may depend upon it, that he is equally disregarded by the boys. (*CW*, I: 458)

Equally, his sense of alienation was conveyed with a markedly grim tone in his letter to Daniel Hodson from Temple Exchange Coffee House on 27 December 1757 (Figure 4). Here his incipient cosmopolitanism is troubled – almost ineffably – by a local allegiance:

> Unaccountable [fond]ness for country, this maladie du Pays, as the french [call] it. Unaccountable, that he should still have an affec[tion for] a place, who never received when in it above civil [contem]pt, who never brought out of it, except his brogue [an]d his blunders; sure my affection is equally ridiculous with the Scotchman's, who refused to be cured of the itch, because it made him unco'thoughtful of his wife and bonny Inverary. But not to be serious, let me ask myself what gives me a wish to see Ireland again? The country is a fine one perhaps? No!—There are good company in Ireland? No; the conversation there is generally made up of a smutty toast or a baudy song. The vivacity supported by some humble cousin, who has just ~~wit vivacity~~ folly enough to earn his—dinner. Then perhaps ther's more wit and [lea]rning among the Irish? Oh Lord! No! there has been more [money] spent in the encouragement of the Podareen mare there [in on]e season, than given in rewards to learned men since [the ti]mes of Usher. (Letter 7)

In this, one of the most substantial letters remaining in the corpus, Goldsmith, newly cosmopolitan but with a longing for home that in himself he finds baffling, measures Ireland's limitations against his own broadened intellectual horizons. His critique of the culture of the minor Irish aristocracy takes particular issue with Ireland's equine obsessions, a sentiment echoed some two centuries later, when Louis MacNeice would memorably say that Irish Big Houses 'maintained

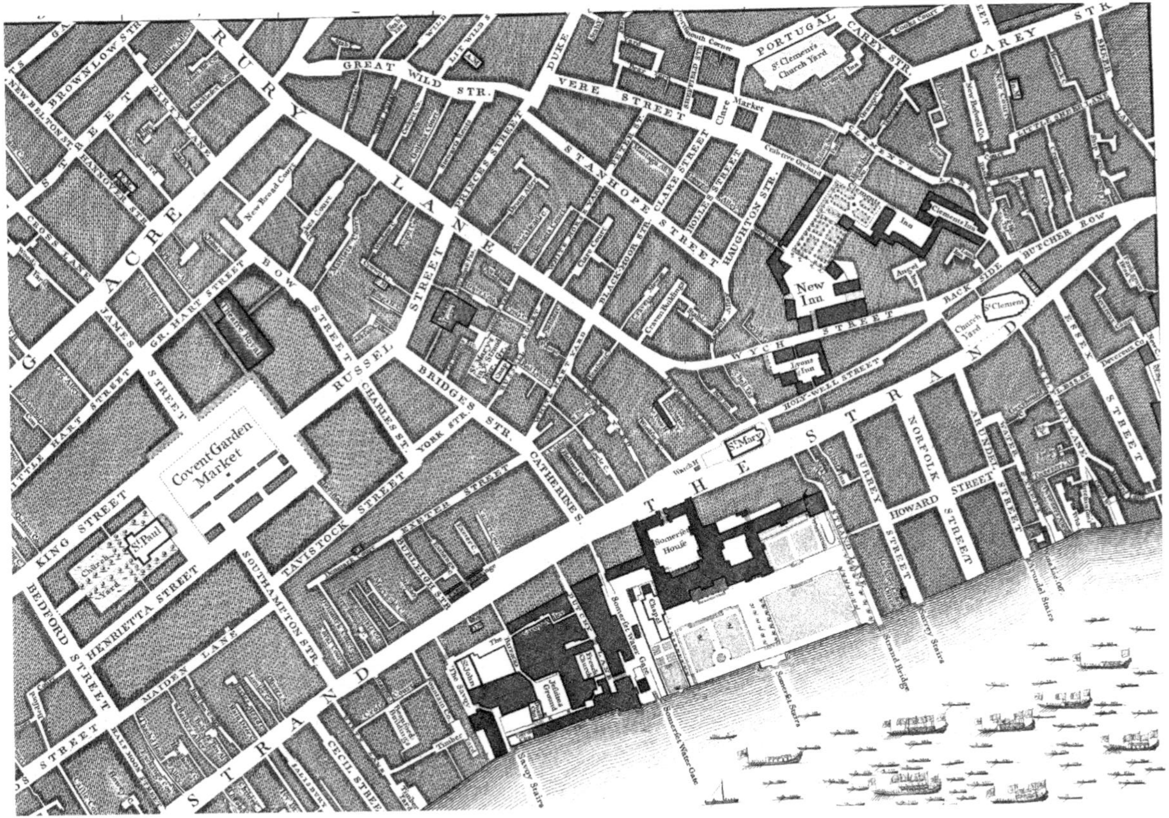

Figure 4 Devereux Court, where Temple Exchange Coffee House was located, can be seen to the east of this map. A short walk from here would have brought Goldsmith to Covent Garden Theatre Royal, or perhaps to Thomas Davies's bookshop on Russell Street, Ralph Griffiths's opposite Somerset House on the Strand, or Thomas Cadell's on the Strand, opposite Catherine Street. Reproduced by permission of the Board of Trinity College Dublin.

no culture worth speaking of – nothing but an obsolete bravado, an insidious bonhomie, and a way with horses'.[19] It is a critique of the sort that Goldsmith would reproduce in the fifth of his satirical Chinese letters, first published in the *Public Ledger* for Thursday 7 February 1760. There, Goldsmith proposed that newspapers are a picture of the genius and the morals of a nation's inhabitants, and he gives a dismaying, if speculative, specimen of Dublin news: 'We hear that there is a benevolent subscription on foot among the nobility and gentry of this country, who are great patrons of merit, in order to assist Black and All Black, in his contest with the Paddaren mare' (*CW*, II: 36). 'Black and All Black' was the nickname (or 'Irish' name) of the horse that had been known to that point as Othello, whereas the Paddereen (or Padreen, or Poddareen, or Padderen) mare was the better-known nickname – she is reputed to have raced with rosary beads around her neck – of Irish Lass. This horse, these horses, seem to represent for Goldsmith something of the stasis of rural Irish gentry when set against the emerging middle-class intellectual bustle of Edinburgh and London.

Isolated and likely rather anxious about his prospects, Goldsmith at this point began to seek out old acquaintance in London. He first sought out Joseph Fenn Sleigh, the doctor and Edinburgh contemporary who had helped him escape the debtors' prison in Sunderland. With Sleigh's help, Goldsmith set himself up as a physician of sorts. Not particularly successful in his medical pursuits (not least due to his rough brogue and the vagueness of his qualifications), Goldsmith supplemented his meagre income by working as a proof-reader in Samuel Richardson's printing establishment in Salisbury Court. While working for Richardson, Goldsmith met Edward Young, the ageing author of *Night Thoughts*, his first encounter with the sort of poetic fame that he would himself acquire with the publication of *The Traveller*. Goldsmith had also reacquainted himself with Dr William Farr, his contemporary at Edinburgh, and with John Beatty of Edgeworthstown, an old room-mate at Trinity College.

Most importantly for his literary career, he was also introduced to the Reverend John Milner, the father of one of his Edinburgh acquaintances, who ran a Presbyterian school in Peckham at which Goldsmith stood in as a teacher. He took his meals with the Milners, and it was in this company that he first met with Ralph Griffiths, the owner of the *Monthly Review*, and the first bookseller to employ Goldsmith as a professional writer. It was due in the main to Goldsmith's knowledge of French that Griffiths's interest in Goldsmith was piqued, and that he took Goldsmith on as an essayist and book-reviewer. Griffiths gave Goldsmith a room over his shop in Paternoster Row, and allowed him a salary of £100 a year.

[19] Louis MacNeice, *The Poetry of W. B. Yeats* (Oxford University Press, 1941), 104–5.

Goldsmith began work in April 1757, reviewing works in English and French. Though his contributions to the *Monthly* were anonymous, their attribution can be confirmed more readily than in the case of his other periodical affiliations, as Griffiths kept a file in which he indicated the authorship of all pieces.[20] While at the *Monthly*, Goldsmith reviewed, most notably, David Mallet's *Remains of the History and Poetry of the Celtes*, John Home's play *Douglas; A Tragedy*, Edmund Burke's *A Philosophical Enquiry into the Origin of Our Ideas of the Sublime and Beautiful*, Tobias Smollett's *Compleat History of England*, and Thomas Gray's *Odes*.

His engagement with these works doubtless influenced his own activities in the theatre, in poetry, in history and in criticism; his activity as a reviewer was a crucial part of his apprenticeship towards a career in those branches of writing. Intriguingly – as far as his nationality and his epistolary writing were concerned – he also reviewed *Letters from an Armenian in Ireland, to his Friends at Trebisond*. A curious piece of work, influenced, as was Goldsmith, by Marana and Montesquieu, *Letters from an Armenian* has been attributed to Viscount Edmund Sexton Pery (1719–1806), a Limerick-born politician and lawyer who had been educated in Trinity College Dublin the decade before Goldsmith. Goldsmith reviewed the book in August 1757; there, he developed the point made in his earlier letter regarding Marana's work, thinking through the device of the Oriental correspondent a little more carefully, as the idea of writing in a similar format, should the opportunity arise, began to insinuate itself.

An Enquiry into the Present State of Polite Learning in Europe (1759)

Griffiths was an intrusive editor, and his alterations to Goldsmith's works proved increasingly irksome to the budding author. Nonetheless, the nature of his work for the *Review*, and the speed at which it was so often completed, set the tone for much of Goldsmith's writerly career. In September 1757, Goldsmith broke off his reviewing arrangement and moved to Salisbury Square, near Fleet Street (Figure 5), but remained close to the Temple Exchange Coffee House and the booksellers.

By early 1758 Goldsmith was planning to write for James and Robert Dodsley a work on 'The Present Taste and Literature in Europe', which combined intellectual and autobiographical insight gleaned from his travels and his reading. It was an initiative which was to prompt a flurry of letters home. In anticipation of the publication of his first book, Goldsmith dispatched (it appears) six letters to Ireland, of which four survive. The letters include some familial and friendly sentiment, but their main purpose was to glean in Ireland subscriptions for his work. He complained to his cousin Edward Mills that Irish printers republished

20 See Benjamin C. Nangle, *The Monthly Review, First Series, 1749–1789: Indexes of Contributors and Articles* (Oxford: Clarendon Press, 1934); and Friedman, *CW*, I: 3–4.

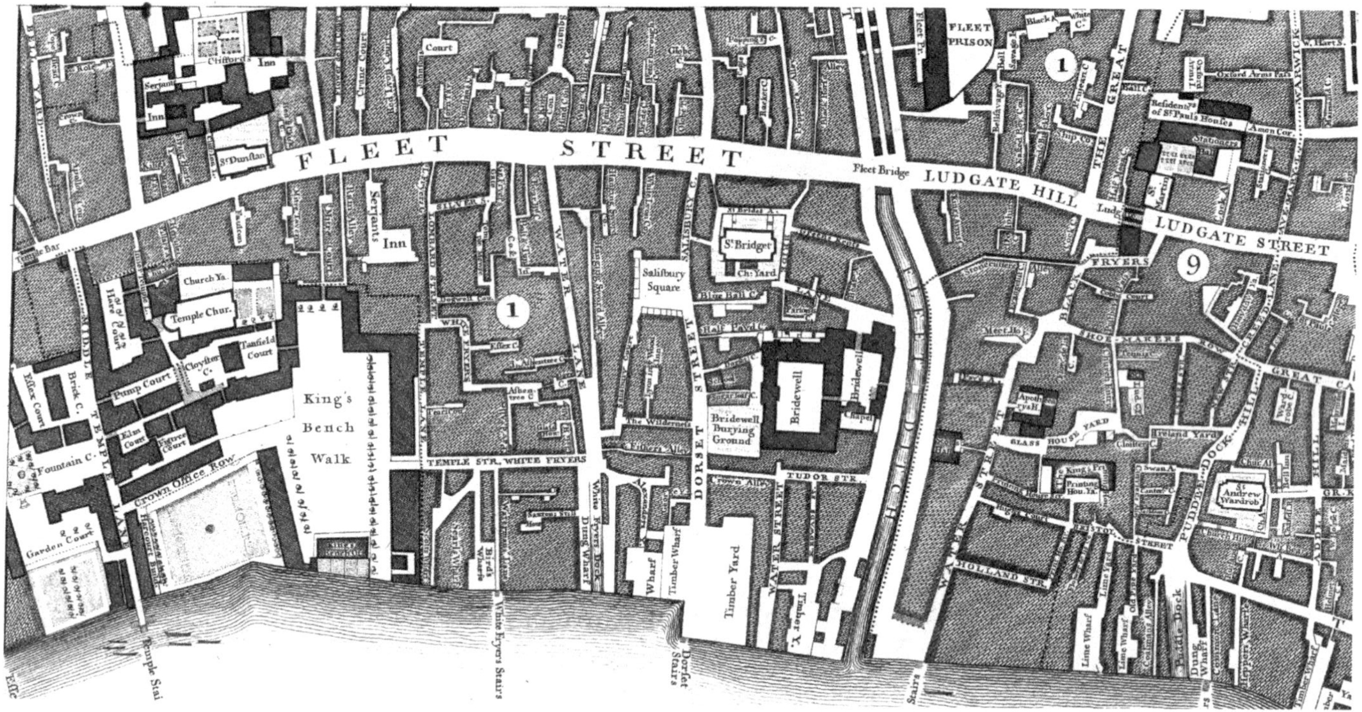

Figure 5 Goldsmith lived for most of his London life in the Temple area on the extreme west of this map. Walking east, down Fleet Street and Ludgate Hill, would have brought him to St Paul's and the considerable book trade in its environs. Reproduced by permission of the Board of Trinity College Dublin.

materials printed in England without any payment to the author; wishing to 'disappoint their avarice', and to earn more from his work than he would otherwise, he wrote to a Dr Radcliff, James Lawder, Bob Bryanton, his brother Henry and Dan Hodson to circulate his proposal to gain subscriptions. His request did not meet with much success. In a letter of 13 January 1759, Goldsmith wrote to his brother Henry of his disappointment at the reception his request had received from friends and relatives in Ireland. The book was to have appeared in February but it would eventually be published in March by the Dodsleys in octavo, priced at 2s 6d, while the Irish copy would sell at 5s 5d. Perhaps the price was the reason his request for Irish subscriptions came to very little.

Goldsmith had good reason to try to generate Irish sales. The British Copyright Act of 1709 made two basic provisions: an author, or the bookseller to whom he had sold his copy, would have exclusive right of publication for twenty-one years, while an author of a book as yet unpublished would have the liberty of printing it for fourteen years, and for fourteen years more if he was still alive. The Act, however, made no mention of Ireland; thus, Irish booksellers could quickly reprint London editions and sell them cheaply, not just in Ireland, but in Britain and, increasingly, as the century wore on, in the American colonies (and the young republic). The grievances of English authors and booksellers led to an Act of Parliament which was passed on 14 June 1739, prohibiting the importation of books composed and first printed in Britain, which meant that books printed in Dublin had to be smuggled into the English market. There is little evidence that smuggled Irish books were an issue after the Act (except, perhaps, in Wales), but by 1759, it was clear that English booksellers were still anxious about the possibility that they could be undercut by the Irish trade. John Whiston of London wrote to fellow booksellers in Cambridge and Oxford in April 1759 indicating that London booksellers had agreed to ban the sale of 'any Scotch or Irish editions of books first printed in England [...] or shall purchase or take in exchange, or bring in by any means, whatsoever, such Scotch or Irish books'.[21] The same clique of London booksellers had raised a fund of £3,150 to defray court expenses and to support the inspection of bookshops across England. Mary Pollard has illustrated that some writers stood to lose out financially because they had not sold the full rights of their work to a London bookseller and retained an interest in the number of copies sold. This may have been the case with Goldsmith's *Enquiry*, and explains his solicitousness in this case. As Pollard notes: 'Once he was in a position to sell his work he does not appear to have been worried about reprints, and much good it would have done him if he had.'[22]

[21] Cited in Richard Cargill Cole, *Irish Booksellers and English Writers, 1740–1800* (Atlantic Highlands, NJ: Mansell, 1986), 3. See also the chapter 'Irish Booksellers and Goldsmith', 114–29.
[22] Mary Pollard, *Dublin's Trade in Books, 1550–1800* (Oxford: Clarendon Press, 1989), 102.

Intellectually ambitious in its own way, an *Enquiry* was at times a floridly composed comparative account of educational and literary cultures across the continent, and across the centuries from the ancient to the contemporary scene. In many of its passages, Goldsmith laments the state of modern writing and criticism, and yet he also recommends the use of vernacular language in writing and in intellectual life. At times the book is ethnocentric, supercilious, straining to appear authoritative on matters which were, in retrospect, the stuff of established prejudices, with Spanish culture, for instance, generally criticized for 'catholic credulity' (*CW*, I: 282). The book reproduces some standard thinking on the influence of climate on culture. Throughout, Goldsmith takes aim at the modern culture of literary criticism, its role in 'the natural decay of politeness' (*CW*, I: 288). Goldsmith also regrets the multiplication of reviews and magazines, and the negative effect of increasing writerly dependence on booksellers: 'There cannot be, perhaps, imagined a combination more prejudicial to taste than this.' The changing literary marketplace has produced a profusion of 'tedious compilations, and periodical magazines', and makes the new breed of dependent, harried author 'little superior to the fellow who works at the press' (*CW*, I: 316). Having worked for Richardson in such a lowly capacity before going on to work for Griffiths, he was well situated to make such comparisons.

An Enquiry was not particularly well received by the critics, except in Tobias Smollett's *Critical Review*, where Goldsmith was, by the time of its publication, ensconced. It was the *Monthly*, almost predictably, which treated the book most unkindly, and with an infusion of personal invective against its erstwhile contributor. Goldsmith's relationship with Griffiths had deteriorated badly by the beginning of 1759, partly because Goldsmith had incurred a debt for clothing – his expensive sartorial tastes were a perennial weakness – for which Griffiths had been the security. Goldsmith needed a suit for his interview at the Surgeons' Hall to obtain a medical post in Coromandel. On 21 December 1758, he had an unsuccessful interview; in any event, news of French victories in India led him to re-think his plans for exotic travel. Goldsmith had in the meantime pawned the clothing and some of Griffiths's books in order to assist his landlord's wife after her husband had been jailed for debt. Trying to explain himself, and denying that he had behaved improperly, he implored Griffiths to withhold 'invective' until the *Enquiry* was published, after which time Griffiths would surely see 'the bright side of a mind when my professions shall not appear the dictates of necessity but of choice' (Letter 13). Though Goldsmith intended that his letter be taken as a declaration of the best intentions, Griffiths did indeed 'spare invective' until Goldsmith's book was published, at which point the *Monthly* viciously attacked it. The review appeared in November 1759, and was penned by William Kenrick with, no doubt,

Griffiths's approval. To Kenrick and the *Monthly*, Goldsmith's book consisted 'Of little else than the trite commonplace remarks and observations, that have been, for some years past, repeatedly ecchoed from Writer to Writer, throughout every country where Letters, or the Sciences, have been cultivated'.

Thus, the book was damned as essentially derivative, its ostensible insights trite. In the final section of the review, Kenrick communicates Griffiths's own grievances at ill-treatment by Goldsmith. Whatever his literary aspiration and pretentions, Goldsmith

> has betrayed, in himself, the man he so severely condemns for drawing his quill to take a purse. We are even so firmly convinced of this, that we dare put the question home to his conscience, whether he never experience the unhappy situation he so feelingly describes, in that of a Literary Understrapper? His remarking him as coming down from his garret, to rummage the Bookseller's shop, for materials to work upon, and the knowledge he displays of his minutest labours, give great reason to suspect he may himself have had concerns in the *bad trade* of book-making. *Fronta nulla fides*. We have heard of many a Writer, who, 'patronized only by his Bookseller,' has, nevertheless, affected the Gentleman in print, and talked full as cavalierly as our Author himself. We have even known one hardy enough, publicly to stigmatize men of the first rank in literature, for their immoralities, while conscious himself of labouring under the infamy of having, by the vilest and meanest actions, forfeited all pretensions to honour and honesty.
>
> If such men as these, boasting a liberal education, and pretending to genius, practise, at the same time, those arts which bring the Sharper to the cart's tail or the pillory; need our Author wonder, that 'learning partakes the contempt of its professors.' If characters of this stamp are to be found among the learned, need anyone be surprized that the Great prefer the society of Fidlers, Gamesters, and Buffoons?[23]

No surprise, perhaps on the back of the *Monthly*'s notice, that the *Enquiry* was not a popular book. It would, however, see a second edition in 1774, for which Goldsmith would receive 5 guineas from James Dodsley, though the book itself would appear some four months after Goldsmith had died. Kenrick's critical hectoring, personal and literary, would span the same period, and he would return periodically to provoke Goldsmith, particularly in the wake of the success of *She Stoops to Conquer* in 1773.

[23] *Monthly Review* 21 (November 1759), 382, 389. '*Fronta nulla fides*' translates as 'Place no trust in appearances.'

Making a Name, 1759–1766

For the *Critical Review*, Goldsmith reviewed, among other items, Arthur Murphy's *The Orphan of China* (1759) – which he criticized for the very Oriental devices that he was himself about to deploy in his Chinese letters – and Richard Brookes's *New and Accurate System of Natural History* (1763), an exercise which would influence his own later endeavours in scientific and natural historical writing. And in February 1759, Goldsmith was introduced to Thomas Percy at the residence of another new friend, Dr James Grainger. Percy had just composed his 'Chinese' novel *Hau Kiou Choaan* (he had the manuscript with him when he met Goldsmith), and was collecting ballads for what would become *Reliques of Ancient English Poetry*. Goldsmith's knowledge of old ballads and songs would no doubt have intrigued him.

As far as correspondence is concerned, Goldsmith composed very little of note – that has survived – between 1762 and 1766. But these were the years in which his name was made, in which he emerged from anonymous drudgery into illustrious friendships and literary fame. It may have been through Smollett that Goldsmith was, around this time, introduced to Samuel Johnson. He also met with John Wilkie, the bookseller for whom he would edit and compose the *Bee*, a periodical whose first issue would be published on 6 October 1759. Generating the columns for such a weekly magazine (32 pages an issue) would have taken up virtually all of Goldsmith's time, and he drew heavily upon French sources to aid in its composition, particularly passages from the fifth volume of the *Encyclopédie*. While he may have felt that this project amounted to little more than hackwork, there was considerable merit in Goldsmith's translations; in any case, borrowing seemed part of the *Bee*'s titular intention to rove and alight upon sources so that they could be transported from flower to flower. The *Bee* petered out at the eighth issue, which along with its other numbers was published in one volume by Wilkie in mid-December. The volume was patronized with faint praise by Kenrick in the *Monthly Review* of January 1760. He affected to write 'with the greatest candour towards an unsuccessful Author', before repeating his earlier critique of Goldsmith's derivation from other sources:

> His stile is not the worst, and his manner is agreeable enough, in our opinion, however it may have failed of exciting universal admiration. The truth is, most of his subjects are already sufficiently worn out, and his observations frequently trite and common. A Writer must, therefore, possess very extraordinary talents, of spirit, humour, and variety of expression, to please, under such disadvantages.[24]

[24] *Monthly Review* 22 (January 1760), 39.

Regardless of Kenrick's condescension, Goldsmith was embarking upon a year of intensive work as a writer for the magazines. He contributed to the *Lady's Magazine* and the *Busy Body*, and Israel Pottinger, who had overseen the *Busy Body*, would publish from late December 1759 the *Weekly Magazine; or Gentleman and Lady's Polite Companion*, with Goldsmith as editor and main contributor. That magazine also contained some of Goldsmith's most Irish material, including his 'Description of the Manners and Customs of the Native Irish' and his memoir of Berkeley (which referenced his uncle Contarine), as well as 'Some Thoughts Preliminary to a General Peace', in which could be found in embryo some of Goldsmith's political principles on the subject of imperial over-extension (principles which would underpin his major poems *The Traveller* and *The Deserted Village*). He also composed two poems for the January issue: his 'Epitaph for Dr. Milner' and 'The Double Transformation', as well as biographical essays.

Early in 1760, Goldsmith met the bookseller John Newbery, though the precise occasion of their meeting remains unclear. Newbery's *Public Ledger* was first published on 12 January 1760 and the instalment of 24 January featured Goldsmith's introductory Chinese letter: the first of the 119 (and eventually 123) ultimately collected as *The Citizen of the World*.[25] The letters satirized the manners, customs and politics of London from the perspective of the Oriental outsider. Goldsmith would supply two letters a week, modelling his approach on Marana, Montesquieu and Horace Walpole, but also drawing quite directly, in the form of translation, from the Marquis d'Argens' *Lettres Chinoises* (1739–42).[26]

Goldsmith was also sporadically composing pieces for Smollett's *British Magazine*. Financially successful by now, if still fiscally careless, he moved from Green Arbour Court to Wine Office Court near Fleet Street by mid-1760. Goldsmith continued to write for the *Public Ledger* all the while, but his enthusiasm for periodical writing was on the wane by mid-1761. In January 1762 he contributed essays to the *British Magazine* and Newbery's new *Lloyd's Evening Post*; in the latter he published 'The Revolution in Low Life' – an adumbration in prose of the argument of *The Deserted Village* – and then ceased writing for periodicals for eleven years. *The Citizen of the World* appeared on 1 May 1762. Perhaps Kenrick was off-duty (the authorship of

[25] For *The Citizen of the World*, Goldsmith added 'The Editor's Preface' and four new letters to the 119 published in the *Public Ledger*. See Friedman's 'Introduction', *CW*, II: ix–xix.

[26] On the models for, and sources of, *The Citizen of the World*, see Martha Pike Conant, *The Oriental Tale in England in the Eighteenth Century* (New York: Columbia University Press, 1908); Hamilton Jewett Smith, *Oliver Goldsmith's The Citizen of the World: A Study* (New Haven: Yale University Press, 1926); Ronald S. Crane and Hamilton Jewett Smith, 'A French Influence on Goldsmith's *Citizen of the World*', *Modern Philology* 19.1 (1921), 83–92; Phillip Harth, 'Goldsmith and the Marquis d'Argens', *Notes and Queries* 198 (1953), 529–30; and David Wei-Yang Dai, 'A Comparative Study of D'Argens' *Lettres Chinoises* and Goldsmith's *Citizen of the World*', *Tamkang Review* 10 (1979), 183–97.

the review is not marked in Griffiths's copy at the Bodleian), but even the *Monthly Review* was kind to the collection, expressing rather tepid regret for its previous treatment of Goldsmith:

> Although this Chinese Philosopher has nothing Asiatic about him, and is as errant an European as the Philosopher of Malmesbury; yet he has some excellent remarks upon men, manners, and things—as the phrase goes.—But the Public have been already made sufficiently acquainted with the merit of these entertaining Letters, which were first printed in *The Ledger*; and are supposed to have contributed not a little towards the success of that Paper. They are said to be the work of the lively and ingenious Writer of An Enquiry into the present State of Polite Learning in Europe; a Writer, whom, it seems, we undesignedly offended, by some Strictures on the conduct of many of our modern Scribblers. As the observation was entirely general, in its intention, we were surprized to hear that this Gentleman had imagined himself in any degree pointed at, as we conceive nothing can be more illiberal in a Writer, or more foreign to the character of a Literary Journal, than to descend to the meanness of personal reflection. It is hoped that a charge of this sort can never be justly brought against the Monthly Review.[27]

Goldsmith's reputation was certainly enhanced by his Orientalist experiment. William Rider, the minor contemporary historian, gave in his anonymously published *Historical and Critical Account of the Lives and Writings of the living Authors of Great Britain* (1762) an early, positive (and brief) assessment of Goldsmith's career to that point, proposing that *An Enquiry into the Present State of Polite Learning in Europe* did honour to Goldsmith's 'Taste and Genius', while the *Bee* 'was greatly admired, both on account of the Elegance of the Stile, in which it is wrote, and the Variety of entertaining Articles which it contains'. Rider was particularly impressed by the *Citizen of the World*, which was 'but little inferior to the *Persian Letters* of the celebrated *Montesquieu*'. A measure of such comparative worth, perhaps, *The Citizen of the World* would be translated into French and German in 1763. Rider concluded that 'whilst he is surpassed by few of his Contemporaries with regard to the Matter which his Writings contain, he is superior to most of them in Style, having happily found out the Secret to unite Elevation with Ease, a Perfection in Language, which few Writers of our nation have attained'.[28] Perhaps as a result of the acclaim Goldsmith's London circle was expanded and, in a sense, consolidated. His acquaintance with Johnson and Joshua Reynolds would grow into firm friendships. In a conversation with James Boswell, on 25 June 1763,

[27] *Monthly Review* 26 (June 1762), 477.

[28] [William Rider], *Historical and Critical Account of the Lives and Writings of the living Authors of Great Britain* (London: Printed for the Author, 1762), 13–14.

Johnson would remark that 'Dr Goldsmith is one of the first men we now have as an author, and he is a very worthy man too. He has been loose in his principles, but he is coming right.'[29]

Goldsmith was beginning to establish himself as an author, perhaps, but had not as yet asserted his own voice. Johnson may have been referring to Goldsmith's political principles, which were to that point largely obscured or contorted by the imperatives of professional writing for different publishers and their constituencies. It was just as likely, however, that Johnson was referring to a general lack of organization and consistency in Goldsmith's thinking and writing. The two problems, perhaps, were related. In the years following, Johnson would see Goldsmith's principles 'coming right' in terms of their general agreement over the status of the monarch, which for both men was an abiding concern. Both men were of a decidedly Tory temperament, certainly averse to unquestioning celebrations of English liberty. Their shared stance is of particular importance given the political turbulence of the 1760s. In May 1762, John Stuart, the third Earl of Bute, was installed as First Minister; he secured a pension for Johnson two months later. Johnson and Goldsmith both may have seen in Bute, the son-in-law of Lady Mary Wortley Montagu, a man of cultural pedigree who could sponsor the sort of cultural reflection and integrity they espoused. Thinking Bute potentially sympathetic, Goldsmith lobbied him to support a projected spell of philosophical travel in the Far East. His request was ignored, dispiritingly for Goldsmith, who was looking to add to his philosophical store. Over the following several years, personal and professional associates of Goldsmith such as Smollett (publisher of the Tory periodical the *True Briton*) and Arthur Murphy (editor of the pro-Bute *Auditor*) were involved in a pamphlet and column war with enemies of Bute, in particular John Wilkes and his supporters Lord Temple and Charles Churchill. A supporter of Britain's adventures in the Seven Years' War, Wilkes attacked Bute for his supposedly generous peace terms with France in the *North Briton*. Issue 45 of that paper likened the Treaty of Paris – which ended the war – with Jacobitism, to which it was deemed an equivalent form of treason. These skirmishes would prefigure the 'Wilkes and Liberty' campaign of the later 1760s.

Though it surrounded him and involved many of his friends and associates, Goldsmith himself stayed out of the pamphlet wars of the 1760s. He was busy enough with his own professional writing, completing four and a half volumes of *Plutarch's Lives* and his biography of Richard Nash in 1762. In October of that year Goldsmith sold to Newbery (along with Benjamin Collins of Salisbury) the rights to the book which would four years later be published as *The Vicar of*

[29] James Boswell, *Life of Johnson*, ed. G. B. Hill and L. F. Powell, 6 vols. (1791; Oxford: Clarendon Press, 1934–50), I: 408.

Wakefield, ultimately one of the most popular and reprinted novels of the later eighteenth and early nineteenth centuries. The *Vicar* was sold due to financial pressure, when Goldsmith was threatened with eviction from Wine Office Court for non-payment of rent. Newbery advanced his third share of the book (£20) and Goldsmith moved with Newbery's assistance, in December 1762, to Canonbury House in Islington, where his domestic needs and purchases were attended to by Elizabeth Fleming, of whom nothing else is known. Newbery would manage Goldsmith's finances more closely, balancing his expenditures against his literary output while he proceeded – among other new projects – with revisions to *The Vicar of Wakefield*.

As he began to emerge from his apprenticeship in the drudgery of hackwork into a more autonomous sphere of action in the mid-1760s, statements of political conviction began to sound more audibly through the hum of conventional sentiment and received wisdom. Pro-monarchical sentiment can be found in parts of his *History of England, in a Series of Letters from a Nobleman to his Son* (1764), in his first major poem *The Traveller, or A Prospect of Society* (1764), and in chapters 19 and 20 of *The Vicar of Wakefield*. To Goldsmith, the new politics, characterized by the jostling of factions for political influence, was a dangerous innovation, one in which private interests would more determinedly overtake the social good.

An History of England, in a Series of Letters was published by Newbery in two volumes on 26 June 1764. In a prefatory address 'To the Publisher', Goldsmith announced that the first fifty-one letters of the sixty-eight 'were written by a Nobleman to his son, at the University. The rest were added, as you will easily perceive, by a much inferior hand; for they were drawn up by me' (*CW*, V: 291). Kenrick, writing in the *Monthly*, took Goldsmith at his (presumably disingenuous) word, commenting: 'we think some of the former Letters much better than some of the last; but, whether they are the labours of the same or a different hand, whether of an honourable Peer or a professed Author, we find it too problematical for us to determine'. Kenrick argued that some of the cultural and political reflection in *An History* might be too subtle to be understood by the schoolboy audience for which it was ostensibly written, adding: 'It is also farther to be doubted, whether a simple narrative of facts, without the intermixture of political observations, and delineation of characters, would not be much more useful, if it were made equally engaging.'[30] Kenrick isolates a particular passage in which Goldsmith describes Walpole's censorious attitude to the theatre and the press, 'which so severely exposed his corruption, and branded his follies'. Kenrick may indeed have had a point about Goldsmith's

[30] *Monthly Review* 31 (October 1764), 245, 248.

political characterizations, as the latter's representation of the culture presided over by Walpole was generally unkind:

> The declining prerogative of the crown might have been an early object of his attention; but, in the sequel, those very measures which he took to increase it, proved to be the most effectual means of undermining it. As latterly all his aims were turned to save himself, and his friends, he undertook to make a majority in the house of commons, by bribing the members; and what was still worse, avowed the corruption. As all spirit of integrity was now laughed out of the kingdom; and as the people were held to duty by no motives of religious obedience to the throne, patriotism was ridiculed, and venality practised without shame.[31]

Similar opinions were expressed in the dedication to *The Traveller*. There, Goldsmith complained to his brother Henry that he saw party and faction as the enemies of poetry – and, by extension, society: 'Party entirely distorts the judgment', he wrote, 'and destroys the taste. When the mind is once infected with this disease, it can only find pleasure in what contributes to encrease the distemper' (*CW*, IV: 246–7). As in culture and in criticism, so it goes, for Goldsmith, in society at large; accordingly, in the poem itself, he proposes to revert from party and factionalism to monarchy:

> When I behold a factious band agree
> To call it freedom, when themselves are free;
> Each wanton judge new penal statutes draw,
> Laws grind the poor, and rich men rule the law;
> The wealth of climes, where savage nations roam,
> Pillag'd from slaves, to purchase slaves at home;
> Fear, pity, justice, indignation start,
> Tear off reserve, and bare my swelling heart;
> 'Till half a patriot, half a coward grown,
> I fly from petty tyrants to the throne.
>
> Yes, brother, curse with me that baleful hour
> When first ambition struck at regal power; (*CW*, IV: 265–6)

The argument against the weakening of regal power was repeated in his prose fiction when, in the nineteenth and twentieth chapters of *The Vicar of Wakefield*, Primrose himself argues for kingly authority, before his peripatetic son George explains that his travels through Europe have proven to him that 'monarchy was

[31] Goldsmith, *An History of England, in a Series of Letters from a Nobleman to his Son*, 2 vols. (London: Printed for J. Newbery, 1764), II: 152, 142–3.

the best government for the poor to live in, and commonwealths for the rich. I found that riches in general were in every country another name for freedom; and that no man is so fond of liberty himself as not to be desirous of subjecting the will of some individuals in society to his own' (*CW*, IV: 121). The protective prerogative of monarchy – and the dangers to the poor of republican forms of government – were abiding convictions in Goldsmith's work, underpinning *The Traveller* just as they would, in a subtler fashion, imbue *The Deserted Village*.

The Traveller was the first publication that appeared with Goldsmith's name attached to it, and he had put much painstaking effort into its composition and revision over the decade since, according to his dedicatory letter to his brother Henry, he had sent a part of the poem from Switzerland. Goldsmith needed Johnson's help in bringing the work to a conclusion, however, and though he contributed key lines towards that end, Johnson could also declare of *The Traveller* as a whole that it signalled the arrival of the best poet since Pope.[32] Johnson's was just one of many positive reviews: the poem was generally acclaimed, and Goldsmith's name was now decisively made. Goldsmith was already one of the original charter members of Johnson's Literary Club, founded by Joshua Reynolds in February 1764 for the purposes of supper and conversation every Monday night in the Turk's Head Tavern in Gerrard Street in Soho.

Though he was very much attuned to Johnson's Toryism, Goldsmith's political worldview could result in fractiousness with other members of the Club. In July 1766, as he was having his portrait painted by Reynolds at the latter's studio in Leicester Square, Goldsmith would leave the room rather than listen to his friends Reynolds and Edmund Burke disparage the king and the king's courtiers. Goldsmith and Burke, reported James Northcote to William Hazlitt many years later, 'had often violent disputes about politics; the one being a staunch Tory, and the other at that time a Whig and outrageous anti-courtier'.[33] The two men had been contemporaries at Trinity College Dublin in the later 1740s. Goldsmith would later decree, in his poem *Retaliation* (1774) that Burke had wasted on party – and on Rockingham's Whigs in particular – a generosity of intellect 'meant for mankind' (*CW*, IV: 353).

His 1766 letters to John Bindley, the MP for Dover, suggest a general weariness with, and wariness of, the sort of ministerial machinations which in his view had resulted from, and continued to contribute to, the diminution of monarchical power. These letters are unusual for Goldsmith in their direct allusion to contemporary political intrigue, though Goldsmith also confessed that he did not fully understand the intricacies of the stratagems currently afoot. He refers disparagingly to John Almon, a radical Liverpool Whig bookseller and political journalist

[32] *Critical Review* 18 (December 1764), 462.
[33] William Hazlitt, *Conversations of James Northcote* (London: Henry Colborn and Richard Bentley, 1830), 40.

(1737–1805), probably best known as an ally of Wilkes, in whose defence he produced *A Letter on Libels, Warrants, Seizure of Papers, etc.* (1764). Almon's affiliation with Wilkes was enough to earn him Goldsmith's disdain. Wilkes's re-election in Middlesex in March 1769 was greatly assisted by John Wheble, editor of the *Middlesex Journal*. Wheble would himself go on to be an ally of Kenrick, printing in 1772 the latter's scurrilous poetic pamphlet *Love in the Suds* (1772), which accused David Garrick of a sexual relationship with Goldsmith's friend, the recently disgraced Irish playwright Isaac Bickerstaff. Literary, critical and political affiliations seemed gradually to align for Goldsmith over the course of the 1760s.

Success and Sociability

The fame brought to Goldsmith on the back of *The Traveller* and *The Vicar of Wakefield* ensured his place at the top table of London's literary world. Of course, his friendship with Johnson and Reynolds played a rather large part in his elevated status as well. But looking at the famous group portrait of the Club painted by James Doyle, the viewer familiar with anecdotal accounts of Goldsmith would not be surprised to find him on the periphery of the group. Seated at the far right of the table, Goldsmith is grim-faced, if not scowling, as Thomas Warton whispers in his ear, perhaps a snide remark on Johnson's *Dictionary* which Warton was known to have disparaged (Figure 6). In any case, Doyle's imagining of the group, with Goldsmith apparently ignored by the conversationalists-in-chief Johnson and Burke, tallies with reports of Goldsmith's awkwardness in company and his inability to measure up to the demands of his peer group's polished verbosity, particularly the account found in Boswell's largely hostile *Life of Johnson*. Here the portrayal of Goldsmith's verbal blunders and bad humour, coupled with his Malvolio-like sartorial excess, suggest a man who invited the ribbings doled out by Johnson and others. Goldsmith emerges from these pages as a clumsy and sometimes envious participant in the polite and waggish sociability of his peers.

The evidence of the letters confirms, in some respects, this peripheral Goldsmith, even as he approached the apex of his fame. A letter to Anne Percy, wife of his friend and confidante Thomas, requests two tickets for an upcoming masquerade ball: 'If she can procure them for him it will be a singular obligation, and make two young Ladies extremely happy.' The letter is undated and Balderston has suggested early January 1768 but we propose a later date of 4 October of that year. Although Balderston's assessment that it must have been written in 1768 is sound, there are, on the basis of Anne Percy's appointment as nurse to Prince Edward and its composition after Goldsmith moved to Brick Court (visible to the far left in Figure 5), a number of factors that support the October date over Balderston's suggestion of early January. Firstly, Goldsmith's polite hope to see Percy over

Figure 6 A group portrait of some of the most eminent members of the Club. Johnson (second from left) seems to be in conversation with Edmund Burke (centre), with the others listening intently. Goldsmith, on the far right of the picture, also appears to be listening to Johnson while Thomas Warton whispers in his ear. William Walker, *Literary Party at Sir Joshua Reynolds*, nineteenth-century stipple engraving after James William Edmund Doyle. Reproduced by permission of Harvard Art Museums.

'this winter' makes a January dating improbable. Secondly, the supplicant tone of the letter, its insistence that this would be a 'singular obligation' and that it would make 'two young Ladies extremely happy' suggests that the letter refers to a significant social occasion. Moreover, masquerades had fallen somewhat out of fashion by this time and the Soho Square operations of Teresa Cornelys – the Queen of balls, masquerades and entertainments – were closed down for refurbishment for the summer of 1768.[34] Therefore, we can say with a degree of confidence that Goldsmith is referring to one of the events held in honour of the visit of King Christian VII of Denmark, brother-in-law to George III, a state visit that inspired

[34] On the decline and revival of the masquerade, see Gillian Russell, *Women, Sociability, and Theatre in Georgian London* (Cambridge University Press, 2007), ch. 2.

enormous public interest in late 1768 and was covered in great detail across the London newspapers.[35]

Goldsmith seems to have conflated two events in the one letter, so, while we can be reasonably confident of the date, we cannot be certain of the particular event to which he is referring. The first event was the grand ball hosted by the Duke and Duchess of Northumberland at Sion House on Friday 7 October, which featured a number of 'Persons of the first Quality and Distinction'.[36] And although it took place in 'a most superb and magnificent rotunda temple' and was decorated with 15,000 lamps, reports indicate that it had no masquerade element.[37] The following Monday, 10 October, saw a spectacular masquerade ball held at the King's Theatre and hosted by King Christian VII, attended by a 'phalanx of fashionable ladies'.[38] There was also a much-publicized shortage of tickets on offer, which even instigated a counterfeiting operation.[39] The lawyer and memoirist William Hickey was entranced by the occasion: 'The *coup d'oeil* upon the first entrance was the grandest and most sublime thing I had ever beheld. This being the only masquerade that had taken place for many years, every body was anxious to see it, and even fifty guineas was advertised in the public papers for a ticket.'[40] In sum, Goldsmith had either requested tickets for the masquerade and mistaken the night, or he had requested tickets for the Friday night ball and mistaken it for a masquerade. We cannot be certain, but happily both alternatives allow us to propose with confidence 4 October for the letter's composition. Prior records that Goldsmith was often listed as being present at masquerades and, as a writer who so often adopted other voices, his interest in the brightly illuminated parade of metropolitan excess bleeds through to his writing. In *The Deserted Village*, his scathing dismissal of such occasions is mediated, perhaps softened, by their visual allure:

> The dome where Pleasure holds her midnight reign,
> Here richly deckt admits the gorgeous train,

[35] See Aileen Ribeiro, 'The King of Denmark's Masquerade', *History Today* 27.6 (1977), 385–9.

[36] *Lloyd's Evening Post* of 7–10 October 1768 provides a detailed account of the entertainments which were 'illuminated with upwards of fifteen thousand lamps'.

[37] Russell, *Women, Sociability, and Theatre in Georgian London*, 40.

[38] *Ibid.* Russell's reading of the event as a response to Wilkesite politics might add another dimension to Goldsmith's eagerness to show he could secure tickets for the event. On the other hand, an important function of the event was to showcase British commerce and industry – specifically, the 'Silk and Fancy Manufactories', a cause for which Goldsmith would not have been sympathetic: *Public Advertiser*, 1 October 1768.

[39] 'It is said that upwards of 2000 counterfeit tickets, for his Danish Majesty's Grand Masquerade Ball and Supper, were sold at from seven guineas to eighteen each; and a number of the above tickets were sold at St. James's end of the town yesterday afternoon at 5s each, all counterfeits': *Lloyd's Evening Post*, 10–12 October 1768.

[40] *Memoirs of William Hickey*, ed. Alfred Spencer, 2 vols. (London: Hurst & Blackett, 1913–25), I: 128.

Tumultuous grandeur crowds the blazing square,
The rattling chariots clash, the torches glare;
Sure scenes like these no troubles ere annoy!
Sure these denote one universal joy! (*CW*, IV: 299)

In the end, the letter requesting tickets invokes a peripheral Goldsmith, a man on the fringes, only able to enjoy the social whirl of mid-Georgian London vicariously, a mirror of his status within the Club. He is likely to be soliciting on behalf of the Horneck sisters, Catherine and Mary, fashionable daughters of a Devonshire family whom he had met through Reynolds. He was very fond of 'Little Comedy' and the 'Jessamy [i.e. fashionable] Bride', as he referred to Catherine and Mary, and the general biographical consensus is that his was a quasi-paternal affection. He was to travel to Paris with them and their mother in the summer of 1770 although, as his letters to Reynolds recount, it would seem this was not a happy experience for any of them. Yet a subsequent request for masquerade tickets in April 1771 for 'some finer people' – when we can be more certain that he is asking on behalf of the pair – reveals that their friendship would recover from its Parisian ebb.[41] And one of the final letters we have in Goldsmith's hand is to Catherine Horneck, who had become Mrs Henry Bunbury in 1771. Goldsmith's jocular response to her teasing verse invitation reveals a warm and intimate friendship that has endured; we might even speculate that her gentle jibe at his 'spring velvet coat' may be an ongoing joke between them with regard to Goldsmith's penchant for ornate coats that dates to that ill-fated Parisian trip when he complained to Reynolds of a silk coat which 'makes me look like a fool'. At the same time, the letter is typically self-deprecating in recognizing that he was always the fool in such social settings and taken advantage of by those more able to discipline their comportment:

... I fret like the devil
To see them so cowardly lucky and civil.
Yet still I sit snugg and continue to sigh on
Till made by my losses as bold as a lion
I venture at all, while my avarice regards
The whole pool as my own. Come give me five cards.
Well done cry the ladies. Ah Doctor that's good.
The pool's very rich. Ah. The Doctor is lood. (Letter 64)

Although there is a danger in overreaching in a reading of this late epistle and taking it as a reflection on his life more generally, a self-recognition does manifest there; it may be wry, weary or simply resigned but it is one that seems

[41] See headnote to Letter 35.

nonetheless devoid of bitterness. Although there were those, from William Kenrick to Washington Irving, who would hint that Goldsmith's feelings towards Catherine veered well beyond the platonic, the letters, in the end, suggest nothing more than affection and respect.

Yet Goldsmith was not always on the periphery of sociability, peering in at others. Leaving aside his participation in Johnson's circle, his innate generosity ensured that he would not be found wanting for companionship. Prior records his habit of hosting suppers in his rooms, jocularly called his 'Little Cornelys', where 'a curious intermixture of characters, and frequently an expensive entertainment, were to be found'.[42] He invited Boswell, his rival for Johnson's attentions, for dinner along with Reynolds and Colman in September 1769, just after a dinner they both attended at bookseller Thomas Davies's house. Similarly, in 1772, when he was staying in Edgeware, he was keen to keep in touch with the events of the city by inviting friends such as Reynolds, Richard Penneck and Isaac Bickerstaff to dine. William Ballantyne, recalling a 'hop' he hosted, offers an intriguing image of 'Dr Goldsmith', who 'was so happy as to dance & throw up his wig to the Ceiling, saying men were never so much like men as when they look'd like boys'.[43]

Bickerstaff was only one of the other Irish writers with whom Goldsmith associated. Robert Nugent, Lord Clare, dedicatee of *The Haunch of Venison*, might well be the best-known, and Norma Clarke's re-examination of Goldsmith has illuminated this aspect of his professional and social lives and provides a tacit reminder that the letters do not offer a complete portrait of Goldsmith by any means. No letters remain to throw light on his relationships with Samuel Derrick, Jack Pilkington, Paul Hiffernan or Edward Purdon, all Irish figures involved in the machinations of London's Grub Street.[44] Although Goldsmith never returned to Ireland, his sense of nationality played heavily on his mind just as much in his successful later life as it had in his earlier, more impoverished years. Letter 29 to Maurice in January 1770 is particularly revealing. His palpable pride and compulsion to boast of his recent elevation to Professor of Ancient History at the Royal Academy and his elite circle of friends give way to a lugubrious indignation that he has been forgotten by those he has left behind. He took particular care to look

42 *P*, II: 511.

43 Letter from Ballantyne to James Asperne, 28 March 1806. Folger Library, Washington DC. PN 2598. M2 C7.

44 Samuel Derrick (1724–69), a writer best remembered for *The dramatic censor; being remarks upon the conduct, characters, and catastrophe of our most celebrated plays* (1752); John Carteret Pilkington (1730–63), writer and son of Laetitia Pilkington (*c.* 1709–50); Paul Hiffernan (1710?–77), a writer and playwright who alternately fought, antagonized and collaborated with Garrick and Samuel Foote in the 1760s, and wrote the amusing *The Recantation and Confession of Doctor Kenrick, LLD* (1772); and Edward Purdon (1729–67), a friend of Goldsmith's from Trinity College Dublin and a minor translator of Voltaire. See Norma Clarke, *Brothers of the Quill: Oliver Goldsmith in Grub Street* (Cambridge, MA: Harvard University Press, 2016).

out for those Irish recently arrived in London, much as other established literary Irishmen such as Edmund Burke and Charles Macklin did, particularly around the Temple where Irish legal students could be found.[45] As John Day, later Judge-Advocate General in Bengal, reminisced:

> The Poet frequented much the Grecian Coffee-house, then the favourite resort of the Irish and Lancashire Templars; and delighted in collecting around him his friends, whom he entertained with a cordial and unostentatious hospitality. Occasionally he amused them with his flute or with whist, neither of which he played well, particularly the latter, but in losing his money, he never lost his temper.[46]

The later letters also show that his efforts extended to his family, in particular his nephew William – the son of Daniel Hodson and Goldsmith's sister, Catherine – for whom he advocated to William Hunter and perhaps other members of the medical community. Although it is unclear how William's medical career played out, we can be certain that Goldsmith's interventions, now that he was a public figure, would have borne some weight.

A Man of Consequence

To note his appointment as Professor of Ancient History to the Royal Academy focuses attention on one aspect of Goldsmith's oeuvre that has to date received inadequate critical attention.[47] History writing was a genre that was very much central to both the cultural and political life of the mid eighteenth century. David Hume's lament on the reception of his important *History of England* testifies to the interest and risk of such ventures: 'I was assailed by one cry of reproach, disapprobation, and even detestation; English, Scotch, and Irish, Whig and Tory, churchman and sectary, freethinker and religionist, patriot and courtier, united in their rage against the man who had presumed to shed a tear for the fate of Charles I and the Earl of Strafford.'[48]

[45] *P*, II: 342–9; Ginger, 281. On Irish legal circles in London, see Craig Bailey, *Irish London: Middle-class Migration in the Global Eighteenth Century* (Liverpool University Press, 2013), and John Bergin, 'Irish Catholics and their Networks in Eighteenth-Century London', *Eighteenth-Century Life* 39.1 (2015), 66–102.

[46] *P*, II: 357–8.

[47] But see Ronald S. Crane and James H. Warner, 'Goldsmith and Voltaire's *Essai Sur Les Mœurs*', *Modern Language Notes* 38.2 (1923), 65–76, and R. W. Seitz, 'Goldsmith and the "Annual Register"', *Modern Philology* 31.2 (1933), 183–94.

[48] Hume, 'The Life of David Hume, Esq., Written by Himself', *The History of England, from the invasion of Julius Cæsar to the revolution in 1688, a new edition*, 8 vols. (London: Printed for T. Cadell, 1778), I: xi.

One might immediately observe that it is indicative of Goldsmith's status in the 1760s that publishers were willing to commission historical works from him when the market was being contested by figures such as Hume and Smollett. Goldsmith followed his *History of England, in a Series of Letters* with a *Roman History* for which Thomas Davies had offered 250 guineas at the end of 1767 or the beginning of 1768. Goldsmith had two years to complete the work but it was published in May 1769, well within the timeframe. Two further editions were to follow in 1770 and 1775, as well as an abridged version 'for the Use of Schools' in 1772. His increased fame notwithstanding, Goldsmith's Grub Street experience had enabled him to spot commercial opportunity: the preface discusses the excessive length and detail of previous Roman histories by Rollin, Crevier, Hooke and Echard, which were 'entirely unsuited to the time and expence mankind usually chuse to bestow upon this subject'.[49] In June 1769, he signed another agreement with Davies to complete a four-volume octavo history of England, again within two years, for £500. Again, Goldsmith was able to produce the work speedily and it was published in August 1771. As Wardle reports, it went through twelve editions in the following fifty years, and twice as many in the one-volume abridgement that he later produced.[50]

Given the time and energy he expended on these writings at this very public stage of his career, and their subsequent longevity, there is considerable scope for a scholarly reassessment of their importance to his achievement and the ways in which they process aspects of Irish history in particular. Edmund Burke's interest in history is well known. And Samuel Johnson's epistolary encouragement in 1755 to Charles O'Conor, the leading writer of the Irish Catholic Enlightenment, to produce a fitting account of Irish literary history confirms that the topic of Irish history was under meaningful consideration within Goldsmith's circle.[51] The publication of O'Conor's groundbreaking *Dissertations on the Ancient History of Ireland* (1753, revised in 1766) and his 1762 assault, in a letter to a London periodical, on Hume's lurid description of Catholic barbarities in 1641 are also events of which Goldsmith was, given his large London Irish circle, surely aware.[52] These debates informed the work of other Irish playwrights with

[49] Goldsmith, *The Roman History, from the Foundation of the city of Rome, to the Destruction of the Western Empire*, 2 vols. (London: Printed for S. Baker and G. Leigh, T. Davies; and L. Davis, 1769), I: ii.

[50] *W*, 220.

[51] 'I have long wished that the Irish Literature were cultivated. Ireland is known by tradition to have been once the seat of piety, and learning; and surely it would be very acceptable to all those who are curious either in the original of nations, or the affinities of Languages, to be further informed of the revolutions of a people so ancient, and once so illustrious': *The Letters of Samuel Johnson*, ed. Bruce Redford, 3 vols. (Oxford: Clarendon Press, 1992), I: 152.

[52] See Robert E. Ward, 'A Letter from Ireland: A Little-Known Attack on David Hume's "History of England"', *Eighteenth-Century Ireland* 2 (1987), 196–7.

Enlightenment tendencies such as Charles Macklin.[53] As critics continue to identify Goldsmith's Irish allegiances as an important way into his oeuvre, the historical writings and his treatment of 1641 and other key events in Anglo-Irish relations demand further scrutiny, particularly as to how they might shape our reading of his canonical works.

Certainly, as Letter 37 to Bennet Langton shows, his historiographical efforts drew considerable public attention. Anticipating Hume's complaint, he wrote in exasperation:

> I have been a good deal abused in the newspapers for betraying the liberties of the people. God knows I had no thoughts for or against liberty in my head. My whole aim being to make up a book of a decent size that as Squire Richard says would do no harm to nobody. However they set me down as an arrant Tory and consequently no honest man. When you come to look at any part of it you'l say that I am a soure Whig.

In a lengthy attack of two and a half columns in the Wilkesite *Middlesex Journal, or, Chronicle of Liberty* of 10–12 September 1771, 'BRUNSWICK' laid out the charges and reveals just how vituperative historiographical debate could be in the contemporary political environment. The writer is 'at a loss to name a punishment adequate to the crime of an historian, who, either through Tory principles, or mercenary views, asserts falsehoods in order to deceive posterity'. Whether Goldsmith was being disingenuous with his surprise at the critique may not be determined but it was certainly true that his elevation in the world of letters came with increased attention as to his political and moral character in the burgeoning newspaper market. His friendship and collaboration with Thomas Percy was the subject of discussion in the *St. James's Chronicle*, where he had to defend himself against a charge of plagiarism in 1767. That Goldsmith chose to take to the press to air his views is a function not only of the press's growing importance and his fame, but also an indication of his confidence.[54] Indeed, there is a tantalizing record of a letter, now believed lost, that Goldsmith wrote to the newspapers in

[53] See Michael Brown, *The Irish Enlightenment* (Cambridge, MA: Harvard University Press, 2016), 338–9, and David O'Shaughnessy, '"Bit, by some mad whig": Charles Macklin and the Theater of Irish Enlightenment', *Huntington Library Quarterly* 80.4 (2017), 559–84.

[54] *The Citizen of the World* betrays some earlier scepticism as to the merit of newspapers: 'You must not, however, imagine that they who compile these papers have any actual knowledge of the politics, or the government of a state; they only collect their materials from the oracle of some coffee-house, which oracle has himself gathered them the night before from a beau at a gaming table, who has pillaged his knowledge from a great man's porter, who has had his information from the great man's gentleman, who has invented the whole story for his own amusement the night preceding' (*CW*, II: 29–30).

November 1773.[55] No longer simply reacting to attacks by others or content to sit on the sidelines of the new politics of which he had complained to Bindley, Goldsmith inserted a paragraph in support of Lord Mayor of London, James Townsend (a friend of Bindley's), as Prior records him telling Shelburne at Drury Lane theatre the night it was published.[56] Townsend had been an enthusiastic supporter of Wilkes but had, along with John Horne (later Tooke), split with him in 1771. He betrayed – and incensed – Wilkes by reneging on an electoral pact, which denied Wilkes the mayoralty. A ferocious paper war ensued in which Goldsmith appears at last to have been compelled to participate. Although the letter has not been located, it seems fitting, in the wake of his most public success with *She Stoops to Conquer*, that Goldsmith felt able, if not obliged, to intervene in affairs of political significance. This new level of engagement emerged more clearly in his posthumously published *The Haunch of Venison* (1774).[57]

Goldsmith and the Theatre

Prior offers about as good and succinct a rationale as any when writing on a dramatist's motivation for attempting to pen a play in the mid-to-late eighteenth century:

> A successful dramatist if shorn of some former honours in our own days, still occupies a large space in the public eye, his reputation spreads more rapidly than that of any other writer, and his name, which is frequently bandied with a familiarity implying regard, forms a passport to the favour of that large class of society, who in a great metropolis find in the amusements of the theatre relaxation from the cares of life. He identifies himself not merely with the literature but with the enjoyments of the people; with one of the most social, and certainly not least intellectual, of their recreations. Like the orator, he has

[55] *P*, II: 482. Prior adds in a footnote that 'This has been sought for in three or four journals without success; the circumstance is unlike his usual habits as he meddled not in city matters, or even in general politics.'

[56] There is an intriguing irony to Goldsmith's alliance with Shelburne as Dennis O'Bryen's *A Friend in Need is a Friend Indeed* (1783), a pointed satiric attack on Shelburne, was a re-imagining of Goldsmith's *The Good Natur'd Man*. See David O'Shaughnessy, 'Making a Play for Patronage: Dennis O'Bryen's *A Friend in Need is a Friend Indeed*', *Eighteenth-Century Life* 39.1 (2015), 183–211.

[57] Frustratingly, large swathes of newspapers from that month are missing from the Burney Collection, including many numbers of the *Westminster Journal* and the *Gazetteer and New Daily Advertiser*. Despite an extensive search of all other newspapers from that month, the letter has not been found. If Goldsmith deployed a pseudonym, as was often the case in the period, the letter, should it be extant, would prove very difficult to identify.

> the gratification of witnessing his own triumphs; of seeing in the plaudits, tears, or smiles of delighted spectators, the strongest testimony of his own powers. The author of a good book hears of his success, but the writer of a good play may night after night witness it.[58]

Added to this, one might also be aware of the considerable financial rewards on offer to a successful piece. The repertory system involved author benefit nights on the third, sixth, and ninth performance of a successful run, whereby the box office receipts less the costs of the house would go directly to the author, which meant that writing for the theatre could prove very rewarding indeed. Goldsmith had eked £60 from the sale of *The Vicar of Wakefield*, hardly a bonanza, and an amount dwarfed by the receipts from his plays. Little wonder that, later in the century, Elizabeth Inchbald would reflect disbelievingly on the sharp financial differences between prose fiction and the drama: 'I was ten months, unceasingly, finishing my novel ... My Health suffered much during this confinement, my spirits suffered more on Publication … and I have frequently obtained more pecunarary advantage by ten days Labour in the Dramatic way.'[59]

Moreover, theatre continued to be a remarkably fertile ground for the literary Irish diaspora. Congreve, Farquhar, Steele and Mary Davys had made a considerable success of the stage earlier in the century and Goldsmith's contemporaries continued this tradition. Writers such as Arthur Murphy, Charles Macklin, Bickerstaff, and, of particular interest to us here, Hugh Kelly had established themselves as London playwrights of note. Always motivated by both financial and reputational concerns and perhaps inspired by his Irish predecessors and contemporaries, it is little surprise then that Goldsmith sought to consolidate his newfound fame by turning to the drama sometime in late 1766 or early 1767, when he wrote his first comedy *The Good Natur'd Man*.

It was one thing, however, to write a comedy, and it was an entirely different proposition to secure its staging – as Goldsmith had noted presciently in his *Enquiry into the Present State of Polite Learning*.[60] Goldsmith, wary of Garrick, who had refused to support him for the position of Secretary to the Society of Arts and Sciences, eventually agreed after the intervention of Joshua Reynolds to a meeting with the

[58] *P*, II: 149–50.

[59] Letter from Inchbald to William Godwin, 3 November 1792. Bodleian Library, Oxford. MS Abinger c.1, fos. 116rv.

[60] 'Yet getting a play on even in three or four years, is a privilege reserved only for the happy few who have the arts of courting the manager as well as the muse: who have adulation to please his vanity, powerful patrons to support their merit, or money to indemnify disappointment. The poet must act like our beggars at Christmas, who lay the first shilling on the plate for themselves' (*CW*, I: 328).

Drury Lane manager.[61] But Garrick was unconvinced and dubious as to the play's prospects. Irate at Garrick's suggested changes to the text, Goldsmith sent the manuscript to George Colman, a former collaborator and employee of Garrick's, who had just acquired a quarter share in Covent Garden Theatre after the retirement of John Rich in 1767. Garrick had taken Colman's defection (and his subsequent poaching of William Powell, a leading actor) rather badly; as Garrick had not in fact rejected the play outright, the situation needed to be handled with some care and Goldsmith's letter to Garrick withdrawing the manuscript from consideration shows a degree of diplomacy and tact rarely remarked upon by contemporaries: 'As I found you had very great difficulties about that piece I complied with his desire, thinking it wrong to take up the attention of my friends with such petty concerns as mine or to load your good nature by a compliance rather with their requests than my merits' (Letter 24).[62] As it happens, Colman would be invited to join the Club just a couple of weeks after the first performance of *The Good Natur'd Man*, suggesting that Johnson had brought his influence to bear rather decisively.

The play was staged on 29 January 1768 against the stiff competition of Hugh Kelly's *False Delicacy*, which was proving an enormous success at Drury Lane. The opening night's audience grumbled at the bailiff scene, unwilling to accept the mixing of vulgar and polite society on the stage, and Goldsmith is supposed to have burst into tears after the opening night party held in his honour by the Club at the Turk's Head.[63] Yet, with ten performances that season (after the excision of the bailiff scene), which included three benefit nights for himself and one performance given by royal command (or command performance), Goldsmith had done quite well. The theatre critic at the *St. James's Chronicle* declared himself pleased and, in comparing Kelly's effort with that of Goldsmith, pre-empts the discussion around laughing and sentimental comedy more usually associated with *She Stoops to Conquer*: 'If the Drury-Lane Comedy is more refined, correct, and sentimental, the Covent-Garden Performance is more bold, more comick, and more characteristic; and if the former, from the chaste Accuracy and duly-tempered Spirit of the Author, has less Need of Pardon, the latter, from having hazarded more, has more Title to Mercy and Forgiveness.'[64]

Goldsmith was also better off to the tune of about £450, including the £50 he made for the play's copyright from William Griffin, a bookseller on Catherine Street on the Strand who played an important part in fostering and supporting Irish writers, a fact that seems to have incensed Goldsmith's nemesis Kenrick.

[61] Thomas Davies, *Memoirs of the Life of David Garrick*, 2 vols. (Boston: Wells and Lilly, 1818), II: 108–9.

[62] The 'desire' in question is that of John Beard, former acting manager of Covent Garden.

[63] For the play's critical reception see *CW*, V: 4–9.

[64] *St. James's Chronicle*, 30 January – 2 February 1768.

The failure of Kenrick's *The Widowed Wife* in 1768 contrasted with the warm reception of Goldsmith's comedy, Bickerstaff's opera *Lionel and Clarissa*, and Murphy's tragedy *Zenobia*, which, as Prior observed, 'seemed to throw the three departments of the drama exclusively into the hands of Irish writers' (*P*, II: 178) Incensed, Kenrick gnashed his teeth and rattled off the following parody of Dryden's 'Epigram on Milton':

> Poor Dryden! what a theme hadst thou,
> Compar'd with that which offers now?
> What are your Britons, Romans, Grecians,
> Compar'd with thorough-bred Milesians?
> Step into G--ff-n's shop, he'll tell ye
> Of G--ds--th, B--k-rs--ff, and K-ll-:
> Three poets of one age and nation,
> Whose more than mortal reputation,
> Mounting in trio to the skies,
> O'er Milton's fame and Virgil's flies;
> While, take one Irish evidence for t'other,
> Ev'n Homer's self is but their foster-brother.[65]

William Griffin would also publish multiple editions of *The Deserted Village* (1770) and the letters provide evidence that Griffin's shop was an important nodal point in Goldsmith's London life, at least after this major poetic success. While in Paris with the Hornecks, he asked Reynolds to check Griffin's shop for incoming letters as Griffin was about to publish the fifth edition of his major poem. Unlike the plays, *The Deserted Village* does not feature in his correspondence, partly a measure of the relative ease he had in getting it published when compared with the challenge of getting his comedies staged. Nonetheless, the publication of the poem, coming soon after the exhibition of Reynolds's portrait of him at the Royal Academy in April 1770, ensured that Goldsmith's star was well and truly in the ascendant.[66] Frances Reynolds candidly observed that it was 'the most flattered picture she ever knew her brother to have painted' and Goldsmith showed his appreciation by dedicating the poem to his dear friend.[67] The poem was an immediate and spectacular success, generating significant column inches in the periodical press as well as a host of responses by subsequent

[65] Kenrick, 'The Poetical Triumvirate. Written in the Year MDCCLXVII', *Poems; Ludicrous, Satirical and Moral* (London: Printed for J. Fletcher, [1768]), 269.

[66] *The Deserted Village* actually appeared on 26 May 1770, the final day of the Royal Academy exhibition.

[67] Cited in *W*, 200–1.

poets, confirming that it was a touchstone for later poets interested in exploring ideas of commercial development, agrarian life, luxury and colonialism.[68] Yet this literary success did not bring with it commensurate financial reward and Goldsmith again looked to the theatre.

She Stoops to Conquer has a remarkable pedigree in Irish theatre history. When Dublin's Gaiety Theatre first opened its doors in 1893, it was with a performance of Goldsmith's comedy. Likewise, when Smock Alley, another Dublin theatre dating from the seventeenth century, reopened in 2012, it too staged *She Stoops to Conquer*. More generally, there have been numerous productions of the play in recent years across the English-speaking world, cementing its status as one of the most popular plays of the eighteenth century. Yet Goldsmith's first reference to it in a September 1771 letter to Langton betrayed little confidence: 'It is not finished but when or how it will be acted, or whether it will be acted at all are questions I cannot resolve' (Letter 37).

Goldsmith's lack of *braggadocio* on the merits of his piece was justified, as various experiences in the run-up to its first performance on 15 March 1773 at Covent Garden testify. For one thing, it proved difficult for him and his friends to decide upon a title – the Larpent manuscript is titled 'The Novel or Mistakes of a Night' and this was just one of many that were considered and then jettisoned.[69] Colman's reaction to the script was decidedly lukewarm: he had only agreed to stage it after Johnson had 'prevailed on [him] at last by much solicitation, nay, a kind of force'.[70] Remarkably, Goldsmith had to write to Garrick yet again to withdraw his manuscript from consideration, although the Drury Lane manager does not seem to have been too upset, supplying, as he did, the prologue.[71] Colman's tepid attitude towards the new play manifested itself in a refusal to sanction expenditure on costumes and a reluctance to galvanize his actors for their parts. Moreover, the play was delayed until quite late in the season, diminishing its chances of a good run. Goldsmith's friend Arthur Murphy, as a letter to Joseph Cradock reveals, had let him down: he had supplied 'rather

68 See *CW*, IV: 277–80, for a survey of contemporary responses. The most notable responses to and re-imaginings of the poem include Philip Freneau, *The American Village* (1772); George Crabbe, *The Village* (1783); Hannah Cowley, *The Scottish Village* (1787); Thomas Dermody, *The Frequented Village* (1807); and, by Goldsmith's grand-nephew Oliver, *The Rising Village* (1825).

69 'The Old House a New Inn', and 'The Belle's Stratagem' were among those also considered. John Larpent (1741–1824) was from 1778 until his death 'examiner of plays', responsible for censoring plays with possible seditious or subversive content. With his wife Anna, he collected play manuscripts submitted for inspection after the Licensing Act of 1737. The Larpent Collection is now housed at the Huntington Library in California.

70 *Life of Johnson*, III: 208.

71 Garrick was also finally invited to become a member of the Club shortly after the performance.

the outline of an Epilogue than an Epilogue' (Letter 49). Despite all these negative auguries and practical obstacles, Goldsmith was determined to proceed. There is no mistaking the shift from authorial pride to outright desperation in his letter to Colman in January 1773. The letter recounts his indignant rejection of Garrick's proposal to have the derivative poet and playwright William Whitehead sit in judgement of the manuscript, but concludes: 'For God sake take the play and let us make the best of it, and let me have the same measure at least which you have given as bad plays as mine' (Letter 47). When it came to it, he found himself unable to attend the opening night (although his Club friends had mustered themselves in supportive numbers at the theatre). William Cooke's story has Goldsmith in St James's Park, too nervous to attend from the outset, before rushing to the theatre to arrive in the middle of the last act. Thankfully, there was no cause for alarm.

This time he wrote to Cradock with pride and relief in equal measure: 'The play has met with a success much beyond your expectations or mine' (Letter 49). The *Public Advertiser* was unequivocal:

> the Applause given to a new Piece on the first Evening of its Representation is sometimes supposed to be the Tribute of partial Friendship. The Approbation on the second Exhibition of Dr. Goldsmith's new Comedy exceeded that with which its first Appearance was attended. Uninterrupted laughter or clamourous Plaudits accompanied his Muse to the last Line of his Play ... the Theatre was filled with the loudest Acclamations that ever rung within its Walls.[72]

It was performed on twelve other nights that season, including a performance on 5 May 'By Command of their Majesties', and had subsequent performances at the Haymarket over the summer. Newspapers reported success around England, in Paris and even farther afield:

> There is hardly a town in England which boasts a play-house, or a village which has a theatrical barn in it, where Tony Lumpkin's drolleries have not been ha! ha'd! at this summer. In our American plantations also, has this mirth exciting comedy been performed. The New York papers, brought by Monday's mail, inform, that 'She Stoops to Conquer' was performed at the theatre in John-street, New York, by the American company, on the 2d of August last.[73]

Crucial to the play's positive reception was the perception that it had been responsible for 'raising the *laughing standard*'.[74] Although the extent to which Goldsmith's

[72] *Public Advertiser*, 17 March 1773.
[73] *Morning Chronicle*, 8 September 1773.
[74] *Morning Chronicle*, 24 April 1773.

comedy had actually done so has been queried by some recent criticism, it was certainly the position that Goldsmith presented to the London public.[75] In an act of canny marketing, Goldsmith published 'An Essay on the Theatre; or, a Comparison between Laughing and Sentimental Comedy' in the first number of the *Westminster Magazine* (1 January 1773), in which he warns against the generic miscegenation that mars much of contemporary sentimental comedy. In his view, such comedy is 'a kind of *mulish* production, with all the defects of its opposite parents, and marked with sterility' (*CW*, III: 213). With no little degree of serendipity, Goldsmith was also fortunate to be able to ride the coat-tails of Samuel Foote's celebrated *The Primitive Puppetshow* (Haymarket, 15 February 1773), which provided a rather caustic view on sentimentalism to a gleeful, if slightly frenzied, London audience, thereby opening the door for the appreciation of his 'laughing' comedy.[76]

She Stoops to Conquer generated just over £500 for Goldsmith on his three benefit nights. Although this was also good news for the Covent Garden coffers, there were personal repercussions for its manager. George Colman was subject to the press's scorn as his hesitation over the comedy – which Goldsmith was not shy about pointing out in the published version's dedication to Johnson – became known to the public. The abuse became so widespread that Colman was forced to retreat to Bath, where he wrote a pleading letter to Goldsmith beseeching him to take him off 'the rack of the Newspapers' (*CW*, V: 101). One wag, for example, trilled mockingly:

> Come, Coley, doff those mourning weeds,
> Nor thus with jokes be flamm'd;
> Tho' Goldsmith's present play succeeds,
> His next may still be damn'd[77]

The letter to Cradock in this edition restores Goldsmith's rather gleeful 'The news papers are now abusing Colman to some purpose' (Letter 49). Evidently, Cradock, who first published the version on which Balderston was obliged to rely, felt that this line revealed a rather vindictive side of Goldsmith that he would rather suppress. He further removed what he felt was a disparaging reference to John Quick, whom no-one, according to Goldsmith, would think of as worthy of delivering the epilogue. Cradock was a little precious, however, as it seems only fair comment to

75 See 'Goldsmith and Sheridan and the Supposed Revolution of "Laughing" and "Sentimental" Comedy', in Robert Hume, *The Rakish Stage: Studies in English Drama 1660–1800* (Carbondale: Southern Illinois University Press, 1983), 312–58.

76 'The Novelty of [the *Primitive Puppet Show*] brought such a crowd to see it that the Haymarket was impassable for above an hour; the doors of the theatre were broke open, and great numbers entered the house without paying any thing for their admission. Several hats, swords, canes, cloaks, &c. were lost among the mob; three ladies fainted away, and a girl had her arm broke in endeavouring to get into the pit': *Gentleman's Magazine* 43 (February 1773), 101.

77 Cited in *W*, 239.

observe that a junior actor – as Quick then was – would not be best placed to perform this prominent task. The architect William Chambers wrote to Goldsmith to congratulate him on the success of the comedy, but he too felt Quick's Lumpkin 'suffers considerably by bad acting'. By the time Cradock began to publish his *Memoirs*, however, Quick had become a theatrical institution. He had first come to public attention through a successful new production of Charles Macklin's *Love à la Mode* in 1767, and had used the part of Tony Lumpkin to consolidate his fame.[78] In any case, Goldsmith was certainly extremely grateful to Quick for his efforts and adapted, as a one-act farce, Charles Sedley's three-act comedy *The Grumbler* for his benefit night some weeks later.[79]

William Kenrick – whose sheer doggedness in hectoring Goldsmith might at least win grudging admiration – felt the need to take him down a peg or two with his attack in the *London Packet*, in which he described the comedy as a '*speaking pantomime*'. But Kenrick's was almost a lone voice. Northumberland wrote to Goldsmith looking for free tickets, and James Boswell, in a carefully contrived missive, wrote to him in what appears to be a flagrant attempt to harvest a letter for literary posterity. In some ways, given their difficult relationship, Boswell's tacit admission that the play was a roaring success gives us the most explicit evidence that contemporaries immediately appreciated the comedy's canonical status. Boswell's letter continues in a remarkably friendly fashion – bordering even on sycophancy – and he manages to refer to the play in all three paragraphs in his desire to elicit a response, even drawing parallels between the arrival of his new daughter and the reinvigoration of the comic strain: 'My little daughter is a fine healthy lively child, and I flatter myself shall be blest with the cheerfullness of your Comick Muse. She has nothing of that wretched whining and crying which we see children so often have; nothing of the *Comedie Larmoyante*.'[80]

The extant letters around *She Stoops to Conquer* offer us a sense of the regard it generated within his own circle. Yet Goldsmith's response to Boswell goes beyond coy modesty. There is an unmistakably bitter vehemence to his insistence 'that the

[78] He would go on to play important parts in Sheridan's *The Rivals* (1775) and *The Duenna* (1776). John O'Keeffe, 'the English Moliere' according to Hazlitt, also made his name acting the part of Tony Lumpkin in Ireland before penning a sequel titled *Tony Lumpkin in Town* (1774) that grabbed the attention of George Colman sufficiently for him to invite O'Keeffe to London.

[79] *The Grumbler* was performed at Covent Garden for one night only on 8 May as an afterpiece to *King Lear*. Quick benefited by £87 6d. Sedley's three-act version (printed posthumously in 1722) was itself a translation of the French original by David-Augustin de Brueys and Jean de Palaprat. See the introduction to Alice Perry, ed., *The Grumbler* (Cambridge, MA: Harvard University Press, 1931) for an account.

[80] *The Correspondence of James Boswell with Certain Members of the Club*, ed. Charles N. Fifer (London and New York: Heinemann and McGraw-Hill, 1976), 25.

stage earning is the dirtiest money that ever a poor poet put in his pocket'. At the moment of his greatest success, he remained firm in marking himself as outside the normal patterns of human sociability, in contrast to the comfort of Boswell's domestic life and indeed the lives of his other friends:

> When I see you in town, and I shall take care to let Johnson, Garrick, and Reynolds know of the expected happiness I will then tell you long stories about my struggles and escapes, for as all of you are safely retired from the shock of criticism to enjoy much better comforts in a domestic life, I am still left the only poet militant here, and in truth I am very likely to be militant till I die, nor have I even the prospect of an hospital to retire to. (Letter 54)

Goldsmith's underlining of 'poet militant' calls our attention to an implied self-comparison with Alexander Pope, a writer he admired enormously.[81] Having recently used Pope's letters extensively in 'The Life of Dr. Parnell' (1770), it seems Goldsmith was taken with Pope's expression of mock petulance to John Gay: 'I am piqued with envy and jealousy at you, and hate you as much as if you had a great place at court; which you will confess a proper cause of envy and hatred, in any Poet militant or unpensioned'.[82] Sardonicism and self-pity mingle here with a very real concern over his parlous financial position: Goldsmith was, at this stage, very much aware of his own weakness in fiscal matters as well as the vagaries of the literary world and its income streams. Such tones and themes can also be detected in his posthumous *Retaliation*, an underappreciated poetic survey of Goldsmith's social circle and an appropriate sign-off from the peripheral insider.

The letters of Goldsmith's final years show no abatement in the range and ambition of his literary projects. He lent books to Hester Thrale Piozzi and it appears that he continued to collaborate with Thomas Percy, sharing at least some initial thoughts on an Irish edition of the *Spectator*. He wrote a letter of introduction for historian John Andrews to publisher John Nourse, and there is an intriguing letter to Garrick to thank him for recruiting Charles Burney for a grand editorial project. According to Burney, Goldsmith planned a 'Dictionary of the Arts and Sciences' 'on the model of the French Encyclopedia' and had also signed up Burke, Reynolds, Garrick and Johnson to contribute articles.[83] Buoyed by the completion and anticipated success of his *History of the Earth, and Animated Nature* (1774), Goldsmith must have seen in this project an opportunity to bring together his literary brilliance with his indefatigable and painstaking talent for compilation

[81] In *The Beauties of English Poesy*, he suggests that *The Rape of the Lock* may be 'the most perfect [poem] in our language' (*CW*, V: 319).

[82] *The Correspondence of Alexander Pope*, ed. George Sherburn, 5 vols. (Oxford: Clarendon Press, 1956), III: 121.

[83] Frances Burney, *Memoirs of Doctor Burney*, 3 vols. (London: Edward Moxon, 1832), I: 271.

and assembly in what would be a synthesis of his polymathic Enlightenment credentials. On a practical note, he had also seen the success of his fellow Irishman, Temple Henry Croker, who had published *The Complete Dictionary of Arts and Sciences* (1766) in three folio volumes. Croker's work had attracted the support of well over a thousand subscribers from all over England and had been printed in London, Cambridge and Dublin. Goldsmith might have imagined such a literary project yielding the financial as well as reputational rewards that could have secured his past, present and future across both Britain and Ireland.

He was dead ten months later, at the age of 45. His demise on 4 April 1774 was ironically hastened by a poor medical decision he took to disregard an experienced apothecary's advice and take large quantities of a quack emetic. When asked whether his mind was at ease, he is supposed to have replied, with his last words, 'No, it is not', less a précis of his literary career, one might imagine, than testimony to his distressed physical state. His friends took the news hard, with Burke breaking down in tears and Reynolds too forlorn to paint for the day when he heard. Even Boswell wrote to Garrick to say 'I have not been much so much affected with any event that has happened of a long time', while Johnson wrote to Bennet Langton: 'Let not his frailties be remembred. He was a very great Man'.[84] William Kenrick was less magnanimous:

By his own Art who justly died
A blundering, artless Suicide;
Share, Earth-worms share, since now he's dead,
His megrim, Maggot-bitten head.[85]

Goldsmith's debts were estimated at about £2,000 which prohibited the large public funeral that Reynolds had initially planned. Goldsmith was buried privately on 9 April at the Temple Burying Ground with only a few close friends in attendance, including his erstwhile rival, Hugh Kelly. Mary Horneck, rather sweetly, requested a lock of his hair as a memento. His friends did organize a monument in Westminster Abbey, for which Johnson wrote a Latin inscription which described him as a 'Poet, Natural Philosopher, Historian / Who left no species of writing untouched'. Obituaries, anecdotes and tributes subsequently began to appear in the press in London and in Dublin. The work of documenting the life of arguably the only eighteenth-century writer who can claim to have produced masterpieces – recognized equally today as they were then – in prose fiction, drama and poetry had begun.

[84] *Correspondence of James Boswell with David Garrick, Edmund Burke, and Edmond Malone*, ed. Peter S. Baker, Thomas W. Copeland, George M. Kahrl, Rachel McClellan and James M. Osborn, with the assistance of Robert Makin and Mark Wolleager (London and New York: Heinemann and McGraw-Hill, 1987), 60; *Letters of Samuel Johnson*, II: 147.

[85] Kenrick, '*On Dr.* Goldsmith', in T. Webb, ed., *A New Select Collection of Epitaphs*, 2 vols. (London: Printed for S. Bladon, 1775), 109.

A NOTE ON THE EDITION

This edition is built on the remarkable endeavours of Katharine C. Balderston. We hope that it is an appropriate advancement on her pioneering scholarship as it seeks to situate Goldsmith's letters in a modern editorial context and to reorient approaches to his life and work.

This volume can be distinguished from Balderston's in a number of ways. Firstly, our edition has sixty-six letters to Balderston's fifty-three. The thirteen additional letters in our edition include three letters published here for the first time (Letters 40, 59 and 66); six letters which, for various reasons, were published after Balderston's edition (Letters 20, 21, 28, 51, 52 and 54); one letter that Balderston categorized as doubtful but which we can now confirm (Letter 56); and three letters to newspapers (Letters 18, 25 and 53). Secondly, we have eschewed the inclusion of seven other 'Doubtful Letters' and 'Mrs Hodson's Narrative' – the account of Goldsmith's early life sent to Thomas Percy by Goldsmith's sister – as appendices. Thirdly, although the majority of letters in both editions share copy-texts, there are a few instances where we have been able to locate manuscripts that Balderston could not, and indeed some cases where the reverse is true.

We have also included a brief contextual headnote to introduce each letter: the aim is to provide a succinct situation of the letter within Goldsmith's circle of acquaintance and his personal circumstances at the moment of composition. Moreover, we have included correspondence directly related to letters written by Goldsmith, when available. This seemed to us the most appropriate and engaging way to manage the limited corpus. There are a small number of letters for which we suggest a different date from Balderston: in such cases, an explanation is offered in the headnote.

The letters are presented here in chronological order. Each letter is headed with the addressee, the date, and the place of writing. Although Goldsmith omitted to include a date in many of his letters, we have been able to establish dates for most on the basis of the letter's content, postmarks, associated incoming correspondence, or other external evidence. Where dates and the location from which the letters were written are uncertain, we indicate this by placing our estimation in square brackets and a rationale in the headnote.

We use the original manuscript for each letter as our source text except when it is lost or no longer extant. We have preserved Goldsmith's spelling and punctuation. False starts and slips of the pen are ignored but significant authorial deletions are shown as strikethrough text. Interlineations and insertions have been incorporated into the main text as per Goldsmith's intentions and we have included words that were scored out by Goldsmith where legible, marking them struck-through. Superscript has been rendered as such. Salutations, closes and signatures have all been rendered approximately as they appear in the original. Headnotes provide biographical and contextual information on the recipient and their relationship to Goldsmith. They also give the following information on the letter insofar as it is available: the copy-text; its first publication; the addressee; postmarks; any pertinent information on the letter's provenance; a comment on the suggested dating; and explanatory and contextual information designed to assist in the understanding of the letter.

Goldsmith's letters vary considerably in length and presentation. There are a number of substantial earlier letters where we get a sense of his exilic sensibility; equally, there are many which comprise just a line or two. His writing can occasionally be hurried but it is generally in a legible hand. Letters tend to appear in clusters that can be associated with particular texts: *An Enquiry into the Present State of Polite Learning in Europe*, *The Good Natur'd Man* and *She Stoops to Conquer* provide the most salient examples.

CHRONOLOGY OF GOLDSMITH'S LIFE AND WORKS

1728 Birth, apparently on 10 November, of Oliver Goldsmith, probably at Pallas, Co. Westmeath, Ireland, fifth child and second son of the Anglican minister the Reverend Charles Goldsmith (*c.* 1693–1747) and Ann Jones (*c.* 1697–1770), daughter of the Reverend Oliver Jones, after whom Goldsmith is named. Charles Goldsmith's sister Jane marries Thomas Contarine (*c.* 1684 – *c.* 1758), a clergyman of Venetian descent who would be a constant support to his nephew Oliver throughout his early years. Contarine's daughter Jane goes on to marry James Lawder.

Oliver's older sister Margaret (b. 1719) dies in childhood. His older sister Catherine (b. 1721) goes on to marry Daniel Hodson, while his older brother Henry (b. 1722) goes on to become a clergyman. Henry's twin sister is Jane. His younger brother Maurice is born in 1736. Charles is born in 1737; John or 'Jack' (b. 1740) dies young.

Charles Goldsmith is appointed curate in Kilkenny West shortly after Oliver's birth. The Goldsmiths subsequently move to Lissoy, to the southeast of Pallas, along the Longford/Westmeath border.

1735–45 Goldsmith is educated through various diocesan schools in the Longford/Roscommon region.

1745–50 Goldsmith studies at Trinity College Dublin. It is a largely unhappy experience but he graduates with a BA in February 1750.

1750–2 Goldsmith works as a tutor in Roscommon. Various efforts are made to emigrate to America and to London but with no success.

1752–4 Goldsmith reads medicine at the University of Edinburgh with financial assistance from relatives, including brother-in-law Daniel Hodson and uncle Thomas Contarine.

1754–5 Goldsmith continues his medical studies at Leiden University in Holland.

1755–6 Goldsmith journeys around Europe, largely on foot, debating and playing music to support himself. He visits Flanders, France, Germany, Switzerland and Italy.

1756–7 Goldsmith arrives in London in February 1756. He works at various jobs: as an assistant to an apothecary, as a physician in Southwark, and as an usher at a boys' school in Peckham in Surrey. He may also have been a proof-reader in Samuel Richardson's printing-house. In 1757 he begins work at the *Monthly Review*, edited by Ralph Griffiths.

1758 Goldsmith plans to travel to Coromandel, on the south-eastern coast of the Indian subcontinent, as a physician with the East India Company but his application to work as a hospital mate is unsuccessful.

1759 Goldsmith begins to contribute, in January, to Tobias Smollett's *Critical Review.* Following the publication of *An Enquiry into the Present State of Polite Learning in Europe* in April, Goldsmith's literary acquaintance comes to include Thomas Percy, Edmund Burke and Samuel Johnson. However, the work is savagely reviewed by William Kenrick, the first attack of a long-running feud. Goldsmith seeks a number of Irish subscriptions for the *Enquiry.* He writes the *Bee*, his own periodical, between October and November.

1759–61 Goldsmith writes essays for a number of periodicals: the *Busy Body*, the *Weekly Magazine*, the *Royal Magazine* and the *Lady's Magazine*. Meets Reverend Thomas Percy. In January 1760 he begins his Chinese letters series in the *Public Ledger*, published by John Newbery. The series continues until August 1761. Goldsmith writes *The Vicar of Wakefield* between 1760 and 1762.

1762 Goldsmith contributes essays to *Lloyd's Evening Post*. His Chinese letters are published as *The Citizen of the World* in May. Newbery contracts him to write what would become *A Survey of Experimental Philosophy*, eventually published two years after the author's death. This work prompts a shift in his writing towards history and popular science. Newbery publishes Plutarch's *Lives*, which Goldsmith had completed with translator Joseph Collyer, and *The Life of Richard Nash*. After some effort by Johnson, Newbery also acquires the rights for Goldsmith's novel *The Vicar of Wakefield*: he promptly resells a third share of the rights to Benjamin Collins and another third to William Strahan.

1764 Goldsmith becomes a founding member, with Joshua Reynolds, Samuel Johnson, David Garrick, Edmund Burke, Christopher Nugent, and others, of the Literary Club. He publishes *An History of England, in a Series of Letters from a Nobleman to his Son* and composes an oratorio libretto titled *The Captivity*. Newbery publishes his major poem *The Traveller, or a Prospect of Society*, dedicated to his brother Henry, in December: it is the first work published under Goldsmith's own name.

1766 *The Vicar of Wakefield* is published in March. Goldsmith develops a friendship with the Horneck sisters, Catherine and Mary, through Joshua Reynolds.

1767 Goldsmith's comedy, *The Good Natur'd Man*, is submitted to George Colman after David Garrick is equivocal about the play's prospects. Goldsmith rebuts an accusation of plagiarism made by Kenrick in a letter to *St. James's Chronicle.*

1768 *The Good Natur'd Man* is performed at Covent Garden in January. Johnson supplies the prologue. William Griffin publishes the play in February. Goldsmith's brother Henry dies in May.

1769 William Griffin contracts Goldsmith to write a natural history. His *Roman History* is published in May. He is appointed Professor of Ancient History at the Royal Academy.

1770 *The Deserted Village* is published in May. It is dedicated to Sir Joshua Reynolds. William Hodson, son of Daniel, arrives in London. Goldsmith tries to find his nephew a place. Goldsmith spends six weeks in France with the Horneck sisters and their mother.

1771 Goldsmith's *History of England, from the Earliest Times to the Death of George II* is published in August. He begins to write *She Stoops to Conquer.*

1772 Goldsmith writes *Threnodia Augustalis* in memory of the Princess Dowager, Augusta, which is performed in February.

1773 *She Stoops to Conquer* is performed at Covent Garden on 15 March with David Garrick providing the prologue. Goldsmith is invited to produce an Irish edition of the *Spectator*. He assaults Thomas Evans in response to an *ad hominem* attack in the *London Packet.* He solicits contributors for a planned 'Dictionary of the Arts and Sciences'.

1774 Goldsmith dies on 4 April having suffered renal infection and fever. His poem *Retaliation*, a satiric riposte to some teasing he received at the Literary Club earlier that year, is published a fortnight after his death. John Nourse publishes Goldsmith's *History of the Earth, and Animated Nature* in July. His *Grecian History* is published shortly after. The second edition of his *History of England* is announced in December.

1776 Goldsmith's *A Survey of Experimental Philosophy*, a two-volume compendium of science, is published. His friends arrange for a monument to be erected in his memory at Westminster Abbey.

LETTERS

1

To Daniel Hodson

[Edinburgh, October–November 1752]

Daniel Hodson, the son of 'a gentleman of good property' from St John's in Roscommon, near Athlone, was Goldsmith's brother-in-law.[1] He eloped with Catherine Goldsmith in 1744, and in so doing occasioned a withdrawal of financial support for Goldsmith's studies at Trinity College Dublin. Hodson was at the time of the elopement a young student of Goldsmith's brother Henry, then curate and teacher at Pallas. Both families were initially aggrieved at the elopement, but would eventually make a settlement. Charles Goldsmith legally engaged himself on 7 September 1744 to pay Hodson £400 in dowry. The Hodsons would earn £40 a year in income from the Lissoy farmland, and £12 in tithes until the Goldsmiths could pay the £400. As a result of this diversion of funds, Goldsmith was admitted to Trinity as a sizar rather than as a pensioner. This letter appears to be the first that Goldsmith sent home to Ireland following his entry to the medical school at the University of Edinburgh in October 1752. It also indicates that, while studying at Edinburgh, Goldsmith's uncle Thomas Contarine would furnish him with £10 a year. The Hodsons and Henry Goldsmith would supply him with £15 between them.

The copy-text is the manuscript in the Huntington Library, California. It was first published by Balderston in 1928. The manuscript is in very bad condition, substantially torn and obscured (see Figure 2). Missing passages were conjecturally added by Balderston, based on the amount of space obscured and the context. We include her suggested insertions.

[__] ance, This country has little or nothing [which I can] give an account of so instead of a D[escription of the] country you must be contented with [an account of the] manner in which I spend my Time, [during the] day I am obligd to attend the Publick L[ectures. At night] I am in my Lodging I have hardly an[y other s]ociety but a Folio book a skeleton my cat and my meagre landlady I pay 22£6 per am[2] for Diet washing and Lodging being the cheapest that is to be got in Edinburgh all things here being much dearer than in Ireland as money is made more Plenty by the Last Rebellion I read hard which is a thing I never could do when the study was displea[s]ing. I have [_______] to three Professors,[3] and bought som[e_______]value of about three more which I w[as___] obligd to buy, besides some cloath[s[4]_______]

My Dr Dan my Freinds sent four guin[eas______] but as I have been promisd fifteen [_______] by my Freinds Exclusive of my Un[cle____] drawn on Mr Constable for ten poun[ds_________ gener]ously contributed to make mine happy [______]

My Dr Brother your afft Freind
Oliver Goldsmith

[______e]very Freind [__] as [____] particularly [me]ntiond Each, there is one on whom I never think without affliction but conceal it from him

Direct to me at Surgeon Sincl[a]irs in the Trunk Close Edinburgh[5]

1 J. J. Kelly, 'The Early Haunts of Oliver Goldsmith', *The Irish Monthly* 7 (1879), 199.

2 £22 6s. The high rent was a consequence of an economic dividend following the defeat of the Jacobite rebellion of 1745, as Goldsmith suggests below. Balderston transcribed this as '22Lb'.

3 Alexander Monro, Andrew Plummer and Charles Alston. Goldsmith elaborates on the qualities of each professor in the following letter.

4 A tailor's account beginning on 24 January 1753 is in the Centre for Research Collections, Edinburgh University Library, La.II.195. It refers to Goldsmith's purchases of drapery materials including white and 'sky-Blew' sattins, shalloons, allapeens, durants, silks and fustians. Goldsmith's debt to this tailor is increased in February and November 1753, amounting to £5 15s 4½d by the year's end, a considerable amount. His tastes in fabrics and clothes were, regardless of his fluctuating circumstances and financial dependencies, extravagant then and later.

5 Trunk Close, or Trunk's Close, was a courtyard near the crossing of Edinburgh's Royal Mile with Leith Wynd. See site no. 48 on William Edgar's 1742 map of Edinburgh (Figure 2).

2

To the Reverend Thomas Contarine

Edinburgh, 8 May 1753

An uncle by marriage, the Reverend Thomas Contarine (*c.* 1684–1758) was also Goldsmith's most reliable financial support while the latter was a student in Dublin, in Edinburgh, and during his Continental travels. The grandson of a Contarini of Venice – one of the city's most noble families, contributing several Doges of the Venetian Republic – Contarine married Charles Goldsmith's sister Jane and became prebend of Oran, near Elphin, where he had a reasonable living, and kept a good library (which was at the disposal of his nephew while he was a student). According to an anecdote and memoir of Berkeley with which Goldsmith furnished the *Weekly Magazine* (1759–60), Contarine recounted to the author (Goldsmith) his witnessing of Berkeley's experimental and dangerous investigation of the effects of hanging in his rooms at Trinity. Much respected in the region, Contarine was also friendly with Charles O'Conor (1710–91), the antiquarian and historian of Gaelic Ireland, at whose house a very young Goldsmith may have met the harper Turlough O'Carolan (1670–1738), about whom Goldsmith would write an essay for the *British Magazine* in July 1760. Contarine's daughter Jane, later Jane Lawder (see Letter 10), would also be a correspondent of Goldsmith's, and he relays his love for his cousin and her husband in his first postscript below.

The copy-text is a facsimile photostat of the manuscript in the Huntington Library, California. The present location of the original manuscript is unknown. It was first published by Prior in 1837. It is addressed 'To | The Rev^{d}. M^{r}. Thos: Contarine | at Kilmore near Carick on | shannon in | Ireland. [Via] London' and postmarked 14 May.

May 8th 1753

My Dr Uncle

In your letter (the only one I receivd from Kilmore) you call me the Philosopher who carries all his goods about him yet how can Such a character fit me who have le[f]t behind in Ireland Every thing I think worth posessing freinds that I love and a Society that pleasd while it instructed, who but must regret the Loss of such Enjoyments who but must regret his abscence from [Ki]lmore that Ever knew i[t] as I did, here as recluse as the Turkish Spy at Parris[1] I am almost unknown to Every body Except some few who attend the Proffesors of Physick as I do, apropos I shall give you the Professors names and as far ~~much~~ as occurs to me their characters and first as most Deserving Mr Monro[2] Professor of anatomy this man has broght the science he Teaches to as much perfection as ~~he~~ it is capable of and not content with barely Teaching anatomy he launches out into all the branches of Physick where all his remarks are new and usefull tis he I may venture to say that draws hither such a number of stu[dents] from most parts of the world Even from Russia, he is [not] only a skilfull Physician but an able Orator and delivers things in the[ir] nature abstruse in s[o] Easy a ma[n]ner that the most unlearn'd may, must understand him, Plumer Professor of chymistry understands his busines well b[u]t delivers himself so ill that He is but little regarded, Alston Professor of Materia medica speaks much but little to the purpose, the

Professors of Theory and Practice say nothing bu[t] what we may find in the books laid before us and speak that in s[o] droneing and heavy a manner that their hearers are not many degrees in a better state than their Patients you see then D^r S^r that monro is the only great man among them so that I intend to hear him another win[t]er and go then to hear Albinus the great Professo[r] at Leyden.[3] I read a science [th]e most Pleasing in nature so that my labours [a]re but a relaxation and I may Truly say the only thing here that gives me Pleasure how I enjoy th[e] Pl[easing] hope of [returni]ng with [skill, and to] find my Freinds stand in no need of my assistance how many happy years do I wish you, and nothing but want of health can take from your happynes since you so well Pursue the paths that conduct to Virtue

I am My Dr Uncle your most oblig^d.
most^t affectionate Nephew
Oliver Goldsmith

PS I draw this time for Six pounds and will draw next october but for four as I was obligd to buy Every thing sinc[e I came to Scot]land Shirts [n]ot Eve[n] Excepted I am a [li]ttle more early ~~than~~ the first year than I shall be for the future for I abso[lu]tely will not Trouble you before the Time heraft[er].

My Best love attend M^r [a]nd Mrs Lawder and heaven preserve them. I am again your Dutifull nephew OG

I have been a month in the Higlands I set out the first day on foot but an ill naturd corn I have got on my Toe has for the future prevented that cheap method of Travelling so the second day I hired a horse of about the size of a ram and he walkd away (Trot he could not) as pensive as his master in 3 days we reachd the Highlands this letter wod be too long ~~to contain~~ if it containd the description I intend giving of that country so shall make it the subject of my next[4]

[1] Originally published in 1684, *L'Espion Turc* was composed by Giovanni Paola Marana, a Genoese political refugee in the French court of Louis XIV, and published several times in translation through the following decades as *The Eighte Volumes of Letters Writ by a Turkish Spy, who liv'd five and forty years, undiscover'd at Paris.* Marana's work was an inspiration for

Montesquieu's *Lettres Persanes* (1721) and Goldsmith's Chinese letters, collected as *The Citizen of the World* (1762).

2 Alexander Monro (1697–1767), surgeon and the first Professor of Anatomy at Edinburgh, and a founder of the Edinburgh medical school. Apprenticed in 1713 to his father, the surgeon John Monro, the younger Monro enrolled in November 1718 as a student at the University of Leiden where he studied clinical medicine and chemistry under Herman Boerhaave. He did not take a degree at Leiden; returning to Edinburgh in 1719, he took up a professorship in anatomy which had been established in 1705 by Edinburgh's town council. With his appointment, the position would become more closely associated with the foundation of a medical school. Monro offered a yearly course on anatomy between 1720 and 1758. By 1751, his popularity as a teacher was such – his style was compelling, non-dogmatic and he taught in English rather than in Latin – that his enrolment neared 200 students of several nationalities. Monro's annual lectures lasted from October to May. See introduction, xxv–xxvi.

3 Andrew Plummer (1697–1756); Plummer was from 1733 the chief teacher of chemistry and chemical pharmacy at the University of Edinburgh. He invented – and his wealth was greatly enhanced by – a widely used 'Plummer's Pill', consisting of a mixture of mercury chloride with antinomy sulphide and guaiacum (a tropical flowering plant) which was originally intended for the treatment of psoriasis, but would eventually be used against syphilis, leprosy, and other causes of lesions and ulceration. Whatever his successes with his famous pill, Goldsmith obviously thought little of his teaching. The doctor and naturalist John Fothergill praised his 'universal knowledge' but conceded that his 'diffidence' hobbled his lecturing style, which was 'Laborious, attentive, and exact'. His modesty was such that 'he spoke to young audiences, upon a subject he was perfectly master of, not without hesitation': Fothergill, *A Complete Collection of the Medical and Philosophical Works* (London: Printed for John Walker, 1781), 643.
Charles Alston (1685–1760) was a physician, botanist and the first professor of botany and *materia medica* at Edinburgh. Born at Eddlewood in the parish of Hamilton, Lanarkshire, Alston entered the University of Glasgow in 1700 but could not graduate because of financial difficulties after the death of his father. He became a servant in the household of the Duchess of Hamilton. After the Jacobite rising of 1715 caused the superintendent of the physic garden at Holyrood to flee, the duchess had him installed in the vacant post. With further application he became King's botanist, a post which he would hold for life. To formalize his qualifications, he returned to Glasgow University and studied for a year under Boerhaave in Leiden in 1718–19. While at Leiden, Alston befriended Monro, and a connection was formed which made possible his teaching post at Edinburgh. Among Alston's key published works were his three dissertations on quick-lime and lime-water (1752, 1755, 1757), *A Dissertation on Botany* (1754) and *Lectures on Materia Medica*, 2 vols. (1770).
Bernard-Siegfried Albinus (1697–1770), German-Dutch anatomist and son of the highly regarded Bernard Albinus (1653–1753). The older Albinus was professor of medicine in Frankfurt before moving to Leiden in 1702, where in 1709 his son would take up his medical and anatomical studies – aged just 12 – under Boerhaave. Albinus would in 1721 succeed his own father as Professor of Anatomy and Surgery, and in 1745 became Professor of the Practice of Medicine. He was a pioneer in the study of the mechanical structure of the skeletal and muscular systems. Alongside Monro, Albinus would become one of the most famous teachers of anatomy in Europe. His works included *Historia Musculorum Hominis* (1734), *Icones Ossium Foetus Humani* (1737), and *Tabulae Sceleti et Musculorum Corporis Humani* (1747). *The Explanation of Albinus's Anatomical Figures of the Human Skeleton and Muscles. With an Historical Account of the Work,* a translation from the Latin of some of his key ideas, was published in London in 1754.

4 The paragraph describing the sojourn in the Highlands is on a separate sheet of paper which suggests that it was added at the end of the trip. The letter referred to is now lost.

3

To Robert Bryanton

Edinburgh, 26 September 1753

Originally from Ballymahon, Co. Longford, Robert Bryanton was a schoolmate of Goldsmith's and subsequently a fellow student at Trinity College Dublin, where he matriculated on 18 November 1746, aged 15, and graduated BA in 1751. The two were also, as indicated here, part of the same social circle at George Conway's inn in Lissoy, a possible model for the Three Jolly Pigeons in *She Stoops to Conquer*. The letter contains rare references to Goldsmith's mother – with whom he seems to have had a fraught relationship before leaving Ireland, probably because of his wayward behaviour – in its opening and in its postscript.

The copy-text is a contemporary copy in an unknown hand of the letter sent to Thomas Percy by Goldsmith's brother Maurice, now in the British Library. It was first published by Percy in 1801. It is addressed to 'Ballymahon | Ireland' (some of the address is torn away). 'Via London' is also written beside the address. Prior printed from another – corrected – copy in his 1837 biography (*P*, I: 139–45). Balderston proposes that Percy's transcript was the most literal; we follow this principle in using it as our copy-text, with words struck through re-introduced. Significant variations from Prior are indicated in the notes below. Towards the end of the letter, sections of lines are missing. Balderston supplies those parts from Prior's suggestions, with some changes. We do likewise, indicating in the notes where those differences occur.

William Shaw Mason refers to a copy in an unknown hand then in the possession of one Mrs McDermott of Ballymahon, which may be the copy now in the library of Trinity College Dublin. This copy also appears to have been the source of the first printed version of the letter published in Dublin in *Anthologia Hibernica* 1 (January–June 1793), 92–4.[1]

My dear Bob — Edinburgh, Sepr ye 26th 1753

How many good excuses (and you know I was ever good at an excuse) might I call up to vindicate my past shamefull silence? I might tell how I wrote a long letter at my first comeing hither, and seem vastly angry at not receiveing an answer; or I might alledge that business, (with business, you know I was always pester'd) had never given me time to finger a pen; but I supress these, & twenty, more, equally plausible[2] & as easily invented, since they might all be attended with a slight inconvenience of being known to be lies; let me then speak truth; An hereditary indolence (I have it from the Mothers side) has hitherto prevented my writing to you, and still prevents my writing at least twenty five letters more, due to my friends in Ireland—no turnspit[3] gets up into his wheel with more reluctance, than I sit down to write, yet no dog ever loved the roast meat ~~meal better th~~ he turns, better than I do him I now address;[4] yet what shall I say now I am enter'd? shall I tire you with a description of this unfruitfull country? where I must lead you over their hills all brown with heath, or their valleys scarce able to feed a rabbit? Man alone seems to be the only creature who has arived to the naturall size in this poor soil; every part of the country presents the same dismall landscape, no grove nor brook lend their musick to cheer the stranger, or make the inhabitants forget their ~~misery~~ poverty; yet with all these disadvantages to call him down to humility, a Scotchman is one of the proudest things alive. the poor have pride ever ready to releive them; if mankind shou'd happen to despise them, they are masters of their own admiration. and that they can plentifully bestow on themselves:[5] from their pride and poverty as I take it results one advantage this country enjoys, namely the Gentlemen here are much better bred, then among us; no such character here as our Fox hunter and they have expresed great surprize when I informed them that some men of a thousand pound a year in Ireland spend their whole lives in runing after a hare, drinking to be drunk, and geting every Girl with Child, that will let them; and truly if such a being, equiped in his hunting dress, came among a circle of scots Gentlemen,[6] they wou'd behold him with the same astonishment that a Country man does King George on horseback;[7] the men here have Gennerally high cheek bones, and are lean, and swarthy; fond of action; Danceing in particular: tho' now I have mention'd danceing, let me say something of their balls which are very frequent here; when a stranger enters the danceing-hall he sees one end of the room taken up by the Lady's, who sit dismally in a Groupe by themselves on the other end stand their pensive partners, that are to be, but no more intercourse between the sexes than there is between two Countrys at war, the Lady's indeed may ogle and the Gentlemen sigh, but an embargo is laid on any ~~other~~ closer commerce; at length, to interrupt hostility's, the Lady directeress or intendant, or what you will pitches on a Gentleman & Lady to walk a minuet, which they perform with a formality that aproaches despondence, after five or six couple have thus walked the Gauntlett, all stand up to country dance's, each gentleman furnished with a partner from the afforesaid Lady directress, so they dance much, say nothing, and thus concludes our assembly; I told a scotch Gentleman that such a profound silence resembled the ancient procession of the Roman Matrons in honour of Ceres[8] and the scotch Gentleman told me (and faith I believe he was right) that I was a very great pedant for my pains:[9] now I am come to the Lady's and to shew that I love scotland and every thing that belongs to so charming a Country Il insist on it and will give him leave to break my head that deny's it that the scotch ladys are ten thousand times finer and handsomer than the Irish to be sure now I see y^m. Sisters Betty & Peggy vastly surprized at my Partiality but tell y^m flatly I don't value them or their fine skins or Eyes or good sense or—a potatoe for I say it and and will maintain it and as a convinceing proof of (I am in a very great passion) of what I assert the scotch Ladies say it themselves, but to be less serious where will you find a language so prettily become a pretty mouth as the broad scotch and the women here speak it in it's highest purity, for instance teach one of the Young Lady's at home to pronounce the Whoar w[u]ll I gong[10] with a beccomeing wideness of mouth and I'll lay my life they'l wound every hearer[11] we have no such character here as a coquett but alass how many envious prudes some days ago I walk'd into My Lord Killcoubry's don't be surpriz'd my Lord is but a Glover,[12] when the Dutchess of Hamilton (that fair who sacrificed her beauty to ambition and her inward peace to a title and Gilt equipage) pass'd by in her Chariot, her batter'd husband or more properly the Guardian of her charms sat beside her[13] strait envy began in the shape of no less than three Lady's who sat with me to find fault's in her faultless form—for my part says the first I think that I always thought that the dutchess has too much of the red in her complexion, Madam I am of your oppinion says the seccond and I think her face has a palish cast too much on the delicate order, and let me tell you adds the third Lady whose mouth was puckerd up to the size of an Issue that the Dutchess has fine lips but she wants a mouth[14] at this every Lady drew up her mouth as If going to pronounce the letter P.[15] but how ill my Bob does it become me to ridicule woman[16] with whom I have scarce any correspondence there are 'tis certain handsome women here and tis as certain they have handsome men to keep them company an ugly and a poor man is society only for himself and such society the world lets me enjoy in great abundance fortune has given you circumstance's and Nature a person to look charming in the Eyes of the fair world nor do I ~~enjoy my~~ envy my Dear Bob such blessings while I may sit down and [laugh at the wor]ld, and at myself—the most ridiculous object in it. but [you see I am grown downright] splenetick, and perhaps the fitt may continue till I [receive an answ] er to this. I know you cant send much news from [Ballymahon, but] such as it is send it all everything you write will be agre[eable and entertai]ning to me,[17] has George Conway put up a signe yet ha[s John Bine]ley[18] left off drinking Drams ~~yet~~ or Tom Allen g[ot a new wig?] but I leave to your own choice what to write but [while Noll Go]ldsmith lives[19] know you have a Friend.

P.S. Give my sincerest regards not [merely my][20] compliments (do you mind) to your agreeable [family] & Give My service to My Mother if you [see her] for as you express it in Ireland I ha[ve a sneaking] kindness for her still.

Direct to me Student of Physick in Edinburgh

1 See William Shaw Mason, *A Statistical Account, or Parochial Survey of Ireland*, 3 vols. (Dublin: at the Faulkner Press, 1815–19), III: 360. The Trinity College copy, in what appears to be a near-contemporary hand, is TCD MS 7398.

2 Prior: 'these and twenty more as plausible'.

3 Prior: 'No turnspit dog'.

4 Prior has a full stop and new paragraph here.

5 Prior has a full stop and new paragraph here. A later iteration of Goldsmith's sense of Scottish national self-regard is recorded by Prior. In early January 1768 Goldsmith dined with several Irish compatriots at his rooms in the Temple. As the conversation turned to literary matters, Goldsmith took to mocking the poetic abilities of Boswell with reference to his Scottish nationality and the patriotic baggage of Scottish song. One Mr Roach, an Irish merchant, recalled Goldsmith's declamation: '"Scotland!" "Ay, ay," said he, "Scotland is ever the burden of a Scotchman's song." "Why," he resumed, "how simple the man must be to write such lines, and call them poetry!"' (*P*, II: 161).

6 Prior: 'Scotch gentry'.

7 Prior has a full stop and new paragraph here.

8 Ceres was an ancient Roman goddess of agriculture and fertility. Torches were carried in her honour at Roman bridal processions, which were, as Goldsmith indicates here, sombre affairs.

9 Prior has a full stop and new paragraph here.

10 Prior adds quotation marks: "Whoar wull I gong?"

11 Prior has a full stop and new paragraph here.

[12] William MacLellan (d. 1762) styled himself Lord Kirkudbright (Kilcoubry). He assumed the title in 1730 on the death of a relation, even though his claim to the title had not been confirmed (his son John would establish the claim in 1773). MacLellan was at this time a glove-maker, known to sell his wares to the fashionable and aristocratic patrons of the old Assembly Rooms in Edinburgh. However, on those nights when the Peers' Ball would take place, he donned a sword and took his seat: assuming a peerage, he socialized with those peers who, on other nights, were his customers.

[13] Elizabeth Gunning, Duchess of Hamilton (1733–90) was originally from Castle Coote in Roscommon. Goldsmith would become more closely associated with the Duchess, probably because of their shared background in the Irish midlands (see following letter). Joshua Reynolds would paint Gunning's portrait in 1760.
James George, 6th Duke of Hamilton (1724–58), was just 29 at this point. Goldsmith is hinting here that his life of debauchery may already have taken its toll. Hamilton met Elizabeth Gunning on Valentine's Day, 1752. In a letter to Horace Mann, 27 February 1752, Horace Walpole described the Duke as 'hot, debauched, extravagant' at the point when he fell in love with Elizabeth Gunning at a London masquerade. Walpole recounted how, at a subsequent assembly at Lord Chesterfield's, Hamilton wooed her at one end of the room while supposedly involved in a card game at the other: his distraction would cost him £1,000. Two nights later, he sent for a parson so that the two could be married instantly; the only ring close to hand for the proceedings was a curtain ring. On 23 March, Walpole wrote again to Mann: 'The world is still mad about the Gunnings: the Duchess of Hamilton was presented on Friday; the crowd was so great, that even the noble mob in the Drawing-Room clambered upon chairs and tables to look at her. There are mobs at their doors to see them get into their chairs; and people go early to get places at the theatres when it is known they will be there': *The Yale Edition of Horace Walpole's Correspondence*, ed. W. S. Lewis, 48 vols. (New Haven: Yale University Press, 1967), XX: 302, 311–12.

[14] Prior places all of the foregoing ladies' remarks between quotation marks.

[15] Prior has a new paragraph here.

[16] Prior: 'women'.

[17] Prior has a full stop and new paragraph here. Also, Prior suggests only that Bryanton's news will be 'agreeable'. Balderston adds 'and entertaining', as the space in the Percy copy suggests.

[18] The Trinity College / *Anthologia Hibernica* copy of the letter has 'John Fineely', which is more likely to be accurate in an Irish midlands context, possibly a variation/misspelling of the Celtic surname Finlay.

[19] Prior: 'While I live'.

[20] Balderston's suggestion for the missing text. For this line Prior has: 'Give my sincere respects (not compliments, do you mind) ...'

4

To the Reverend Thomas Contarine

[Edinburgh, *c.* December 1753]

Goldsmith gives here an account of his medical plans and intuitions to his uncle, indicating also that he is about to travel to the Continent to study further with some of the most eminent professors there. Though he suggests that Paris will be his next port of call, Goldsmith would instead travel to Leiden. His path may have been decided for him by some of the incidents referred to in the letter following.

The copy-text is the manuscript in the Beinecke Library, Yale. It was first published by Prior in 1837.[1]

My D^{rst} Uncle,

after having spent two winters in Edinburgh, I now prepare to go to France the tenth of Next February, I have seen all that this country can Exhibit in the medicall way, and therefore intend to visit Paris, where the great M^{r}. Farhein Petit and Du Hammell du monson,[2] instruct, their pupils in all the branches of medecine: they speak French[3] and consequently, I shall have much the advantage of most of my countrymen, as I am perfectly acquainted with that language, and Few who leave Ireland are so, since I am upon so pleasing a Topick as self aplause give me leave to say that the circle of science which I have run thro before I undertook the study of Physick, is not only usefull, but absolutely necesary to the making a skillfull Physician such sciences enlarge our understanding sharpen our sagacity, and what is a practitioner without both but an Empirick, for never yet was a disorder found Entirely the same in two patients, a Quack unable to distinguish the particularities in Each disease, prescribes at a venture, if he finds such a disorder may be calld by the generall name of feve[r] for instance, he has a set of remedies, which he applies to cure it. nor does he desist till his medecines are run out or his patient has lost his life, but the skillfull Physician distinguishes the symptoms, manures the sterility of nature or prunes her luxuriance, nor does he depend so much on the efficacy of medecines as on their proper application. I shall spend the Spring and Summer in Paris and the begining of next winter go to Leyden, the Great Albinus, is still alive there and twill be proper to go tho only to have it said, that we have studied in so famous an university; as I shall not have another opertunity of receiving money from your Bounty till my return to Ireland so I have drawn for the last sum that I hope I shall Ever Trouble you for, tis twenty pounds. and now, D^{r} S^{r} let me here acknowledge the humility of the Station in which you found me let me tell how I was despisd by most and hatefull to myself. poverty, hopeless poverty, was my lot, and melancholly was beginning to make me her own, when you, but

I stop here, to enquire how your health goes on how does my cousin Jenny and has she recoverd her late complaint how does my poor Jack Goldsmith I fear his disorder of such a nature as he wont easily recover I wish my Dr Sir you wod make me happy by another letter before I go abroad for there I shall hardly hear from you, I shall carry just thirty three pounds to france with good store of clothes, shirts, &c &c and that with oeconomy will serve; I have spent more than a fornight every second day at the Duke of Hamiltons, but it seems they lik'd more as a Jester than as a companion so I disdaind so servile an employment twas unworthy my ~~Employment~~ calling as a Physician.[4]

I have nothing new to add from this country, and I beg, D^{r} S^{r} you will Excuse this letter so filld with Egotisms, I wish you may be reveng'd on ~~my~~ me by sending an answer fill'd with nothing but an account of your self.

I am Dr Uncle your most
Devoted Oliver Goldsmith

Give my—how shall I Express it,
Give my earnest love to M^{r} and Mrs Lawder

[1] Balderston relied on Prior's version in which spelling and punctuation were considerably different from the original manuscript, of which sight had been lost after it was sold at Sotheby's in 1904. It re-emerged in the 1970s in the F.W. Hilles acquisition in the Beinecke Library at Yale University.

[2] Antoine F. Ferrein (1693–1769) was Professor of Medicine and Surgery in the Collège Royale in Paris. In 1742 he became a member of the Académie des Sciences, the learned society founded by Louis XIV in 1666 to facilitate and encourage scientific research. Ferrein was a pioneer in the understanding of the physiology of the voice, and coined the term 'vocal cords' (*cordes vocales*).
Antoine Petit (1722–94) was Professor of Anatomy, Surgery and Childbirth, who would succeed Ferrein in the chair of anatomy in 1768 at the Jardin du Roi. Subsequently the Jardin des Plantes, the Jardin du Roi in Paris was founded by Louis XIII's physician in 1626 as a medicinal herb garden. George-Louis Leclerc, the Comte de Buffon (1707–88), a major source for Goldsmith's later writings in natural history, became the curator in 1739.
Henri-Louis Duhamel du Monceau (1700–82) was a French physician and botanist, elected to the Académie des Sciences in 1738.

[3] By this, Goldsmith probably means that the classes were given in French, and not in Latin, as per other Continental medical schools.

[4] Goldsmith had become a regular guest at the Hamiltons' Edinburgh residence. Balderston (18) suggests that his role there seems to have been something akin to that of entertainer or

flatterer, and the experience may be the source of the complaint by the Man in Black in Letter 27 of *The Citizen of the World*: 'Poverty naturally begets dependance, and I was admitted as a flatterer to a great man. At first I was surprised, that the situation of a flatterer at a great man's table could be thought disagreeable; there was no great trouble in listening attentively when his lordship spoke, and laughing when he looked round for applause' (*CW*, II: 116).

5

[To Daniel Hodson]

[Edinburgh, *c.* December 1753]

The copy-text is the manuscript in the Taylor Library at Princeton University, which consists of the lower part of a folio sheet with writing on both sides. It was first published by Balderston in 1928. Balderston notes that it was probably torn away and preserved for the signature. The recipient, not indicated on the original manuscript, was probably Dan Hodson. In Letter 1 to Hodson, Goldsmith writes in a similar tone regarding his circumstances, and there is also the shared connection to Contarine. The date is conjectural: the postscript refers to the previous letter in a way which implies that it was reasonably recent.

... share of my native assurance I shew'd my Talent and acquird the name of the facetious Irish man, I have either dined [o]r sup'd at His Graces[1] this fortnight every second day, as I did not pretend to great things and let em into my circumstances and manner of thinking very freely they have recomended me to Mr Thos Coelehit[2]

[...]

[al]ways sangui[ne but now I express my] ambitions—adieu

Oliver Goldsmith

I have wrote My Uncle Contarine a long letter relative to the above mentiond afair I wish you coud see it as it is much fuller than this[3]

1 At the house of the Duke and Duchess of Hamilton, to whom Goldsmith refers in the previous letter.

2 Unidentified.

3 Probably Letter 4, the previous letter, which refers to Goldsmith's relationship with the Hamiltons. However, the reference is not substantial enough to be considered a longer treatment of that 'affair', so it may be that Goldsmith is referring to another topic addressed in a missing part of this letter, or to another letter to Contarine regarding the Hamiltons, now lost.

6

To the Reverend Thomas Contarine

Leiden, [*c.* 6 May 1754]

Contrary to his claim to Percy that he had received his medical degree at the age of 20, this letter indicates that Goldsmith had not received it by the age of 26, though he clearly still had intentions of so doing. The letter also discourses upon ideas of national character and the contemporary demand for travel accounts, with which Goldsmith would later engage in his periodical and natural historical writings, and in *The Traveller, or a Prospect of Society* (1764). He also evokes the cosmopolitan qualities of Leiden, a major centre of medical education and commerce.

The copy-text is the manuscript in the British Library. It was first published, with some omissions, by Percy in 1801. It was addressed 'To | The Revd Mr Thos: Contarine | [K]ilmore near | Carrick on Shannon | in | Ireland'. It is postmarked 6 May and above the postmark is recorded 'this lett^{r} is charg'd 1^{s}–8^{d}'. The portions in square brackets are worn away in the manuscript and are supplied from a contemporary copy, made by Catherine Hodson, also in the British Library.

Dr Sr Leyden

I suppose by this time I am accus'd of Either neglect or ingratitude and my silence imputed to my usual slowness of writing but believe me S^{r} when I say that till now I had not an opertunity of sitting down with that ease of mind, which writing requird, you may see by the top of this letter that I am at Leyden but of my Journey hither you must be inform'd. some time after the receipt of your last I embarkd for Burdeaux on board a scotch ship calld the St Andrew, ~~Cap~~John Watt Master the ship made a Tolerable apearance and as another inducement I was let to know that six agreeable passengers were to be my company, well we were but two days at sea when a Storm drove us into a Citty of England call'd Newcastle upon Tyne we all went ashoar to refresh us after the fatigue of our voyage seven men and me we were one day on shore and o[n th]e following e[ve]ning as we were all verry merry the room door bursts open enters a Serjeant and twelve Grenadiers with their bayonets screwd and put us all under the Kings arrest, it seems my company were Scotch men in the French service and had been in Scotland to enlist Soldiers for the French King. I endeavourd all I could to prove my inocence however I remain'd in prison with the rest a Fortnight and with difficulty got off even then, Dr Sr keep this all a secret or at least say it was for debt[1] for if it were once known at the university I shoud hardly get a degree. but hear how providence interposd in my Favour the ship was gone on to burdeaux before I got from prison and was wreckd at the mouth of the Graronne, and every one of the crew were drownd it happen'd the last great storm, there was a ship at that time ready for Holland I embarkd and in nine days thank My God arrivd safe at Rotterdam, from whence I Traveld by land to Leyden ~~from~~ whence I now write. You may Expect some account of this country and tho I am not as yet well qualified for such an undertaking, yet shall I endeavour to satisfie some part of your Expectations. nothing sur[pri]zes me more than the books every day publishd, descriptive of the manners of this country any young man who takes it into his head to publish his travells visits the countries he intends to describe passes thro them with as much inattention as his valet de chambre and consequently not having a fund himself to fill a vollume he applies to those who wrote before him and gives us the manners of a country not as he must have seen them but such as they might have been fifty years before, ~~but~~ the modern dutch man is quite a different creature from him of former times, he in every thing imitates a French man but in his easy disingagd air which is the result of keeping polite company, the dutch man is vastly ceremonious and is perhaps exactly what a French man might have been in the reign of Lewis the 14th. such are the better bred but the downright Hollander is one of the oddest figures in Nature upon a head of lank hair he wears a half cock'd Narrow leav'd hat lacd with black ribon, no coat but seven waistcoats and nine pairs of breeches so that his hips reach almost up to his armpits this well ~~clad~~ cloathd ~~man~~ vegetable is now fit to see company or make love but what a pleasing creature is the object of his apetite why she wears a large friez cap with a deal of flanders lace and for every pair of breeches he carries she puts on two petticoats, is it not surprizing how things shoud ever come close enough to make it a match, when I spoke of love I was to be understood not in a—in short I was not to be understood at all, a Dutch Lady burns nothing about her Phlegmatick admirer but his Tobacco. you must know Sr every woman carries in her hand a Stove with coals in it which when she sits she sn[ug]s under her petticoats and at this chimney Dozing Strephon[2] lights his pipe. I take it that this continuall smoaking is what gives the man the ruddy healthfull complexion he generally wears by draining his superfluous moisture while the woman deprivd of this amusement overflows with such visciditys[3] as teint the complexion and gives that paleness of visage which Low fenny grounds and moist air conspire to cause A dutch woman and a Scotch will well bear an opposition the one is pale & fat and the other lean and ruddy the one walks as if she were stradling after a go cart and the other takes too Masculine a stride, I shall not endeavour to deprive either country of its share of beauty but must say that of objects on this earth an English farmers Daughter is most charming every woman there is a complete beauty, while the higher class of women want many of the requisites to make ~~her~~ them even Tolerable. Their pleasures here are very dull tho very various you may smoak you may doze: you may go to the Italian comedy as good an amusement as either of the former this entertainment always brings in Harlequin who is generally a Magician and in consequence of his Diabolicall art performs a thousand Tricks on the rest of the persons of the drama who are all fools. I have seen the pit in a roar of laughter at his humour when with his sword he Touches the glass another was drinking from, 'twas not his face they laughd at for that was maskd, they must have seen something vastly queer in the wooden sword that neither I nor you Sr were you there cou'd see, In winter, when their cannalls are frozen every house is forsaken and all People are on the ice sleds drawn by horses and skating are at that time the reigning amusements they have boats here that slide on the ice and are driven by the winds when they spread all their sails they go more than a mile and an half a minite their motion is so rapid that the Eye can scarce accompany them ~~nothing~~ Their ordinary manner of Travelling is very cheap and very convenient they sail in coverd boats drawn by horses and in these you are sure to meet people of all nations here the Dutch slumber the French chatter and the English play cards, any man who likes company may have them to his Taste for my part I generally detatchd myself from all society and was wholy Taken up in observing the face of the country, nothing can Equall its beauty wherever I turn my Eye fine houses elegant gardens statues grottoes vistas present themselvs but enter their Towns and you are charmd beyond description no no[th] ing can be more clean [or beau]tifull. Scotland and this country bear the highest contrast there Hills and rocks intercept every prospect here tis all a continu'd plain there you might see a well dresd Dutchess issuing from a dirty close and here a dirty Dutch man inhabiting a Palace, the Sotch may be compard to a Tulip planted in dung but I never see a dutch man in his own house, but I think of a magnificent Egyptian Temple dedicated to an ox. Physick is by no means Taught here so well as in Edinburgh and [in] all Leyden there are but four British students[4] all nescsarys being so extreamly Dear and the Professors so very Lazy (the chymicall Professor[5] excepted) that we dont much care to come hither I am [no]t certain how long my stay here may be however I expect to [have] the hapiness of seeing you at Kilmore if I [can next March.] Direct to me if I am honourd with a letter from you to Madam De Allion's in Leyden Thou Best of Men may heaven guard and preserve you and those you Love

Oliver Goldsmith

1 An account of this episode was given in Glover's *Life of Dr Goldsmith* (1774): 'It was in the beginning of the year 1754, that he quitted Edinburgh; but he had no sooner reached Sunderland, than he was arrested for the amount of his bond; but he was happily relieved from his distress, by the humanity of Dr. Sleigh and Mr. Laughlin Maclane' (4). On the point of the Sunderland incident, Prior records that Goldsmith had stood as a guarantor for the debts of one Kennedy, a fellow student at Edinburgh, and that the arrest in the north-east was at the suit of the tailor with whom Kennedy had incurred the bad debt. Maclane or Maclean and Dr Joseph Fenn Sleigh (1733–70), contemporaries and mutual friends of Goldsmith and Edmund Burke at Trinity College, and Goldsmith's fellow students at Edinburgh, then delivered Goldsmith from the bailiffs, allowing him to take a ship from Newcastle to Holland to begin his studies at Leiden. John Ginger argues that Goldsmith's letter to Contarine was intended to scramble the narrative: the imputation of keeping Jacobite company was potentially injurious to his medical studies and so, begging discretion in general, he tells this tale so as not to appear financially or otherwise irresponsible. See John Ginger, *The Notable Man: The Life and Times of Oliver Goldsmith* (London: Hamilton, 1977), 81.

2 Strephon was a conventional name in seventeenth- and eighteenth-century pastoral poetry given to pastoral or rustic male lovers. Strephon laments his lost lover Urania in the opening lines of Sir Philip Sydney's *Arcadia*. The character was given an urban environment in Jonathan Swift's scatological poems 'The Lady's Dressing Room' (1732) and 'Strephon and Chloe' (1734). Goldsmith's 'dozing' figure of that name is an image of his own devising.

3 Viscid or phlegmatic humours, bringing about a pallid appearance.

4 One of these students would have been one Dr Ellis, who was Percy's informant on Goldsmith's Leiden years and whose anecdotes were further recorded by Matthew Weld Hartsonge of Dublin, who in turn was Prior's source (*P*, I: 169–71). According to Prior, Ellis was, like Goldsmith, a Trinity graduate. He travelled to Leiden for two to three years to attend the university and returned to Dublin to study further. He settled in Monaghan where he practised as a physician, returning to Dublin upon being appointed Clerk to the Irish Parliament. He died in 1791.

5 Jerome (or Heronymus) David Gaubius (1705–80), Boerhaave's student, and successor as Professor of Chemistry at Leiden in 1729. His degree at Leiden was earned with a thesis on psychosomatic medicine. Boswell would write (in Latin) to – and visit – Gaubius in May 1764 to glean solutions for his hypochondria. Gaubius informed him that his hypochondria would pass after the age of 30 (it did not). In *An Enquiry into the Present State of Polite Learning*, Goldsmith would single Gaubius out as the Dutch intellectual deserving 'the highest applause' (*CW*, I: 286), and would record a conversation with him in which were compared the universities of Leiden and Edinburgh. Gaubius supposed that medical teaching in Edinburgh was superior because the professors there were paid less by the university, whereas higher pay at Leiden had disposed the faculty to opulence, making them lazy (see *CW*, I: 309).

7
To Daniel Hodson
London, 27 December 1757

This is Goldsmith's first known letter home following his arrival in February 1756 in London and gives an account of the beginnings of his career in writing, providing reviews for Ralph Griffiths's *Monthly Review* from April 1757. The letter conveys his sense of financial embarrassment and his conflicted mental state, critical of his home country's limitations but disturbed by an inexplicable homesickness. That he was writing the letter from Temple Exchange Coffee House helps explain his nostalgia for home as Goldsmith mixed with Irish students of the law who socialized there. The coffee house was located on Fleet Street, near Temple Bar.

The copy-text is the manuscript in the British Library. It was first published, with omissions, by Percy in 1801. It is addressed 'To | Daniel Hodson Esqr. At Lishoy near Ballymahon, Ireland'. The bracketed portions are worn away in the manuscript; like Balderston, we have taken Percy's readings of those portions where they are likely to have been accurate and have noted where Balderston diverges. We have, in a few instances, ventured suggestions where none have been offered to date.

Dear Sir

It may be four years since my last letters to Ireland, and to y[ou in partic]ular. I received no answer; probably because you never wrote [to me. My] Brother Charless, however, informs me of the fatigue you w[ere at in] soliciting a subscription to assist me, not only among my [friends and relations,] but acquaintance in general. Tho' my pride might feel so[me repug]nance at being thus relieved, yet my gratitude can suffer no [diminu]tion. How much am I obliged to you, to them, for such generos[ity,] (or why should not your virtues have the proper name) for such charity to me at that Juncture. Sure I am born to ill fortune to be so much a debtor and so unable to repay! But to say no more of this; too many professions of gratitude are often considered as indirect petitions for future favours; let me only add, that my not receiving that supply was the cause of my present establishment at London. You may Easily imagine what difficulties I had to encounter, left as I was without Friends, recommendations, money, or impudence, and that in a Co[untry] where my being born an Irishman was sufficient to keep me [unem] ploy'd. Manny in such circumstances would have had recou[rse to] the Friar's cord, or suicide's halter. But with all my fol[lies I] had principle to resist the one, and resolution to com[bat the] other.

I suppose you desire to know my present situation, a[nd since][1] there is nothing in it, at which I should blush, or mankind [could censure, I] see no reason for making it a secret; in short, by a v[ery little] practice as a Physician and a very little reputation a[s an author][2] I make a shift to live. Nothing more apt to introduce us to the gates of the muses than Poverty; but it were well if she only left us at the door; the mischief is, she sometimes chooses to give her company during the entertainment, and Want, instead of being gentleman-usher, often turns master of the Ceremonies. Thus upon hearing, I write, no doubt, you immagine, I starve, and the name of an Author naturally reminds you of a garret, in this particular I do not think proper to undeceive my Friends; but whether I eat or starve, live in a first floor or four pair of stairs [attic] high, I still remember them with ardour, nay my ve[ry coun]try comes in for a share of my affection.[3] Unaccountable [fond]ness for country, this maladie du Pays, as the french [call] it. Unaccountable, that he should still have an affec[tion for] a place, who never received when in it above civil [contem]pt,[4] who never brought out of it, except his brogue [an]d his blunders; sure my affection is equally ridiculous with the Scotchman's, who refused to be cured of the itch, because it made him unco'thoughtful of his wife and bonny Inverary.[5] But not to be serious, let me ask myself what gives me a wish to see Ireland again? The country is a fine one perhaps? No! There are good company in Ireland? No; the conversation there is generally made up of a smutty toast or a baudy song. The vivacity supported by some humble cousin, who has just ~~wit vivacity~~ folly enough to earn his—dinner. Then perhaps ther's more wit and [lea]rning among the Irish? Oh Lord! No! there has been more [money] spent in the encouragement of the Podareen mare[6] there [in on]e[7] season, than given in rewards to learned men since [the ti]mes of Usher.[8] All their productions in learning amount [mayb]e[9] to, perhaps a translation, or a few tracts in labo[rious[10] div]inity, and all their productions in wit, to just nothing at all. [Why the P]lague then so fond of Ireland! Then all at once be[cause y]ou, my dear friend, and a few more, who are exceptions [to the g]eneral picture, have a residence there. This it is that gives me all the pangs I feel in seperation. I confess I carry this spirit sometimes to the souring the pleasures I at present possess. If I go to the Opera where Signora Colomba[11] pours out all the mazes of melody; I sit and sigh for Lishoy fireside, and Johnny armstrong's last good night from Peggy Golden.[12] If I climb Flamstead hill where nature never exhibited a more magnificent prospect; I confess it fine but then I had rather be placed on the little mount before Lishoy gate, and take in, to me, the most pleasing horizon in nature. Before Charless came hither, as my thoughts sometimes found refuge from severer studies among my friends in Ireland I fancied to myself strange revolutions at home, but I find it was the rapidity of my own motion that gave an immaginary one to objects really at rest.[13] No alterations there; some friends, he tells me, are still lean but very rich, others very fat but still very poor, nay all the news I hear from you, is that you and Mrs. Hodson sally out in visits among the neighbours, and sometimes make a migration from the blue bed to the brown.[14] I could from my heart wish that you and She and Lishoy and Ballymahon and all of you would fairly make a migration into Midlesex; tho' upon second thoughts this might be attended with a few [in]conveniencies; therefore as the Mountain will not come to Mahomet, why Mahomet shall go to the Mountain, or to speak plain english as you can not conveniently pay me a visit, if next Summer I can contrive to be absent six weeks from

London I shall spend three of them among my friends in Ireland.[15] But first [belie]ve me my design is purely to visit, and neither to cut a [figure] nor levy contributions, neither to excite envy or [solicit charit]y;[16] in fact my circumstances are adapted to neither. [I am too] poor to be gazed at and too rich to need the assistance [of others.][17] You see, Dear Dan, how long I have been talking about [myself,] but attribute my vanity to my affection; as every man is [pleasing] to himself,[18] and as I consider you as second self, I imaggine [you will] be consequently pleased with these instances of egotism. Charless is furnished with every thing necessary, but why [ask a] stranger to assist him? I hope he will be improved in his [lot against] his return. Poor Jenny![19] But it is what I expected, My mother too has lost Pallas![20] My Dear Sir, these things give me real uneasiness and I could wish to redress them. But at Present there is hardly a Kingdom in Europe in which I am not a debtor. I have already discharged my most threatening and pressing demands, for we must be just before we can be grateful. For the rest I need not say (you know I am)

Your Affectionate Kinsman
Oliver Goldsmith

Temple Exchange Coffee house December the 27th 1757
Near Temple Bar. Where you may direct an answer.

1 Percy: 'As' for 'a[nd since]'.
2 Percy: 'as a poet'; 'author', Balderston suggests, fits the space more convincingly.
3 The first, or ground floor, was the most expensive; attic accommodation was cheaper. John Trusler, *The London Adviser and Guide: Containing every Instruction and Information useful and necessary to Persons living in London, and coming to reside there* … (London: printed for the author, 1786), 2.
4 Percy: 'common civility'.
5 Inveraray, on the western shore of Loch Fyne in Scotland, was the ancestral home of the Duke of Argyll.
6 The Podareen mare was the nickname of Irish Lass, owned by the Archbold family, who won the Royal Plate at the Curragh in 1745 and 1748. Goldsmith was in Dublin in these years, and news of these races would have circulated generally in city and countryside. Horse racing in Ireland was in a phase of accelerated development when Goldsmith was young. Landowners organized meetings on their land – probably a source of Goldsmith's dismay at the priorities of the minor gentry, whose passion for horses was a long-standing cultural tendency. In Goldsmith's formative period, and in his native region, new race-courses were established at Roscommon, and at Ballymore and Castlepollard in County Westmeath, illustrating the appeal of the sport to the Protestant ascendancy. See James Kelly, *Sport in Ireland, 1600–1840* (Dublin: Four Courts, 2014), 42–73.

7 Percy: 'one', not '[in on]e'.

8 James Ussher (1581–1656), scholar, author and Church of Ireland Archbishop of Armagh, was born and educated in Dublin, where he was one of the first students to enter Trinity College when it opened in 1594. He graduated with a BA in 1598 and an MA in 1601. He was ordained a deacon in the Church of Ireland in 1602, and was Chancellor of St Patrick's Cathedral in 1605. By 1607 Ussher was Professor of Theological Controversies at Trinity, and built up a substantial library. He made book-buying trips to England in 1603, 1606, 1609 and 1612, which enabled him to make contacts with English antiquarians and collectors such as Thomas Bodley and William Camden. Ussher was awarded the degree of Doctor of Divinity in 1612 (he would become Vice-Chancellor in 1615 and Vice-Provost in 1616). His antiquarian research was largely informed by theological questions. In 1631 he published his *Discourse of the Religion Anciently Professed by the Irish and British* which, while scholarly, also projected contemporary disputes into the ancient Irish past (it had been previously published in 1622 as an appendix to another work). Between 1625 and 1656 he was Archbishop of Armagh and Primate of All Ireland. Ussher is perhaps most famous to posterity as the author of *Annales Veteris Testamenti* (1650), a history of the world derived from a literal reading of the Old Testament in which he deduced that creation commenced at 6 p.m. on 22 October 4004 BC.

9 Percy omitted '[mayb]e'.

10 Percy omitted 'laborious'.

11 Signora Columba Mattei (fl. 1754–63), a noted singer and actress, was also, from 1758 to 1763, manager of the King's Theatre in London. In 1757, she was particularly in the public eye, playing the title role in Tomaso Albinoni's *Zenobia* that year, which is where Goldsmith may have seen her perform. Goldsmith writes of her exceptional status in an otherwise mundane British operatic scene in the *Bee* 8 (24 November 1759) ('Of the Opera in England'): 'To say the truth, the opera, as it is conducted among us, is but a very humdrum amusement; in other countries, the decorations are entirely magnificent, the singers all excellent, and the burlettas or interludes, quite entertaining; the best poets compose the words, and the best masters the music, but with us it is otherwise; the decorations are but trifling, and cheap; the singers, Matei only excepted, but indifferent' (*CW*, I: 506). He continues: 'Signora Matei is at once both a perfect actress and a very fine singer. She is possessed of a fine sensibility in her manner, and seldom indulges those extravagant and unmusical flights of voice complained of before' (*CW*, I: 507). However, Goldsmith goes on to compare the achievement of Matei in the high operatic arts with the singing of ballads by dairy-maids in his youth in Ireland. Nostalgia and homesickness confer superiority on the latter (see below).

12 In the *Bee* 4 (27 October 1759) ('A Flemish Tradition'), Goldsmith discusses the songs and stories which 'instruct and amuse' the lower orders. Among such cultural artifacts, Goldsmith lists 'the adventures of Robin Hood, the hunting of Chevy-chace, and the bravery of Johnny Armstrong, among the English' (*CW*, I: 420). He refers again to Johnny Armstrong in the *Bee* 2 (13 October 1759) ('Happiness, in a Great measure, Dependent on Constitution'), where the song forms part of his reminiscences: 'My present enjoyments may be more refined, but they are infinitely less pleasing. The pleasure the best actor gives, can no way compare to that I have received from a country wag, who imitated a quaker's sermon. The music of the finest singer is dissonance to what I felt when our old dairy-maid sung me into tears with Johnny Armstrong's Last Good Night, or the Cruelty of Barbara Allen' (*CW*, I: 385). 'Johnny Armstrong's Last Good Night' was a so-called 'Riever' or border ballad, which told of the adventures of raiders along the Anglo-Scottish border in the fifteenth and sixteenth centuries. Johnny Armstrong was one such border raider, captured and hanged with several of his men at Caerlanrig Castle in 1530. The ballad records the duplicity of the King who had in a letter promised Armstrong safety should he attend at his court, a ruse to trick him into capture. The song records that he resists, and is run through from behind by one of the King's men.

13 Very similar sentiments are expressed in Letter 63 of *The Citizen of the World*: 'In every letter I expect accounts of some new revolutions in China, some strange occurrence in the state, or

disaster among my private acquaintance. I open every pacquet with tremulous expectation, and am agreeably disappointed when I find my friends and my country continuing in felicity. I wander, but they are at rest; they suffer few changes but what pass in my own restless imagination; it is only the rapidity of my own motion gives an imaginary swiftness to objects which are in some measure immoveable' (*CW*, II: 261).

14 This pastoral image of neighbourliness untroubled by social upheaval is reproduced in the first chapter of *The Vicar of Wakefield*: 'We had no revolutions to fear, nor fatigues to undergo; all our adventures were by the fire-side, and all our migrations from the blue bed to the brown' (*CW*, IV: 18). The precise sense of the reference to the blue and brown beds is obscure but Goldsmith seems to be gently mocking the stasis of the Hodsons' life by suggesting that changing the colour of their bedclothes passes for notable incident in Ireland.

15 Goldsmith, in fact, never returned to Ireland.

16 Percy: 'solicit favour'.

17 Percy: 'to need assistance'.

18 Percy: 'fond of himself'.

19 This is Jane Goldsmith, Oliver's sister, who had, it seems, misguidedly married a Mr Johnson, possibly under the impression that he was possessed of a greater fortune than he had.

20 This may refer to the loss of the Goldsmiths' home at Pallas, rented by Goldsmith's grandparents on his mother's side. Half of the property had already been lost upon the death of Goldsmith's maternal grandfather. See *P*, I: 9n. It is not clear how the rest of the property was lost.

8

To Edward Mills

London, 7 August [1758]

Edward Mills was Goldsmith's cousin, the son of Charles Goldsmith's sister. Mills did not respond in any way to Goldsmith's request, as the later letter to Henry Goldsmith shows. This letter is introduced with thoughts upon what would become a quintessentially Goldsmithian opposition of ambition and domestic contentment. Mills, it seems, had forsaken a career at the bar in Dublin – or, more probably and profitably, London – and there is a little needling, possibly, in Goldsmith's imagining his cousin's lost glories as enhancing his own. Mills has chosen instead his own smaller circle of acquaintance, the 'cultivation of his paternal acres'. There is an awkwardness of tone in this letter as Goldsmith tries to establish, or re-establish, a connection with Mills only to set up his own request that Mills help to collect Irish subscriptions for Goldsmith's forthcoming *Enquiry into the Present state of Polite Learning in Europe*, which would be published anonymously in April 1759. Dated 7 August, this is the first letter of a series which Goldsmith wrote to relatives and friends in Ireland seeking such subscriptions in order to preempt Irish piracy.

The copy-text is the manuscript in the British Library. It was first published by Percy in 1801. It is addressed 'To Edward Mills Esqr. | near | Roscommon | Ireland' and postmarked 17 August. The bracketed portions, worn away in the manuscript, are supplied by Percy, except where otherwise noted.

D[r] S[r].

You have quitted, I find, that plan of life which you once Intended to pursue, and given up ambition for domestic tranquillity: Were I to consult your satisfaction alone in this change I have the utmost reason to congratulate your choice, but when I consider my own I cant avoid feeling some regret, that one of my few friends has declin'd a pursuit in which he had every reason to expect success. The truth is, like the rest of the world I am self-interested in my concern and do not so much consider the happiness you have acquir'd as the honour I have probably lost in the change. I have often let my fancy loose when you were the subject, and have imagined you gracing the bench or thundering at the bar, while I have taken no small pride to myself and whispered all that I could come near, that that was my cousin. Instead of this it seems you are contented to be merely an happy man to be esteem'd only by your acquaintance, to cultivate your paternal acres; to take unmolested a nap under one of your own hawthorns, or in Mrs. Mills' Bedchamber which even a Poet must confess is rather the most comfortable place of the two.

But however your resolutions may be altered with respect to your situation in life I persuade my self they are unalterable with regard to your friends in it. I can't think the world has taken such entire possession of that heart (once so susceptible of friendship[)] as not to have left a corner there for a friend or two; Nay I flatter myself that even I have a place among the number. This I have a claim to from the similitude of our dispositions, or setting that aside I can demand it as my right by the most equitable law in nature, I mean that of retaliation for indeed you have more than your share in mine. I am a man of few professions, and yet this very instant I can't avoid the painful apprehension that my present professions (which speak not half my feelings) should be considered only as a pretext to cover a request, as I have a request to make. No, my dear Ned, I know you are too generous to think so, and you know me too proud to stoop to mercenary insincerity. I have a request it is true to make but, as I know to whom I am a petitioner, I make it without diffidence or c[on]fusion. It is in short this: I am going to publish a book in London Entituled an Essay on the present State of Taste and Literature in Europe. Every work publish'd here the

Printers in Ireland republish there, without giving the Author the least consideration for his Coppy. I would in this respect disappoint their avarice, and have all the additional advantages that may result from the sale of my performance there to myself. The book is now printing in London, and I have requested Doctor Radcliff, Mr Lawder, Mr Bryanton, My Brother Mr Henry Goldsmith, and Brother in Law Mr Hodson to circulate my proposals among their acquaintance; the same request I now make to you, and have accordingly given directions to Mr Bradley bookseller in Dame street[1] to send you an hundred proposals. Whatever subscriptions pursuant to those proposals you may receive, when collected, may be Transmitted to Mr. Bra[dley who] will give a receipt [for the] money, and be accountable f[or t]he books. I shall not [by a] paltry apology excuse myself for putting you to this troubl[e. Were] I not convincd that you found more pleasure in doing good-n[atured] things than uneasiness at being employd in them I should [not have] singled you out on this occasion. It is probable you would c[omply with] such a request if it tended to the encouragement of any [man of] learning whatsoever, what then may not he expect who [has] Ties of family and friendship to enforce his.
I am Dear Sir your Most a[ffectionate]

Friend and humble servant
Oliver Goldsmith

London Temple Exchange
Coffee house Temple Bar.
August the 7th 17[58.][2]

[1] Hulton Bradley (d. 1778) was apprenticed in 1751 to his father Abraham, who operated at the Two Bibles on Dame Street in Dublin. Abraham Bradley had published the second Irish edition of Shakespeare's *Works* in 1739, but gradually became busier with affairs of state after he became the King's Stationer in 1749. From 1751 to 1777, he was printer to the Irish House of Commons. It appears as though his son Hulton took over the family's concern in literary matters from around 1758 or 1759. On 8 May 1759, he announced in the *Dublin Journal* a subscription edition of Goldsmith's *Enquiry* at the price of 5s 5d. Goldsmith had informed his brother Henry that he intended to send 250 copies of the London edition to Ireland for Bradley to sell. There is no trace of any contemporary Dublin edition of the book. See Mary Pollard, *A Dictionary of Members of the Dublin Book Trade 1550–1800* (London: Bibliographical Society, 2000), 48.

[2] The last two figures of the date, worn away in the manuscript, were incorrectly given by Percy as '59'. As Balderston explains, Percy first visited Goldsmith on 3 March 1759, and mistakenly recorded that Goldsmith was then in the process of writing his *Enquiry*. As the book was published in April 1759, he would, in March, have been working on the proofs.

9

To Robert Bryanton

London, 14 August 1758

The copy-text is the manuscript in the Royal Irish Academy in Dublin. It was first published by Prior in 1837. It is addressed 'To | Robert Bryanton Esqr At | Ballymahon | Ireland.' It is postmarked 15 and 17 August.

Balderston uses Prior's copy of this letter, a transcript of the original manuscript given him by the owner, the Reverend Robert Handcock (1770–1848), of Dublin. Prior, and thus Balderston, introduced paragraphing, punctuation and other emendations which were not in the original, which have been reversed below, though we have taken Prior as our guide where the text is worn away. The *Hibernian Chronicle* (1 Jan. 1795) reported that Handcock, of Marlborough Street, Dublin, had recently married a Miss Bryanton of Frederick Street, Dublin. Robert Handcock was, thus, Robert Bryanton's son-in-law. Prior notes 'that portions of the paper being worn away by time, a few sentences now imperfect, are attempted to be supplied from the context, and it is hoped, with a near approach to accuracy. The passages thus introduced are inclosed within brackets' (*P*, I: 263). His suggestions for illegible passages are retained here.

D^{r}. Sir.

I have heard it remark'd, (I believe by yourself), that they who are drunk or out of their wits fancy every body else in the same condition; Mine is a friendship that neither distance nor time can efface, which is probably the reason that for the soul of me I can't avoid thinking yours of the same complexion; and yet I have many reasons to be of a contrary opinion, else why in so long an absence was I never made a partner in your concerns, to hear of your successes would have given me the utmost pleasure; and a communication of your very disappointments would divide the uneasiness I too frequently feel for my own; indeed my Dear Bob you don't conceive how unkindly you have treated one whose circumstances afford him few prospects of pleasure except those reflected from the happiness of his friends. However, since you have not let me hear from you I have in some measure disappointed your neglect by frequently thinking of you. Every day do I ruminate the calm anecdotes of your life from the fire-side to the easy chair; recall the various adventures that first cemented our friendship, the school the college or the tavern, preside in fancy over your cards, am displeasd at your bad play when the rubber goes against you tho' not with all that agony of soul as when I once was your partner. Is it not strange, that two of such like affections should be so much separated and so differently employd as we are? You seem plac'd at the centre of fortune's wheel and let it revolve never so fast are almost insensible of the [mo]tion; I seem to have been tied to the circumference, and [turned] disagreeably round like an whore in a whirlgigg. [I sat do]wn with an intention to chide, and yet methinks [I have forgot] my resentment already, the truth is, I am a [simpleton with r]egard to you; I may attempt to bluster, [but like] Anacreon, my heart is respondent only to softer affections.[1] And yet now I think on't again I will be angry—God's curse, Sir, who am I? Eh! What am I? Do you know whom you have offended? A man whose character may one of these days be mentioned with profound respect in a German Comment or Dutch Dictionary. Whose name you will probably hear ushered in by a Doctissimus Doctissimorum, or heelpiec'd with a long lattin termination. Think how Goldsmithius, or Gubblegurchius or some such sound as rough as a nutmeg grater, will become me? Think of that. God's curse, Sir who am I? I must own my illnatured cotemporaries have not ~~yet~~ hitherto paid me those honours, ~~hitherto~~ I have had such just reasons to expect. I have not yet seen my face reflected in all the lively display of red and white paint on any sign posts in the subburbs. Your handkerchief weavers seem as yet unacquainted with my merits or Physiognomy and the very snuff-box makers ~~seem to~~ appear to have forgot their respect. Tell them all from me they are a set of Gothic, barbarous ignorant Scoundrells. There will come a day, no doubt there will, I beg you may live a couple of hundred years longer only to see the day, when the Scaligers and Daciers[2] of the age will vindicate my character, give learned editions of my labours, and bless the times with copious comments on the Text you shall see how they will fish up the heavy scoundrels who disregard now, or will then offer to cavil at my productions. How will they bewail the times that suffered so much genius to lie neglected. If ever my works find their way to Tartary or China I know the consequence. Suppose one of your Chinese Owanowitzers instructing one of your Tartarian Chianobacchi you see I use Chinese names to show my own erudition, as I shall soon make our Chinese talk like an Englishman to [show his][3] This may be the subject of the lecture. "Oliver [Goldsmith flou]rish'd in the eighteenth and nineteenth c[enturies. He lived] to be an hundred and three years old[, and in that] age may justly be stiled the sun of [literature] and the Confucius of Europe. [Many of his earlier writings, to the regret of the][4] learned world, were anonymous and have probably been lost because united with those of others. The first avowed piece the world has of his is Entituled an Essay on the Present State of taste and literature in Europe a work well worth its weight in Diamonds. In this he profoundly explains what learning is and what learning is not. In this he proves that blockheads are not men of wit and yet that men of wit are actually blockheads." — But as I chuse neither to tire my Chinese Philosopher, nor you, nor myself I must discontinue the oration in order to give you a pause for admiration, and I find myself most violently disposed to admire too. Let me then, stop my fancy to take a view of my future self, and as the boys say, light down to see myself on horseback. Well now I am down, where the Devil is, I,. Oh, Gods Gods! here in a Garret writing for bread, and expecting to be dunned for a milk score! However, Dear Bob, whether in penury or affluence, serious or gay I am ever wholly thine.

Oliver Goldsmith.

Lond. Temple Exchange Coffee house
Temple bar. Augst. 14 1758.

Give my — no not compliments neither, but something [like the][5] most warm and sincere wish that you can conceive [to your] mother, Mrs Bryanton. To Miss Bryanton. To yo[urself] and if there be a favourite dog in the family, let me [be remem]berd to it.

P.S. As Perhaps you may not take the Chin[...][6]

1 In 'To his Lyre', the Greek lyric poet Anacreon (*c.* 582–*c.* 485 BC) eschews singing of war in favour of love and desire. Love, friendship and revelry were among his primary themes.

2 Julius Caesar Scaliger (1484–1558), an Italian scholar and physician (and defender of Aristotelianism) who spent much of his career in France.
André (1651–1722) and his wife Anne (1654–1720) Dacier, French classical scholars who defended the ancients against the moderns. Goldsmith refers to Scaliger and the Daciers together in the *Bee* 4 (27 October 1759) ('Miscellaneous'). In a similarly defiant, or mock-defiant, tone, he envisions the posthumous reception and assessment of his work: 'If the present generation will not hear my voice, hearken, O posterity, to you I call, and from you I expect redress! What rapture will it not give to have the Scaligers, Daciers, and Warburtons of future times commenting with admiration upon every line I now write, working away those ignorant creatures who offer to arraign my merit with all the virulence of learned reproach' (*CW*, I: 416).

3 An indication that Goldsmith was already contemplating the design of his Chinese letters, or *The Citizen of the World*.

4 This section is obliterated in the original manuscript, and the words given here are as conjectured by Prior.

5 Prior suggests, incongruently, the word 'the' here; it was more likely to have been 'like the'. Balderston did not include either postscript; Prior, the first only.

6 The rest of the manuscript is torn away. Goldsmith may have been about to continue his thoughts on China and Chinese writing. Though he had indicated his intention to do so in the previous letter to Mills, Goldsmith does not in the main body of this letter ask for Bryanton's help in soliciting Irish subscriptions for *An Enquiry*. It is possible that Goldsmith may have introduced the matter in this postscript but that is conjecture.

10

To Jane Lawder

London, 15 August 1758

Jane Lawder was Goldsmith's cousin, and the daughter of Thomas Contarine. The cousins, who by Catherine Hodson's account were fond of each other as children, seem to have fallen out in the years preceding this letter, possibly while Goldsmith was on his Continental travels. Over that period, Contarine's health, physical and mental, had declined. Goldsmith's communications in the meantime may have consisted of letters asking for a continuation of financial support from the Lawders, though Goldsmith was, ostensibly, no longer dependent on his uncle. Whatever the cause of their falling out, Goldsmith was clearly troubled by it. In the following letter to Dan Hodson, he asks his sister Catherine for information regarding the Lawders, indicating that he had also asked his brother Charles to write to him with similar information, which was never furnished. The Lawders seem not to have responded to his letters, including this one, nor did they inform him of the small legacy that Contarine had left him when he died (which was probably in 1758). He would only refer to that legacy, writing to Maurice twelve years later (Letter 29), in which he records, more generally, the kindness of the Lawders to the Goldsmiths.

The copy-text is the manuscript in the Free Library of Philadelphia. It was first published by Prior in 1837. It is addressed 'To | Mrs. Jane Lawder at Kilmore near Carrick | on Shannon | Ireland.' It is postmarked 17 August. There is some addition marked on the envelope as well with the amounts of '5/4 | 8 | 4 | [=] 6/4'. This is too expensive to be postage so it may be related to the purchase of a copy of *An Enquiry into the Present State of Polite Learning in Europe*, Irish copies of which were priced at 5s. 5d.

If you should ask, why in an interval of so many years, you never heard from me, permit me, Madam, to ask the same question, I have the best excuse in recrimination. I wrote to Kilmore from Leyden in Holland, from Louvain in Flanders, and Rouen in France, but receivd no answer. To what could I attribute this silence but to displeasure or forgetfulness. Whether I was right in my conjecture, I do not pretend to determine, but this I must ingenuously own, that I have a thousand times in my turn endeavoured to forget them whom I could not but look upon as forgetting me. I have attempted to blot their names from my memory, and I confess it, spent whole days in efforts to tear their images from my heart; could I have succeeded you had not now been troubled with this renewal of a discontinued correspondence; but as every effort the restless make to procure sleep serves but to keep them waking, all my attempts contributed to impress what I would forget deeper on my imagination. But this is a subject I would willingly turn from, and yet for the soul of me I can't till I have said all; I was, madam, when I discontinued writing to Kilmore in such circumstances that all my endeavours to continue your regards might be attributed to wrong motives, my letters might be regarded as the petitions of a beggar and not the offerings of a friend, while all my professions instead of being considered as the result of disinterested esteem might be ascribed to venal insincerity. I believe, indeed, you had too much generosity to place them in such a light, but I could not bear even the shadow of such a suspicion; the most delicate friendships are always most sensible of the slightest invasion and the strongest jealousy is ever attendant on the warmest regard. I could not, I own, I could not continue a correspondence where every acknowlegement for past favours might be considered as an indirect request for future ones, and where it might be thought I gave my heart from a motive of gratitude alone when I was conscious of having bestowed it on much more disinterested principles.

It is true this conduct might have been ~~folly~~ simple enough, but yourself must confess it was in character. Those who know me at all, know that I have always been actuated by different principles from the rest of Mankind, and while none regarded the interests of his friends more, no man on earth regarded his own less. I have often affected bluntness to avoid the imputation of flattery, have frequently seem'd to overlook those merits too obvious to escape notice, and pretended disregard to those instances of good nature and good sense which I could not fail tacitly to applaud; and all this lest I should be rank'd among the grinning tribe who say very true to all that is said, who fill a vacant chair at a tea table whose narrow souls never moved in a wider circle than the circumference of a guinea, and who had rather be reckoning the money in your pocket than the virtue in your breast; all this, I say, I have done and a thousand other very silly, though very disinterested things in my time, and for all which no soul cares a farthing about me. Gods curse, Madam, is it to be wondered that he should once in his life forget you who has been all his life forgetting himself.

However it is probable you may one of those days see me turn'd into a perfect Hunks[1] and as dark and intricate as a mouse-hole. I have already given my Lanlady orders for an entire reform in the state of my finances; I declaim against hot suppers, drink less sugar in my tea, and cheek my grate with brick-bats.[2] Instead of hanging my room with pictures I intend to adorn it with maxims of frugality, these will make pretty furniture enough and won't be a bit too expensive, for I shall draw them all out with my own hands and my lanlady's daughter shall frame them with the parings of my black waistcoat; Each maxim is to be inscrib'd on a sheet of clean paper and wrote with my best pen, of which the following will serve as a specimen. "Look Sharp. Mind the mean[3] chance. Money is money now.[4] If you have a thousand pound, you can put your hands by your sides and say you are worth a thousand pounds every day of the year. Take a farthing from an hundred pound and it will be an hundred pound no longer."[5] Thus which way so ever I turn my eyes they are sure to meet one of those friendly Monitors, and as we are told of an Actor[6] who hung his room round with looking glasses to correct the defects of his person, my appartment shall be furnished in a peculiar manner to correct the errors of my mind.

Faith! Madam, I heartily wish to be rich, if it were only for this reason, to say without a blush how much I esteem you, but alass I have many a fatigue to encounter before that happy time comes; when your poor old simple friend may again give a loose to the luxuriance of his nature, sitting by Kilmore fireside recount the various adventures of an hard fought life, laugh over the follies of the day join his flute to your harpsicord and forget that ever he starv'd in those streets where Butler and Otway starv'd before him.[7]

And Now I mention those great names My Uncle—He is no more that soul of fire as when once I knew him. Newton and Swift grew dimn with age as well as he.[8] But what shall I say; his mind was too active an inhabitant not to disorder the feeble mansion of its abode, for the richest jewels soonest wear their settings. Yet who but the fool would lament his condition, he now forgets the calamities of life, perhaps indulgent heaven has given him a foretaste of that tranquillity here which he so well deserves hereafter.

But I must come to business, for business as one of my maxims tells me must be minded or lost, I am goin to publish in London A Book entituled the Present state of Taste and Literature in Europe; The Booksellers in Dublin republish every performance there without making the author any consideration I would in this respect disappoint their avarice and have all the profits of my labours to myself. I must therefore request Mr. Lawder to Circulate among his friends and acquaintance an hundred of my proposals which I have given the Bookseller Mr Bradley in Dame Street directions to send him, if in pursuance to such circulation he should receive any subscriptions I entreat when collected they may be sent to Mr. Bradley's as aforsaid who will give a receipt and be accountable for the work or a return of the subscription. If this request, (which if complied with will in some measure be an encouragement to a man of Learning,) should be disagreable or troublesome I would not press it, for I would be the last man on earth to have ~~his my~~ my labours go a begging; but if I know Mr Lawder and sure I ought to know him, he will accept the employment with pleasure, all I can say if he writes a book I will get him two hundred subscribers and those of the best witts in Europe. Whether this request is complied with or not I shall not be uneasy, but there is one Petition I must Make to him and to you which I solicit with the warmest ardour and in which I cannot bear a refusal I mean Dr Madam, That I ~~am~~ may be always

your Ever affectionate and obliged
Kinsman ~~and that I may be~~
~~in fact~~ Oliver Goldsmith

You see how I blot and blunder
when I am asking a favour.

Temple Exchange Coffee house near
Temple Bar. Lond. Aug[st] 15th 1758.

1 Miser. In Letter 27 of *The Citizen of the World*, the Man in Black records a period of frugality during which he 'began to get the character of a saving hunks that had money; and insensibly grew into esteem' (*CW*, II: 119).

2 'Cheeks' were side-pieces put into the fire-place to narrow the fire, saving fuel.

3 Goldsmith intends the proverbial 'main chance', but spells 'main' as 'mean' to give the word an Irish accent.

4 See the *Bee* 3 (20 October 1759) ('On the Use of Language'): 'To say the truth, Sir, money is money now' (*CW*, I: 398).

5 See Letter 27 of *The Citizen of the World*: 'I have contracted a friendship with an alderman, only by observing, that if we take a farthing from a thousand pound it will be a thousand pound no longer' (*CW*, II: 119–20).

6 Balderston (*BL*, 46n1) suggests that the actor in question is Thomas Sheridan (1719?–88), manager of the Smock Alley Theatre in Dublin when Goldsmith was a student at Trinity. See also the *Bee* 2 (13 October 1759) ('On our Theatres'): 'I am told his apartment was hung round with looking-glass, that he might see his person twenty times reflected upon entering the room; and I will make bold to say, he saw twenty very ugly fellows whenever he did so' (*CW*, I: 391).

7 Though pensioned by Charles II, Samuel Butler (1613–80), author of *Hudibras* (1663–78), died at Covent Garden in near-poverty. Equally, Thomas Otway (1652–85), playwright and author of *The Orphan* (1680) and *Venice Preserv'd* (1682), died destitute at Tower Hill, London. In Letter 84 of *The Citizen of the World*, Goldsmith writes that 'the sufferings of the poet in other countries is nothing when compared to his distresses here, the names of Spencer and Otway, Butler and Dryden, are every day mentioned as a national reproach, some of them lived in a state of precarious indigence, and others literally died of hunger' (*CW*, II: 343–4).

8 Both Isaac Newton (1642–1727) and Jonathan Swift (1667–1745) suffered from mental health issues later in life.

11

To Daniel Hodson

[London, *c.* 31 August 1758]

This is the penultimate known letter to refer to subscriptions for *An Enquiry into the Present State of Polite Learning in Europe*. Goldsmith also explains to Hodson his intention to work as a physician with the East India Company, in one of its coastal Coromandel factories in southeastern India, in which were produced silk and cotton textiles, and gunpowder.

The copy-text is the manuscript in the British Library. It was first published by Percy in 1801. It is addressed 'To | Daniel Hodson Esqr at Lishoy near | Ballymahon. | Ireland'. It is postmarked 31 August. On the verso of the second page, with the address, there is a note from a family friend: 'Killishee, Septemr 18th 1758. Mr. Piers's best Complim^{ts} to ~~the~~ his friends at Lisshoy. He is obliged to them for the Treat Noll's letter has afforded him – Every line speaks the writer and is a better picture of him than a Bindon cou'd give us of him – I ~~shall~~ long to see his book whatever it is – And desire I may have the honour of being among the Subscribers to it.' It is likely that Hodson had passed the letter around among family and friends to encourage subscriptions for *An Enquiry*, and that in this instance Mr Piers had responded positively. The Bindon to whom Mr Piers refers in his note is Francis Bindon (*c.* 1690–1765), who painted several well-known likenesses of Swift, with whom he was friendly, between 1735 and 1740.

The bracketed portions are worn away in the manuscript, and are given here as suggested by Percy.

D^{r}. Sir

You can't expect regularity in a correspondence with one who is regular in nothing. Nay were I forc'd to love you by rule I dare venture to say I could never do it sincerely. Take me then with all my faults let me write when I please, for you see I say what I please and am only thinking aloud when writing to you. I suppose you have heard of my intention of going to the East Indies. The place of my destination is one of the factories on the coast of Coromandel and I go in quality of Physician and Surgeon for which the Company has sign'd my warrant which has already cost me ten pounds. I must also pay 50 £b for my passage ten pound for Sea stores, and the other incidental expences of my equipment will amount to 60 or 70 ₤b more. The Sallary is but triffling viz 100 ₤b per ann. but the other advantages if a person be prudent are considerable. The practice of the place if I am rightly informed generally amounts to not less than one thousand pounds per ann. for which the appointed Physician has an exclusive privelege, this with the advantages resulting from trade with the high interest which money bears viz 20 per cent, are the inducements which persuade me to undergo the fatigues of sea the dangers of war and the still greater dangers of the climate, which induce me to leave a place where I am every day gaining friends and esteem and where I might enjoy all the conveniencies of life. I am certainly wrong not to be contented with what I already possess triffling as it is, for should I ask myself one serious question what is it I want? What can I answer? My desires are as capricious as the big bellied woman's who longd for a piece of her husband's nose. I have no certainty it is true; but why can't I do as some men of more merit who have liv'd upon more precarious terms? Scaron us'd jestingly to call himself the Lord Marquis of Quenault[1] which was the name of the bookseller who employ'd him, and why may not I assert my privelege and quality on the same pretensions? Yet upon deliberation, whatever airs I may give myself on this side of the water, my dignity I fancy would be evaporated before I reach'd the other. I know you have in Ireland a very indifferent Idea of a man who writes for bread, tho Swift and Steel did so in the earlier part of their lives.[2] you Imagine, I suppose, that every author by profession lives in a garret, wears shabby cloaths, and converses with the meanest company; but I assure you such a character is entirely chimerical. Nor do I believe there is one single writer, who has abilities to translate a french novel, that does not keep better company wear finer cloaths and live more genteely than many who pride themselves for nothing else in Ireland.[3] I confess it again my Dear Dan that nothing but the wildest ambition could prevail on me to leave the enjoyment of that refind conversation which I sometimes am admitted to partake in for uncertain fortune and paltry shew. You can't conceive how I am sometimes divided, to leave all that is dear gives me pain, but when I consider that it is possible I may acquire a genteel independance for life, when I think of that dignity which Philosophy claims to raise it above contempt and ridicule, when I think thus, I eagerly long to embrace every opportunity of separating myself from the vulgar, as much ~~by my~~ in my circumstances as I am in my sentiments already. I am going to publish a book for an account of which I refer you to a le[tter] which I wrote to my Brother Goldsmith. Circulate for me among your acquaintance an hundred proposals which I have given orders may be sent to you. and if in pursuance of such circulation you should receive any subscriptions let them when collected be transmitted to Mr Bradley who will give a receipt for the same. I am very much pleasd with the accounts you send me of your little son;[4] if I do not mistake that was his hand which subscrib'd itself Gilbeen Hardly.[5] There is nothing could please me more than a letter filld with all the news of the country, but I fear you will think that too troublesome. you see I never cease writing 'till a whole sheet of paper is wrote out, I beg you will immitate me in this particular and give your letters good measure. You can tell me, what visits you receive or pay, who has been married or debauch'd, since my absence what fine girls you have starting up and beating of the veterans of my acquaintance from future conquest. I suppose before I return I shall find all the blooming virgins I once left in Westmeath shrivelled into a parcel of hags with seven children a piece tearing down their petticoats. Most of the Bucks and Bloods whom I left hunting and drinking and swearing and getting bastards I find are dead. Poor devils they kick'd the world before them. I wonder what the devil they kick now?

Dear Sister I wrote to Kilmore I wish you would let me know how that family stands affected with regard to me.[6] My Brother Charless promis'd to tell me all about it but his letter gave me no satisfaction in those particulars. I beg you and Dan would put your hands to the oar and fill me a sheet with somewhat or other, if you can't get quite thro your selves lend Billy or Nancy the pen and let the dear little things give me their nonsense. Talk all about yourselves and nothing about me. You see I do so. I know not how my desire of seeing Ireland which has so long slept has again revivd with so much ardour. So weak is my temper and so unsteady that I am frequently tempted, particularly [when low] spirited, to return home and leave my fortune tho' just [now it is be]ginning to look kinder. But It shall not be. In five or si[x years] I hope to indulge these transports, I find I want constitution, [and a] strong steady disposition which alone makes men great, I [will how] ever correct my faults since I am conscious of them. I [hope] brother Charles is setted to business. I see no probability of h[is succeeding in] any other method of proceeding.[7] ~~Maurice I find wan~~[ts] ~~I am sorry for it. But what can be done since he neith~~[er can write nor] ~~spell with tolerable propriety. As for going with m~~[e that is im]~~possible his verry passage expences and all would cost one hundred pounds. If he would accustom himself to write and spell I will end~~[ea]~~vour to procure him some employment in London. In about two months with diligence and care he might gain a tolerable proficiency in those qualifications and if when so qualified he would send me a specimen of his performance which I might show to his employer I hope I will get him some thing or other unless he might think it beneath him to stoop to little things in the beginning. What money may be necessary to carry him to London shall be supply'd him by a correspondent at Chester,~~[8] ~~and his prudence and submissive behaviour in this station may be a means of his meeting something better in time to come, Or if I succeed according to my expectation where I am going, of my sending for him to live with me.~~ Pray let me hear from my Mother since she will not gratify me herself and tell me if in anything I can be immediately servicable to her. Tell me how My Brother Goldsmith and his Bishop agree.[9] Pray do this for me for heaven knows I would do anything to serve you.

1 The impecunious French poet, comic novelist and dramatist Paul Scarron (1610–60) was employed by the bookseller Toussaint Quinet, and referred to the profit from his works as his 'Marquisat de Quinet'.

2 Jonathan Swift and Richard Steele (1672–1729), Irish authors. In Swift's case, Goldsmith is probably referring to that phase of the author's career, between 1710 and 1714, when he wrote propaganda for the Tories in the *Examiner*. On the other side of the political divide, Steele contributed to the creation of periodical culture with his work for the *Tatler* (1709–11), the *Spectator* (1711–14) and the *Guardian* (1713). Though such work could hardly be called writing for bread in the economy that prevailed in mid-century Grub Street, Goldsmith is conveying something of his predicament to his Irish acquaintance with a vague and general reference to Irish authors.

3 A receipt at the Beinecke in Yale, undated but signed, recorded that 10 guineas had been paid to Goldsmith by Ralph Griffiths 'for the translation of a book entituled Memoirs of My Lady B', a translation of Charlotte-Anne Charbonnier de la Guesnerie's *Memoires de Milady B.* (1760). This work had been given up as lost by Balderston and Friedman; however, Arthur Freeman revealed in 2006 that the book existed and that it had evaded scholars for three reasons: it was published with a different title by a different publisher, to whom Griffiths had sold the rights, in two volumes, the first of which was incorrectly dated. *Memoirs of Lady Harriot Butler* was published by R. Freeman in 1761, but the date of the first volume was given on the title page as MDCCXLI and not MDCCLXI. See Arthur Freeman, 'New Goldsmith?' *Times Literary Supplement* 5411 (15 December 2006), 15.

4 William Hodson, to whom Goldsmith would become a friend and mentor, as evidenced in Letters 30, 31, 36 and 45.

5 Unidentified.

6 A reference to the previous letter to Jane Lawder.

7 Balderston (54n2) speculates that Goldsmith's youngest brother Maurice may have struck through the following passage before sending the letter to Percy in 1776.

8 Possibly the Doctor Keay of Chester referred to in Letter 15 to Mrs Johnson, below. His relationship to Goldsmith is unclear.

9 Goldsmith's brother Henry, a clergyman (see following letter). Goldsmith is here inquiring about his brother's relationship with Edward Synge (1691–1762), the Church of Ireland Bishop of the Diocese of Elphin between 1740 and 1762. He was asking, perhaps, because of his own experience with Synge: after his graduation from Trinity College Dublin, he had been suggested to the Bishop for a living in the church by his uncle Contarine. Goldsmith's interview did not go well, however, supposedly because of his youth and inexperience. In a footnote, Percy added the local tradition that Goldsmith was refused 'either because he had neglected the professional studies, or from a (perhaps exaggerated) report of irregularities at college': 'The Life of Dr. Oliver Goldsmith', I: 9.

12

To the Reverend Henry Goldsmith

[London, *c.* 13 January 1759]

Henry Goldsmith (1722–68) was Oliver's older brother and the sibling to whom he looked for guidance in his youth. Henry had acted as a peacemaker with his brother's tutor Theaker Wilder during Goldsmith's troublesome early Trinity years, and Goldsmith would stay with Henry, a clergyman, upon his return from Dublin in 1751–2. In the dedication to *The Traveller, or a Prospect of Society* (1764), Goldsmith indicated that he had sent a draft of part of that poem to Henry from Switzerland, probably in 1755. The letter below features lines of verse; Henry may, therefore, have been a sounding board for Goldsmith's earlier poetic efforts, though no other examples of such correspondence are extant. Henry died unexpectedly, and much to his brother's sorrow, in 1768. Hence, Goldsmith dedicated his second major poem, *The Deserted Village* (1770), to Joshua Reynolds: 'The only dedication I ever made was to my brother, because I loved him better than most other men. He is since dead. Permit me to inscribe this Poem to you' (*CW*, IV: 285).

The copy-text is the manuscript in the British Library. It was first published by Percy in 1801. It is addressed 'To | The Rev^{d}. Henry Goldsmith, at Lowfield, near | Ballymore in Westmeath; | Ireland.' It is postmarked 13 January.

Dear Sir,

Your Punctuality in answering a man whose trade is writing, is more than I had reason to expect; and yet you see me generally fill a whole sheet which is all the recompence I can make for being so frequently troublesome. The behavior of Mr Mills and Mr Lawder is a little extraordinary, however their answering neither you nor me is a sufficient indication of their disliking the employment which I assign'd them. As their conduct is different from what I had expected so I have made an alteration in mine. I shall the beginning of next month send over two hundred and fifty books which is all that I fancy can be well sold among you. And I would have you make some distinction in the persons who have subscrib'd. The money which will ammount to sixty pounds may be left with Mr. Bradley as soon as possible I am not certain but I shall quickly have occasion for it. I have met with no disappointment with respect to my East India Voyage nor are my resolutions altered, tho' at the same time I must confess it gives me some pain to think I am almost beginning the world at the age of thrty one.[1] Tho' I never had a day's sickness since I saw you yet I am not that strong active man you once knew me. You scarce can conceive how much eight years of disappointment anguish and study have worn me down. If I remember right you are seven or eight years older than me, and yet I dare venture to say that if a stranger saw us both he would pay me the honours of seniority. Immagine to yourself a pale melancholly visage with two great wrinkles between the eye brows, with an eye disgustingly severe and a big wig, and you may have a perfect picture of my present appearance. On the other hand I conceive you as grown fat sleek and healthy, passing many an happy day among your own children or those who knew you a child. Since I knew what it was to be a man this is a pleasure I have not known. I have passd the days among a number of cool designing beings and have contracted all their suspicious manner, in my own behaviour. I should actually be as unfit for the society of my friends at home as I detest that which I am oblige'd to partake of here. I can now neither partake of the pleasure of a revel nor contribute to raise its jollity, I can neither laugh nor d[rin]k, have contracted an hesitating disagreeable manner of speaking, and a visage that looks illnature itself, in short I have thought myself into settled melanchollly and an utter disgust of all that life brings with it. Whence this romantic turn that all our family are possessed with, whence this love for every place and every country but that in which we reside? For every occupation but our own, this desire of fortune and yet this eagerness to dissipate! I perceive my dear Sir that I am at intervals for indulging this splenetic manner and following my own taste regardless of yours. The reasons you have given me for breeding up your son[2] a scholar are judicious and convin[cing] ~~and~~ I should however be glad to know for what particular profession he is design'd? If he be assiduous, and divested of strong passions, (for passions in youth always lead to pleasure) he may do very well in your college, for it must be ownd that the industrious poor have good encouragement there, perhaps better than in any other in Europe. But if he has ambition, strong passions, and an exquisite sensibility of contempt, do not send him there, unless you have no other trade for him except your own.[3] It is impossible to conceive how much may be done by a proper education at home. A boy, for instance, who understands perfectly well Latin, French, Arithmetic and the Principles of the civil law, and can write a fine hand, has an education that may qualify him for any undertaking. And these parts of learning should be carefully inculcated let him be designed for whatsoever calling he will. Above all things let him never touch a romance, or novel, those paint beauty in colours more charming than nature, and describe happiness that man never tastes.[4] How delusive, how destructive therefore are those pictures of consummate bliss, they teach the youthful mind to sigh after beauty and happiness which never existed, to despise the little good which fortune has mixed in our cup, ~~and~~ by expecting more than she ever gave. And in general take the word of a man who has seen the world, and studied human nature more by experience than precept, take my word for it I say that books teach us very little of the world.[5] The greatest merit, and the most consummate virtue that ever grac'd humanity in a state of poverty would only serve to make the possessor ridiculous,[6] they may distress but cannot relieve him. Avarice in the lower orders of mankind is true ambition, avarice is the only ladder the poor can use to preferment. Preach, then my dear Sir, to your son, not the excellence of human nature, nor the disrespect of riches, but endeavour to teach him thrift and œconomy. Let his poor wandering uncles example be plac'd in his eyes. I had learn'd from books to love virtue, before I was taught from experience the necessity of being selfish. I had contracted the habits and notions of a Philosopher, while I was exposing myself to the insidious approaches of cunning; and often, by being even from narrow finances charitable to excess, I forgot the rules of justice, and placd myself in the very situation of the wretch who thank'd my bounty.[7] When I am in the remotest part of the world tell him this and perhaps he may improve by my example. But I find myself again [falling] into my gloomy habits of thinking.[8] ~~Prithee why does not Maurice send me his writings. I would wish him in a way of getting his bread. If he should want about five pounds to carry him up to London Pray let him have it when you receive it for me and if the Poor lad wants cloaths I believe mine will fit him so let not that retard his diligence. I don't want to have him here in order to make him unhappy; I have taken a chambers in the temple~~[9] ~~and he shall lodge with me until something is provided, for places of the sort for which I intend him, every day open.~~ My Mother I am informed is almost blind, even tho' I had the utmost inclination to return home I could not, to behold her in distress without a capacity of relieving her from it, would be too much to add to my present splenetic habit. Your last letter was much too short, it should have answered some queries I had made in my former. Just sit down as I do, and write forward 'till you have filld all your paper, it requires no thought, at least if I may judge from the ease with which my own sentiments rise when they are addressd to you. For believe me my head has no share in all I write my heart dictates the whole. Pray give my love to Bob Bryanton and entreat him from me not to drink. My Dear Sir give me some account about poor Jenny. Yet her husband loves her, if so she cannot be unhappy. I know not whether I should tell you, yet why should I conceal those triffles, or indeed any thing from you, there is a book of mine will be publish'd in a few days. The life of a very extraordinary man, No less than the great Mr. Voltaire.[10] You know already by the title that it is no [mo]re than a catchpenny. However I spent but four weeks on the whole performance for which I received twenty pound. When publish'd I shall take some method of conveying it to you, unless you may think it dear of the postage which may ammount to four or five shillings, however I fear [y]ou will not find an equivalence of amusement. Your last letter, I repeat it, was [t]oo short, you should have given me your opinion of the design of the heroicomical poem which I sent you. You remember I intended to introduce the hero of the Poem as lying in a paltry alehouse you ~~are~~ may take the following specimen of the manner; which I flatter myself is quite original. The room [in] which he lies may be described somewhat this way.[11]

[A] Window patch'd with paper lent a ray,
That feebly shew'd the state in which he lay.
The sanded floor, that grits beneath the tread
The humid wall with paltry pictures spread.
The game of goose was there expos'd to view,[12]
And the twelve rules the Royal Martyr drew.[13]
The seasons, fram'd with listing, found a place,[14]
And Prussia's Monarch shew'd his lamp black face.[15]
The morn was cold he views with keen desire,
A rusty grate unconscious of a fire.
An unpaid reck'ning on the [fre]eze was scor'd,
And five crack'd teacups dress'd the chimney [board]

And Now immagine after his soliloquy the landlord to make his appearance in order to Dun him for the reckoning,

Not with that face so servile and so gay
That welcomes every stranger that can pay,
With sulky eye he smoak'd the patient man
Then pull'd his breeches tight, and thus began, &c. All this is taken you see from Nature. It is a Good remark of Montaign's that the wisest men often have friends with whom they do not care how much they play the fool.[16] Take my present follies as instances of regard. Poetry is much an easier and more agreeable species of composition than prose, and could a man live by it, it were no

unpleasant employment to be a Poet. I am resolvd to leave no space tho' I should fill it up only by telling you what you very well know already, I mean that I am your most affectionate friend and Brother.

Oliver Goldsmith.

1 This statement suggests that Goldsmith was born in 1727. Though his year of birth was subsequently torn away in the Goldsmith family bible, 1728 is the year given by Percy, Prior, and William Shaw Mason. It may be that Goldsmith is here thinking of himself as being in his thirty-first year.

2 The younger Henry Goldsmith was in his infancy when this letter was written. He would enter the British Army as an ensign in 1778, becoming a lieutenant in the 54th Regiment of Foot in 1775. Wounded fighting for the British in the American War of Independence, he married the daughter of a rebel family who tended to him; when the war was over, they settled and raised a family in Nova Scotia. He died in New Brunswick in 1811. His son Oliver, the poet's grand-nephew and namesake, published 'The Rising Village: A Poem' in 1825, an optimistic re-working of *The Deserted Village* which would become a foundational text in the Canadian canon. See E. H. Fairbrother, 'Lieut. Henry Goldsmith: the Poet's Nephew', *Notes and Queries* 12.4 (July 1918), 177–8; see also *P*, II: 564–9.

3 The sentiments in these lines about the passions and fragile intellectual endeavour of youth are reproduced in chapter 10 ('Of the encouragement of learning') of *An Enquiry into the Present State of Polite Learning in Europe*: 'A lad whose passions are not strong enough in youth to mislead him from that path of science, which his tutors, and not his inclinations, have chalked out, by four or five years perseverance, will probably obtain every advantage and honour his college can bestow' (*CW*, I: 308); 'If the author be, therefore, still so necessary among us, let us treat him with proper consideration, as a child of the public, not a rent-charge on the community. And, indeed, a *child* of the public he is in all respects; for while so well able to direct others, how incapable is he frequently found of guiding himself. His simplicity exposes him to all the approaches of cunning, his sensibility to the slightest insidious invasions of contempt. Though possessed of fortitude to stand unmoved the expected bursts of an earthquake, yet of feelings so exquisitely poignant, as to agonize under the slightest disappointment' (*CW*, I: 315).

4 See Letter 83 of *The Citizen of the World*: 'It was a saying of the ancients, that a man never opens a book without reaping some advantage by it. I say with them, that every book can serve to make us more expert except romances, and these are no better than instruments of debauchery. They are dangerous fictions, where love is the ruling passion' (*CW*, II: 340).

5 See Letter 67 of *The Citizen of the World*: 'A youth who has thus spent his life among books, new to the world, and unacquainted with man but by philosophic information, may be considered as a being, whose mind is filled with the vulgar errors of the wise; utterly unqualified for a journey through life, yet confident of his own skill in the direction, he sets out with confidence, blunders on with vanity, and finds himself at last undone' (*CW*, II: 276).

6 See chapter 10 of *An Enquiry into the Present State of Polite Learning*: 'If the profession of an author is to be laughed at by stupids, it is better sure to be contemptibly rich, than contemptibly poor. For all the wit that ever adorned the human mind will at present no more shield the author's poverty from ridicule, than his high topped gloves conceal the unavoidable omissions of his laundress' (*CW*, I: 314).

7 See the *Bee* 3 (20 October 1759) ('On Justice and Generosity'): 'A man, therefore, who has taken his ideas of mankind from study alone, generally comes into the world with an heart melting at every fictitious distress. Thus he is induced by misplaced liberality, to put himself into the indigent circumstances of the person he relieves' (*CW*, I: 408).

8 Once again, Maurice may have struck through the section following before sending the letter to Percy in 1776.

9 Goldsmith's statement here is fanciful. He was still living in Green Arbour Court at this time and could not afford to take lodgings at the Temple until 1764, though he may have taken a temporary residence in the Temple around the time of this letter.

10 Goldsmith's life of Voltaire was never published in book form, though it was advertised as such in the *Public Advertiser* (7 February 1759): 'Speedily will be published, Memoirs of the Life of Monsieur de Voltaire; with Critical Observations on the Writings of that celebrated Poet, and a new Translation of the Henriade'. It was advertised again in the same paper by John Wilkie, Goldsmith's collaborator on the *Bee*, on 23 May 1760. The work would eventually be published in ten monthly instalments between February and November 1761 in the *Lady's Magazine*, which Goldsmith may have edited for a time. See *CW*, III: 225–6.

11 The lines of poetry below are given again, slightly modified, in Letter 30 of *The Citizen of the World* (*CW*, II: 129). Some of these images recur in *The Deserted Village*, ll. 227–36: 'the nicely sanded floor'; 'The twelve good rules, the royal game of goose'; the 'broken tea-cups, wisely kept for shew, / Ranged o'er the chimney, glistened in a row' (*CW*, IV: 296).

12 A rudimentary children's game intended to teach addition, played with counters on a board divided into sixty-three compartments. In every fourth or fifth compartment a goose was depicted. If a thrown dice landed on a picture of a goose, the player would move forward by two times the number on the dice.

13 Moral maxims attributed to Charles I: '1. Urge no healths; 2. Profane no divine ordinances; 3. Touch no state matters; 4. Reveal no secrets; 5. Pick no quarrels; 6. Make no comparisons; 7. Maintain no ill opinions; 8. Keep no bad company; 9. Encourage no vice; 10. Make no long meals; 11. Repeat no grievances; 12. Lay no wagers': *Maxims, Morals, and Golden Rules*, 4th edn (London: James Madden & Co., 1844), 10. See also Kevin Sharpe, 'Private Conscience and Public Duty in the Writings of Charles I', *The Historical Journal* 40.3 (1997), 643–65.

14 Prints depicting the seasons were popular; Balderston notes that four mezzotint sets of 'Seasons' were published around 1759 (64n4).

15 Frederick the Great of Prussia was popular in Britain in 1758–9, due to his successes in the Seven Years' War, though Goldsmith presents that popularity cynically in his essay 'On the Instability of Worldly Grandeur' in the *Bee* 6 (10 November 1759), in which an Islington alehouse keeper regularly changes the sign at his alehouse according to the fashion of the day. The sign of the King of Prussia, more recently raised, 'may probably be changed in turn for the next great man that shall be set up for vulgar admiration' (*CW*, I: 470). In *The Citizen of the World*'s version of these poetic lines, Frederick is – perhaps ironically – replaced by 'brave prince William'. Friedman suggests that this William is William Augustus, third son of George III, the Duke of Cumberland, who had signed an unfavourable neutrality pact with the French in 1757 (*CW*, II: 129n4). The lamp-black face suggests that such portraits of Frederick and William took the form of silhouettes.

16 This may be a corrupted reference to Montaigne's suggestion, following Cato, in 'De l'art de conférer', *Essais* III.8: 'A cette sorte de discipline regardoit le vieux Caton, quand il dict que les sages ont plus à apprendre des fols que les fols des sages' (*The Montaigne Project: Villey Edition of the Essais* online) [It was this sort of teaching that the elder Cato had in mind when he said that wise men have more to learn from fools than fools from wise men].

It may also refer to a less aphoristic passage from 'De trois commerces', *Essais*, III.3: 'Mais cette mollesse de jugement, dequoy je parle, m'attache par force à la solitude: voire chez moy, au milieu d'une famille peuplée et maison des plus fréquentées. J'y voy des gens assez, mais rarement ceux avecq qui j'ayme à communiquer; et je reserve là, et pour moy et pour les autres, une liberté inusitée. Il s'y faict trefve de ceremonie, d'assistance et convoiemens, et telles autres ordonnances penibles de nostre courtoisie (ô la servile et importune usance!); chacun s'y gouverne à sa mode; y entretient qui veut ses pensées: je m'y tiens muet, resveur et enfermé, sans offence de mes hostes' [But that softness of judgement, of which I speak, forcefully attaches me to solitude: even at home, amongst a large family in a much-visited house. Here I see many people but rarely those whose conversation I enjoy; and I reserve here, for myself and others, an unusual liberty. Here there is a suspension of ceremony, in admittance and ushering out, and other such prescriptions of courtesy (servile and intrusive customs!); there everyone behaves as he likes; and if he wants can entertain his thoughts: I stay silent, dreamy and withdrawn, without offending my guests].

13
To Ralph Griffiths
[London, January 1759]

Ralph Griffiths (1720?–1803) was Goldsmith's first bookseller, with whom he had a fraught relationship. Griffiths established the *Monthly Review* in 1749, and erected over the door the sign of the Dunciad, the reference to Alexander Pope's excoriating satire and an indication that his reviewers would be unforgiving in their assessments. Griffiths worked closely with his wife Isabella, who also wrote for and helped to edit the *Monthly*. Mrs Griffiths was a critic of Goldsmith's work, and had a tendency to interfere with it, as recorded by Percy: 'In this Thraldom he lived 7 or 8 months Griffith and his wife continually objecting to everything he wrote & insisting on his implicitly submitting to their corrections.'[1]

Goldsmith had begun to work for Tobias Smollett's *Critical Review* – which was, in Griffiths's view, an adversary – in late 1758. Though estranged, Goldsmith was looking for work from Griffiths at the same time, agreeing to do four reviews in return for Griffiths acting as security for a new suit which Goldsmith required to present himself at an ill-fated interview at Surgeons' Hall for a medical position in India. Goldsmith promised to return the suit or furnish the written material; however, he pawned the clothing and Griffiths's books, ostensibly to aid his landlord's wife, after his landlord was jailed for debt. When Griffiths heard of this affair, he wrote angrily to Goldsmith demanding the suit, books or money, in such a threatening manner as to have provoked the letter below, in which Goldsmith seeks to explain himself. The letter may have had a softening effect on Griffiths. Though he would authorize William Kenrick's brutal and personal attack on the *Enquiry* in the *Monthly Review* of November 1759 (see Introduction, xxxvi–xxxvii), Griffiths would contract Goldsmith to translate *Memoires de Milady B.* in 1760; and the review of *The Citizen of the World* in the *Monthly Review* in June 1762 contained a somewhat mealy-mouthed apology to the 'lively and ingenious' author:

we were surprized to hear that this Gentleman had imagined himself in any degree pointed at, as we conceive nothing can be more illiberal in a Writer, or more foreign to the character of a Literary Journal, than to descend to the meanness of personal reflection. It is hoped that a charge of this sort can never be justly brought against the Monthly Review.[2]

The copy-text is the manuscript in the Victoria and Albert Museum. It was first published by Prior in 1837. The letter is endorsed by Griffiths 'Rec'd in Jany. 1759' which supplies the date. Balderston proposes that the letter was written after the preceding letter to Henry. The 'three or four weeks' referred to in the second sentence probably alludes to the time which had elapsed since Goldsmith's unsuccessful interview (on 21 December 1758) at Surgeons' Hall. This dates the letter in mid-January, and probably after the letter to Henry in which he betrays none of the anxiety evident here.

Sir,

I know of no misery but a gaol to which my own imprudencies and your letter seem to point. I have seen it inevitable this three or four weeks, and by heavens, request it as a favour, as a favour that may prevent somewhat more fatal. I have been some years struggling with a wretched being, with all that contempt which indigence brings with it, with all those strong passions which make contempt insupportable. What then has a gaol that is formidable, I shall at least have the society of wretches, and such is to me true society. I tell you again and again I am now neither able nor willing to pay you a farthing, but I will be punctual to any appointment you or the taylor shall make; thus far at least I do not act the sharper, since unable to pay my debts one way I would willingly give some security another. No Sir, had I been a sharper, had I been possessed of less good nature and native generosity I might surely now have been in better circumstances. I am guilty I own of meanessess which poverty unavoidably brings with it,[3] my reflections are filld with repentance for my imprudence but not with any remorse for being a villain, that may be a character you unjustly charge me with. Your books I can assure you are neither pawn'd nor sold, but in the custody of a friend ~~for whom~~

from whom my necessities oblig'd me to borrow some money, whatever becomes of my person, you shall have them in a month. It is very possible both the reports you have heard and your own suggestions may have brought you false information with respect to my character, it is very possible that the man whom you now regard with detestation may inwardly burn with grateful resentment, it is very possible that upon a second perusal of the letter I sent you, you may see the workings of a mind strongly agitated with gratitude and jealousy, if such circumstances should appear at least spare invective 'till my book with Mr. Dodsley[4] shall be publish'd, and then perhaps you may see the bright side of a mind when my professions shall not appear the dictates of necessity but of choice. You seem to think Doctor Milner[5] knew me not. Perhaps so; but he was a man I shall ever honour; but I have friendship only with the dead! I ask pardon for taking up so much time Nor shall I add to it by any other professions than that I am Sir your Humble serv^{t}.

Oliver Goldsmith.

P.S. I shall expect impatiently the result of your resolutions.

1 Katharine C. Balderston, *The History and Sources of Percy's Memoir of Goldsmith* (Cambridge University Press, 1926), 16.

2 *Monthly Review* (June 1762), 477.

3 See Letter 83 of *The Citizen of the World*: 'a man being possessed of more than he wants, can never be subject to great disappointments, and avoids all those meannesses which indigence sometimes unavoidably produces' (*CW*, II: 339).

4 A reference to his *Enquiry into the Present State of Polite Learning in Europe*, which would be published, anonymously, around 4 April 1759 by Robert and James Dodsley.

5 The Reverend John Milner (d. 1758), the father of one of Goldsmith's Edinburgh acquaintances, who ran a Presbyterian school in Peckham, at which Goldsmith stood in as a teacher. It was through the Milners that Goldsmith first met with Ralph Griffiths. Milner was a noted scholar of the Latin and Greek languages, and author of *A Practical Grammar of the Latin Tongue* (1729), *A Practical Grammar of the Greek Tongue* (1734), *The Accidents of Words in the Latin Tongue* (1742), and *An Abstract of Latin Syntax* (1743). Several of his sermons were published through the 1740s and 1750s. He died in 1758.

14

To Mrs. Johnson

[London, 1758–1762]

The identity of Mrs Johnson is unknown and the nature of the business involving a guinea is unclear. The dating of the two notes to this Mrs Johnson is highly conjectural. Balderston suggests that the use of 'Mr. Goldsmith' in the first note indicates that it was written before 1763, around which time Goldsmith began routinely to refer to himself as 'Dr. Goldsmith' (*BL*, 70n2). However, it is also possible that Dr Keay referred to in the second note here is the Chester correspondent mentioned in Letter 11 of August 1758, which suggests an earlier date.[1] Splitting the difference, so to speak, Balderston suggests the summer of 1760. It would appear that Mrs Johnson and Dr Keay were correspondents through whom Goldsmith carried out unspecified miscellaneous tasks and transactions: Mrs Johnson in London, Dr. Keay in Chester, which was, along with Holyhead, one of two major ports for traffic with Ireland.

The copy-text is the manuscript in the Houghton Library, Harvard University. It was first published by Balderston in 1928. It is endorsed on the verso, in another hand, 'To Mrs. Johnson'.

Mr. Goldsmith's best respects to Mrs. Johnson will pay a Guinea or whatever she thinks proper either of his own or her appointing only letting him know to whom or for what: He will wait on Mrs. Johnson if she thinks proper this evening at six, or if, as she intended she will call upon him he will be very proud of that honour. A line or two by the bearer will not be amiss.

[1] 'T. Keay, M.D. Chester' is listed as a subscriber to Priscilla Pointon, *Poems on several occasions. By Miss Priscilla Pointon, of Lichfield* (Birmingham, 1770).

15

To Mrs. Johnson

[London, 1758–1762]

See headnote to previous letter.

The copy-text is a facsimile of the manuscript in the sale catalogue of *The Library of Jerome Kern, New York City, Part 1, A–J* (1929), 198. A copy of the catalogue is housed at the Rosenbach of the Free Library of Philadelphia. Balderston accessed this letter in the private collection of A. S. W. Rosenbach, then of New York. The catalogue records, as does Balderston, that the letter is endorsed on the reverse 'To Mrs. Johnson'. Balderston also notes that, along with the endorsement, there is a partially illegible memorandum in an eighteenth-century hand: 'There is a 3 or 400 pds worth of things brought in to the House which [ ] no person.'

Dear Madam

I sent word to Doctor Keay of Chester to pay Faulkener a guinea I receiv'd no answer from him but I believe it is paid.[1] I shall write again tonight. If you chuse I will return you the guinea

I am your
humble servant
Oliver Goldsmith

[1] Possibly the Dublin publisher George Faulkner (*c.* 1703–75), who visited London annually. Goldsmith certainly knew him later in life, as Letter 29 testifies. For Doctor Keay, see previous letter.

16

To John Newbery

[London, early summer 1762]

Of a farming family background in Berkshire, John Newbery (bap. 1713, d. 1767) was apprenticed to the printer William Carnan in Reading and would inherit a share of his mentor's business when Carnan died in 1737. He set up as a bookseller in St Paul's Churchyard in London in 1743 and would become famous for his innovative ventures in children's literature. Newbery founded in January 1760 the *Public Ledger* in which Goldsmith's Chinese letters were first published in 1760–1; he would also publish the collected Chinese letters as *The Citizen of the World* in 1762. When Goldsmith was arrested for debt in 1762, Newbery purchased a third share in the novel which would be published four years later as *The Vicar of Wakefield*. He would also publish Goldsmith's *History of England* and *The Traveller, or a Prospect of Society* in 1764.

The copy-text is the manuscript in the Free Library of Philadelphia. It was first published by Prior in 1837. It is addressed 'To Mr. Newbery, St. Paul's Church Yard'. Balderston dates it in the early summer. '1762' is pencilled onto the manuscript by an unknown hand, but it seems fair to date it in the summer of that year for the reason given in Balderston: there exists a receipt of 5 March 1762 from Goldsmith to Newbery – also in the Free Library of Philadelphia – in which Goldsmith writes: 'Receivd from Mr Newbery eleven guineas and an half for an abridgment of Plutarch's lives' (see *BL*, 71n2). That receipt was for the first two volumes, while the second of these letters refers to another payment – of 12 guineas – which would have been for the third and fourth volumes. Balderston gives this pair of letters in a different order; given the sequence of references to the fourth and fifth volumes, however, and the reference in the second letter to his being 'still not quite recovered', we suggest that they were marginally more likely to have been composed in the order we give here.

Sir

One Volume is done namely the fourth; When I said I should be glad Mr Collier would do the fifth for me, I only demanded it as a favour, but if he cannot conveniently do it, tho I have kept my chamber these three weeks and am not yet quite recovered yet I will do it.[1] I send it per bearer, and if the affair puts you to the least inconvenience return it, and it shall be done immediately. I am, &c.

The Printer has the Copy of the rest. O.G.

[1] Joseph Collyer (1714/15–76) was a translator who had a shop in Plough Court in London. He translated works by Voltaire, Plutarch and Bodmer. See following letter.

17

To John Newbery

[London, early summer 1762]

See headnote to previous letter.

The copy-text is the manuscript in the Free Library of Philadelphia. It was first published by Prior in 1837.

D[r] Sir,

As I have been out of order for some time past and am still not quite recovered, the fifth volume of Plutarch's lives remains unfinish'd, I fear I shall not be able to do it, unless there be an actual necessity and that none else can be found, If therefore you would send it to Mr Collier[1] I should esteem it a kindness, and will pay for whatever it may come to. N.B. I received twelve guineas for the two Volumes.

I am Sir your obliged
humble serv[t]
Oliver Goldsmith,

Pray let me have an answer.

1 The abridgement of *Plutarch's Lives* which Goldsmith had contracted with Newbery was published in seven volumes from May to November 1762. Goldsmith acknowledged receipt of 11½ guineas for the work. It would appear from the letter and receipts that Goldsmith completed four volumes, but that Collyer was tasked with the fifth. Friedman notes that the work was advertised on 15 June 1774 as the work of Goldsmith and Joseph Collyer. See previous letter.

18

To *Lloyd's Evening Post*

London, 17 November 1762

Goldsmith's biography of Richard Nash (1674–1761) was published anonymously on 14 October 1762. A second edition followed on 9 December. *The Life of Richard Nash, Esq; Late Master of the Ceremonies at Bath* was compiled and composed by Goldsmith from Nash's papers and the anecdotes of Nash's executor George Scott. Nash, also known as Beau Nash, was a social celebrity famed for generous extravagance, and the *Life* – an engaging, anecdotal and, at times, critical narrative of Nash's life – is perhaps Goldsmith's best-known biographical work. It was not particularly well received however. The *Monthly* and *Critical* reviews deemed its subject matter, and its manner, trivial, while in its issue of October 1762, the *St. James's Magazine* took additional issue with its apparent attribution to ageing actor James Quin (1693–1766) of a letter to an unnamed nobleman indicating Quin's supposed designs on Nash's position as Master of Ceremonies at Bath in October 1760, a matter of months before the latter's death. Quin's supposed letter was mediated to Nash, Goldsmith reported, by a third party, and was thus found among Nash's papers – hence its inclusion in the *Life*. Goldsmith did not explicitly endorse Quin's authorship of the letter, but its inclusion was read as a tacit attribution. The *St. James's Magazine* reviewer deemed the attribution an absurdity, and his review was followed with a letter to the editor with an epigram ridiculing Goldsmith for his alleged folly.

Just over three weeks later a letter to the editor appeared in *Lloyd's Evening Post* defending the author of the *Life of Nash*. Signed 'A. B.', this letter, Arthur Friedman has all but conclusively demonstrated, was composed by Goldsmith (see *CW*, III: 392–4), and thus we include it here.[1] The grounds given by Friedman for its inclusion are several: the penultimate paragraph of the letter was slightly altered and included as a footnote in the second edition of the *Life* just two weeks after the letter appeared in *Lloyd's*. It is likely, therefore, that the paragraph had been prepared and copy for the new edition dispatched before the letter appeared in the newspaper. Friedman also noted that Goldsmith was writing for no other periodicals at the time, having published five essays in *Lloyd's* over the first half of 1762. It was also unlikely that anyone else would have composed the letter. The *Life of Nash* was published anonymously, and no-one else would have had any particular cause to defend its author, nor would anyone outside of Goldsmith's circle have had particular cause to defend it so ardently. The letter also betrays a familiarity with the research which made the *Life* possible: its anecdotal, epistolary and archival sources. Finally, Friedman compellingly cites parallels, given in our notes below, between the letter and Goldsmith's thoughts on factionalism in the republic of letters, as expressed in his *Memoirs of M. de Voltaire* and Letter 20 of *The Citizen of the World*.

The copy-text is *Lloyd's Evening Post*, 22–24 November 1762, where it was first published. Balderston did not include letters to newspapers in her edition.

To the EDITOR *of* LLOYD'S EVENING POST.

Sir,

IT has long been a doubt with me, (which I would gladly have solved either by you or the publick) whether literature and learned men have suffered most by ignorance or malevolence; that is, whether the disregard which has been paid to the Republick of Letters by the generality of mankind, or the party disputes which have always subsisted, and carried on with asperity by the writers themselves, have been most injurious to Science and the Muses. – – – If this question was confined to poetry, and what the French call the *Belles Lettres*, it would admit of no dispute; for these people are always together by the ears, and behave to each other so scandalously, that if Plato were living, and presided over them, he would either banish them the society, or confine them in the stocks. Success will ever excite among these people envy and detraction;[2] and in this they descend even to the *Petitesse* of science, as the French call it. The little books for children, written by Mr. Newbery, have not escaped censure and abuse, though they have done so much service to the rising generation;[3] and the Editor of the Life of Nash has been lately attacked, in a very ungentleman-like manner, and for no other reason, perhaps, but because the book has attracted the notice of the publick, and met with an uncommon sale.

But the Author of that Piece of criticism (if it may deserve this name) is the more inexcusable, as it seems to be written with a view of giving the publick an unfavourable opinion of a work which he had not read, or which he read partially, and with a design to misrepresent the Author's meaning. To elucidate this matter, and to give the publick a proper Specimen of this Author's candour, I shall insert that part of his Paper respecting the letter said to be attributed to Mr. Quin:

"Of all the curiosities in this work (says the Author) the letter so strangely attributed to Mr. Quin is the greatest. Bad spellers, it is observable, however unlike they make the words to the manner they ought to be written in, endeavor to bring them as near as possible to the common pronunciation. But this before us seems to be *artificially* ill spelt, and labouring to be wrong. Surely no person can suspect a letter of this kind to be original from a man, of whom the *first Personages* in the kingdom have condescended to become scholars, and learn to deliver themselves with strength and propriety. But the matter, the manner, the spelling, are equally absurd, and the letter carries its own refutation along with it."

Not satisfied with this, our Critic writes an epistle to himself, in order to introduce what he calls an Epigram; with both of which we shall oblige the reader.

"Sir,

"As you have taken upon you a kind of literary jurisdiction, I must beg leave to lay an information before you, against the Editor of the Life of Richard Nash, of Bath, Esq;—If you will give yourself the trouble of turning to page 161 of this Book, you will find there a supposed letter from Mr. Quin, in which he makes interest to a supposed Lord, to supersede Mr. Nash, as Master of the Ceremonies at Bath. Now, Sir, can it possibly be supposed, by any man of sense, or common justice, that Quin, who quitted the stage at the height of his reputation, to be free from restraint, should endeavor to supplant poor Nash in his most troublesome and ridiculous employment? Or that he, who gave such force to Shakespear's wit and humour, and sets the table on a roar with his own, could be capable of writing such nonsensical stuff, as that supposed letter contains?—These are the considerations which produced the following Epigram:

EPIGRAM

To the EDITOR *of* NASH'S *Life.*

"Think'st thou that Quin, whose parts and wit
Might any station grace,
Could e'er such ribbald stuff have writ,
Or wish'd for Nash's place?[4]
With scorn we read thy senseless trash,
And see thy toothless grin,
For Quin no more cou'd sink to Nash,
Than thou can'st rise to Quin."

This he thought very ingenious; but a Barber's boy, who shaved me this morning, was of a contrary opinion, and said, though he knew the Author, and was well assured he was a fortnight about it, 'twas but a poor piece of business. Then begging pen and ink he sate down and wrote the following answer:

The BARBER'S BOY'S EPIGRAM, *in the Style and Spirit of the above.*

Labourious ——,[5] why all this spleen?
With satire why so free?
He who can't rise to mighty Quin
May dwindle down to *thee.*

Had the Author of this criticism read the paragraph which immediately precedes the letter complained of, he would have seen that the Editor of the Life of Nash did not believe it was written by Mr. Quin. The paragraph I mean is in page 159, of the first edition, and is verbatim as follows:

'Even his place of Master of the Ceremonies (if I can trust the papers he has left behind him) was sought after. I would willingly be tender of any living reputation; but these papers accuse Mr. Quin of endeavouring to supplant him. He has even left us a letter, which *he supposed* was written by that Gentleman, soliciting a Lord for his interest upon the occasion. As I chuse to give Mr. Quin an opportunity of disproving this, I will insert the letter, and, to shew the *improbability* of its being his, with all its faults, both of style and spelling. I am the less apt to believe it written by Mr. Quin, as a Gentleman, who has mended Shakespear's Plays so often, would surely be capable of something more correct than the following. It was spent, *as it should seem*, from Mr. Quin to a Nobleman, but left open for the perusal of an intermediate friend. It was this friend who sent a copy of it to Mr. Nash, who caused it to be instantly printed, and left among his other papers.'

Nor is this all that appears in behalf of the Editor; for in the next paragraph that follows this letter, are these words:

'Here Nash, if I may be permitted the use of a polite and fashionable phrase, was *humm'd*;[6] but he experienced such rubs as these, and a thousand other mortifications, every day.'

Now can any one who has read these two paragraphs, and is not wilfully blind, suppose that the Editor thought the letter in question was written by Mr. Quin, or that it would give any uneasiness either to him or his friends? The letter, as I am in formed, was really found among Mr. Nash's papers, and was inserted to shew what artifices were used by those who had more levity than good-nature, to impose upon a poor old man, and to embitter his last moments.

The reader will observe, that I have omitted the name of this Critic, and the title of the pamphlet in which his piece was inserted: The first was done out of tenderness to the character of a man, who may in time learn a more prudent behaviour; and the name of the pamphlet was omitted for no other reason but because it was thought altogether unworthy of publick notice.

Yours, etc.
A. B.

Bedford-Coffee-house,
Nov. 17, 1762.

[1] See also Oliver W. Ferguson, 'The Materials of History: Goldsmith's *Life of Nash*', *PMLA* 80.4 (1965), 372–86: 381.

[2] In his *Memoirs of M. de Voltaire*, Goldsmith writes: 'There is perhaps no situation more uneasy than that of being foremost in the Republic of letters. If a man, who writes to please the public, cannot, at the same time, stoop to flattery, he is certainly made unhappy for life. There are an hundred writers of inferior merit continually expecting his approbation, these must be all applauded, or made enemies, the public must be deceived by ill-placed praise, or dunces provoked into unremitting persecution. This undertribe in the literary commonwealth perfectly understand the force of combinations, are liberal in their mutual commendations, and actually enjoy all the pleasures of fame without being so much as known to the public. While the man of eminence is regarded, as an outcast of their society, a fit object at which to level all their invective, and every advance he makes towards reputation, only lifts his head nearer to the storm; till at last he finds, that, instead of fame, he has been only all his life earning reproach, till he finds himself possessed of professing friends and sincere enemies' (*CW*, III: 243).
Letter 20 of *The Citizen of the World* contains similar sentiments: 'every member of this fancied republic is desirous of governing, and none willing to obey; each looks upon his fellow as a rival, not an assistant in the same pursuit. They calumniate, they injure, they despise, they ridicule each other: if one man writes a book that pleases, others shall write books to shew that he might have given still greater pleasure, or should not have pleased' (*CW*, II: 85).

[3] John Newbery was the publisher of *The Life of Richard Nash* and a principal shareholder in *Lloyd's Evening Post*. Goldsmith would praise Newbery's publications for children again in his preface to Charles Wiseman's *Complete English Grammar* (1764) as 'happily adapted to delight and rectify the growing mind, and lead it up to truth, through the flowery paths of pleasure' (*CW*, V: 311). Though it was published by W. Nichol, Newbery had an interest in Wiseman's *Grammar*. Goldsmith also praises Newbery in *The Vicar of Wakefield*, where he makes a cameo appearance as 'the philanthropic bookseller in St. Paul's church-yard, who has written so many little books for children: he called himself their friend; but he was the friend of all mankind' (*CW*, IV: 94).

[4] A space is given between two quatrains in the original in the *St. James's Magazine*, but not in Goldsmith's reproduction in *Lloyd's Evening Post*.

[5] The name of the critic is omitted here and throughout for reasons which Goldsmith gives towards the end of the letter.

[6] 'Humm'd', in this context, implies that dissent or dissatisfaction was murmured.

19

To James Dodsley

London, 10 March 1764

James Dodsley (1724–97), bookseller, was the younger brother and colleague of Robert Dodsley (1704–64). Their imprint, founded by Robert in 1735 at Tully's Head in Pall Mall in London, became one of the more prestigious publishing concerns of its time. Robert published Edmund Burke's *Philosophical Enquiry into the Origins of our Ideas of the Sublime and Beautiful* (1757), which Goldsmith reviewed in the *Monthly Review*. In April 1759, the Dodsleys published Goldsmith's *Enquiry into the Present State of Polite Learning in Europe* and Samuel Johnson's philosophical Orientalist fable *Rasselas*. James Dodsley would also pay Goldsmith 10 guineas for a share of his oratorio *The Captivity* in October 1764 (John Newbery bought the other share).

The copy-text is the manuscript in the Free Library of Philadelphia. It was first published by Forster in 1848. It is addressed 'To Mr. John Dodesley in Pall Mall.'

Gray's Inn[1]

Sir

I shall take it as a favour if you can let me have ten guineas via bearer, for which I promise to account. I am sir your humble servant,

Oliver Goldsmith

March 10th, 1764

P.S. I shall call to see you on Wednesday next with copy[2] &c.

[1] The address given here is the only evidence for Goldsmith's place of residence between his leaving Canonbury House in Islington, on 25 December 1763, and his returning there on 29 March 1764.

[2] Probably a history of England which Goldsmith wrote for Dodsley at some point in 1764, and which, as Balderston notes, Dodsley included in *The Geography and History of England done in the manner of Gordon's and Salmon's Geographical and Historical Grammars*, an anonymous volume published the following year (*BL*, 73n3). The authorship of the book is evidenced by Goldsmith's receipt to Dodsley, also in the Free Library of Philadelphia: 'Received from Mr. James Dodsley thirty guineas for writing and compiling an history of England August 8th. 1764.—Oliver Goldsmith'.

20

To John Bindley

[London, early July 1766]

John Bindley (*c.* 1735–86) of Whitefriars, London, and Caversham, near Reading, started in business with his father as a distiller; upon becoming secretary to the Board of Excise, he made his share of the business over to his brother James. He was appointed commissioner of the Excise by the Earl of Bute, who was then prime minister, in February 1763. A friend of Charles Townshend (1725–67), politician, Bindley sought a seat in Parliament in 1764; he was returned on the government interest on 23 December 1766 as MP for Dover.[1] In the general election of 1768, Bindley stood for Reading but was defeated. His financial situation deteriorated and he was bankrupt within a couple of years. In an obituary for his brother James in 1818 in the *Gentleman's Magazine*, it was recorded that John Bindley 'had great talents, with a vivacious turn of mind, and united a peculiar aptitude for financial concerns to an ease and pleasantness of conversation, which, in his progress through life, obtained for him many friends'.[2] The friendship between Goldsmith and the Bindleys seems new, and the tone in the letters to John is familiar and giddily ironic.

The two letters to Bindley were written in July 1766. The second letter is at the end dated 12 July by Goldsmith. It is likely that very little time elapsed between the two letters. Balderston reconstructs the letters' contexts as follows: Goldsmith may have visited Bindley's new home – its newness to the Bindleys might explain the many references to thatching and cultivation – in mid-to-late June, before attending a social gathering at Dr George Fordyce's house on Monday 23 June where Bindley's absence was lamented (it may have been Fordyce who introduced Goldsmith to Bindley in the first instance).[3] During the week following, Goldsmith misdirected a letter to Bindley at West hatch, and the mistaken name of the location becomes a running – not to say tedious – joke in the letter. Bindley may have written to Goldsmith in the meantime asking about the authorship of *A History of the Late Minority*, a new edition of which had been advertised for 29 June 1766 in the *Gentleman's Magazine* (36, 288). The first letter was probably rewritten and dispatched to Bindley in the first week of July (there is a reference to a fortnight elapsing since the gathering at Fordyce's). Bindley's response would then have been sent in time for Goldsmith to respond by 12 July.

The copy-text is the manuscript in the Beinecke Library, Yale University. It was first published in 1964 by Balderston in the *Yale University Library Gazette*, the year after Yale had acquired the two Bindley letters from a private collection in Australia.[4] It is addressed 'To | John Bindley Esqr. At West—not quick— | hatch near Woodford Bridge in the | County of Essex called by the ancients | Wessex. # a note. | # vide Polydore Virgil, &c.'[5]

Dear Sir,

You have removed the thatch'd house; you have done quite right. You have not done any thing to the piece of water; you have done very wrong. You talk to me much about vinegar, and quicksilver and stuff. I see youre no conjuror. When you think of those things a little deeply you will alter your opinions, just as in the affair of the thatch'd house. I wrote you a long letter to prove that I was right, but by a small mistake in the direction, the letter went wrong.[6] It is thus in all my other experiments, the theory is always true, but there is some error in the application. Indeed you do me the justice to own it yourself. If we missed when I was down with you, I can ascribe the failure only to the fault of the weather, which you know we both complain'd of, and when the weather is wrong every thing is wrong with an English man. But in the affair of the thatch'd house, there you own I was infallible. I shall be very glad to see the thatch'd house as soon as I can, and if you will permit me I will on the first opportunity take a post chaise with an umbra,[7] and dine with you at quick hatch, West hatch I mean. You talk of the stage coach, there again you are wrong, a stage coach to one who takes a jaunt for pleasure! I had as lief carry a chair for my own amusement. I could tell you such stories of a stage coach as would make your hair stand on end, about nurses, and cook maids, and parsons, and a mad pastry cook, but no more of that. As for the life enclosed I am obliged to you for it, whose ever life it is, it is humorous, natural, and pretty, and I don't believe you wrote it. I am resolved ~~not~~ to allow neither you, nor Mrs Bindley, one good quality, 'till you acknowledge my skill as an Alchemist, a projector, and even a conjuror if I think proper to claim the title. For instance I will deny that you have the smallest share of wit, or she the least pretensions to beauty, I will deny that you are a well bred man, or that she knows how to make her company happy at ~~Quick hatch~~, West hatch.[8] In short you shall have neither sense, virtue, nor good manners between you till I am fairly reinstated in all my philosophical claims from Metaphysics to cookery. The Pamphlet you were talking of was neither written by Cooper or Burke, but as I am told by Guthrie.[9] I should be sorry to see any one enter the lists with him, for a Grubstreet writer never thinks his pamphlet succeeds untill it is answered. As for my friends, my very good friends the ministers, with whom I am so well acquainted, you may tickle them if you please. The writing of pamphlets is at present fallen very low, the history of the minority was written by one Almon a little halfwitted Bookseller,[10] the most ignorant impudent thing upon earth, he wanted me to sell him my name once, and what was worst of all the book was to be of his own writing. I can tell you one thing, that something is going forward, the old ministry are very close at it, not yet left town, who knows what this may produce? I am sure neither you nor I do?[11] At least

I can answer for myself, and as for you, the thatch'd house for that. Ill make the thatch'd house one of the most unfortunate jobs of your whole life. Upon the strength of that alone I will for the future claim a complete superiority of taste. I will talk of myself eternally before you, and will possitively, and punctually come once a year to see it, and make the proper alterations that I see fit. Ill think of a mottoe for it. We thought much about you at Fordyce's last Monday sennight,[12] you did not come according to your promise, there again you were wrong. Just this moment I have received a message from a great man, what it means I don't know, but I am to wait for him tomorrow morning, I suppose to be served in my usual way, to be prais'd, and then to be forgotten. God bless you all at West hatch, Mrs Bindley, the child, your Brother, and you; tell your brother I have not forgot the jaunt he promisd me to Cambridge. I am Dear Sir your most obedient servant and
sincere friend

Oliver Goldsmith.

1 Cited in Lewis Namier and John Brooke, *The History of Parliament: The House of Commons 1754–1790*, 3 vols. (London: Secker & Warburg, 1985), II: 92.
2 *Gentleman's Magazine* 88 (1818), 631.
3 George Fordyce (1736–1802) was of an eminent Scottish family and he entered the medical school at the University of Edinburgh in 1754. He went on to study in London and Leiden before settling in Essex Street, the Strand, where he would lecture on chemistry and physic. These lecture courses were very successful; he taught thousands of pupils over about thirty years while publishing on medicine. He was a friend of Joshua Reynolds, David Garrick, Edward Gibbon and Richard Brinsley Sheridan, and he was elected to the Club in 1774, proposed by Goldsmith and Johnson.
4 See Katharine C. Balderston, 'New Goldsmith Letters', *Yale University Library Gazette* 39 (1964), 71–2.
5 An antiquarian joke. In AD 823, Essex ceased to be a kingdom in itself and was for a time subsumed into the larger domain of Egbert, King of Wessex. Polydore Virgil (*c.*1470–1555) was an Italian humanist who settled in England and composed *Anglica Historia* in 1513; it was printed in 1534. To the northeast of London, Woodford Bridge was historically an agrarian village in Epping Forest in Essex. It became a place of fashionable residence for wealthy Londoners in the eighteenth century.
6 He had directed the letter to Quick hatch. The correct address was West hatch.
7 An uninvited, and in this case unidentified, visitor who attends in the company of an invited guest. Goldsmith may be referring coyly to a female friend.
8 Another, indecipherable, word is deleted here.
9 William Guthrie (1708–70), historian and moderate Whig political writer. It is unclear which pamphlet Goldsmith and Bindley are discussing. Goldsmith makes no reference to the topic, and no pamphlets have been attributed to Guthrie in 1765 or 1766.

10 John Almon, bookseller and political journalist (1737–1805), wrote and had published late in 1765 *The history of the late minority: Exhibiting the conduct, principles, and views, of that party, during the years 1762, 1763, 1764, and 1765*. Almon was an associate of John Wilkes, the famous liberal to whose philosophy Goldsmith harboured a Tory aversion. On the political climate that Goldsmith alludes to in this letter, see Introduction, xli–xlv.

11 Rockingham's ministry, to which Edmund Burke had been a key advisor, had ended on 7 June. Goldsmith is alluding to a general confusion about Rockingham's successor. William Pitt, who had been at the head of government previously from 1756 to 1761, would not be formally brought in until the end of July, so Goldsmith is indicating, possibly on Burke's information, that Pitt and Newcastle ('the old ministry') were staying in London – though Parliament had been suspended on 6 June – with a view to being re-installed.

12 A week. The Club met once a week on Monday nights. It may have been that the meeting at Fordyce's took place at an earlier point in the evening, preceding the appointed time of the Club. Goldsmith's attendance at the Club was, as Johnson wrote to Bennet Langton in March 1766, 'very constant': Bruce Redford, ed., *The Letters of Samuel Johnson*, 5 vols. (1992–4), II: 17.

21

To John Bindley

[London], 12 July 1766

See headnote to previous letter. Goldsmith and Bindley continue their exchange here with Goldsmith noting Bindley's younger brother's illness. James Bindley (1739–1818) was a book collector and a fellow of Peterhouse, Cambridge (1762–8). Goldsmith writes of him: 'I never knew any one so short a time whose mind I fancy'd more like my own, that is in other words that I loved better.' The younger Bindley assisted Edmond Malone with the third edition of Boswell's *Life of Johnson* (1799). He was also a friend of John Nichols, who described him in the fourth volume of *Illustrations* as a 'kind-hearted and intelligent Bibliographer'.[1] James Bindley suffered with ill health through much of his life.

The copy-text is the manuscript in the Beinecke Library, Yale University. It was first published in 1964 by Balderston in the *Yale University Library Gazette*, the year after Yale had acquired it from a private collection in Australia.[2] Below Goldsmith's signature at the foot of the letter 'Author of the *Traveller* & other *works of genius*' is written in a different, later hand.

Dear Sir

You tell me I forgot to date my letter. I did that by design for if ever my letters come before a court of justice, as they want a date no body can take any hold of them. What do you think of me there? Now I will give you a receipt to make a conjuring box! Take four penny worth of half pence and rivet them together at the edge. Then let there be an hole in the bottom of these here halfpence to hold a die, or a conjurors ball no matter which, then you have a little tin box with which you cover the half pence, while the halfpence cover the die, and so taking the cover off and putting it on you can conjure. This I keep as a secret except upon particular occasions. Am I any body now? You are going to build two houses an hot house and a cold house. Ill be hanged but the one is an oven and the other a drain. I find however the pot pourri has succeeded, but the truth is, it was Mrs Bindley that was my operator, and I entreat that you may be kept away from the jar. I fancy you will shortly have something else to mind, for I learn there is a long string of new ministers coming in, and others going out, when I get a list I will send it to you, and perhaps the news papers will inform you of it first.[3] I am heartily sorry for your brothers illness, for with great truth I may say that I never knew any one so short a time whose mind I fancy'd more like my own, that is in other words that I loved better. I have not as yet been able to wait upon him at King Street but will go there tomorrow, those slow fevers I do not at all like, and I wish~~d~~ he would spend more time at West Hatch. It is certainly a charming place and I believe healthy too. I dont think I can go down as I had some intentions, some plaugey[4] thing or other is ever coming in my way, so that I am eternally busy without doing any thing. There are however twenty things there I should be glad to see. Mrs Bindley, little Betsy, and the young gentleman that wants to see a live author. Beside this I should be glad to see the thatchd house, the garret that is to be a library, the pond, yourself, the ox-park, and the strawberry bed. You tell me the wood is clear'd away from the ox park, that I believe, and that the fields look as green as grass, that I deny. How could you assert a thing of this kind. Ill make an oration against it in the true style of the arts and Sciences. Mr Chairman Sir. I entirely agree with the gentleman that his fields are very green, but when he asserts they are as green as grass there I humbly think he wants precision. There are several kinds of grasses Mr Chairman, Linnæus gives us a catalogue of twenty five kinds, and all these kinds are green, but then Sir on the other hand there are several kinds of herbs that are not green at least in the flower.[5] There is the crowfoot for instance there are several types of crowfoot, one of them is called Geranium Roberti and this has a yellow blossom, and great quantities of this grow in the fields in question so that it gives them a yellowish greenish sort of a look so they are not quite as green as grass. I therefore move Sir for the greater precision that before the word fields, the words grass of be inserted, and then the whole paragraph will run elegantly thus, All the wood is removed from the ox park, and the grass of the fields looks as green as grass, which is very true. All of this is lost upon you if you have never attended the arts and sciences.

You write in paragraphs. Ill have my paragraphs too.

By these inns and outs we shall have statesmen shortly as plenty as the crowfoot in your meadows.

You had a mind to puzzle me in the affair of the houses, now Ill puzzle you in my turn. What kind of pen and ink did I use in writing this query?[6] Answer me that if you can? Now I think I have answerd all your letter, which youl find tedious I am afraid but no matter for that. My best and sincerest respects to Mrs Bindley, and I remain dear Sir your friend and humble servant

Oliver Goldsmith.

I'll date this letter purely to
try your fidelity. July 12th 1766.

1 John Nichols, *Illustrations of the Literary History of the Eighteenth Century. Consisting of Authentic Memoirs and Original Letters of Eminent Persons*, 9 vols. (London: Printed for the Author, 1822), IV: vii.
2 Balderston, 'New Goldsmith Letters', 71–2.
3 See note to previous letter.
4 *Sic*: plaguey?
5 Carl Linnaeus (1707–78), Swedish, botanist, physician and zoologist who pioneered a taxonomical approach to the natural world in his *Systema Naturae* (1735), a major source for Goldsmith's eight-volume *History of the Earth, and Animated Nature* (1774).
6 This question is shakily scrawled in crude, over-inked script, which gives a 'bold' effect to the question.

22

To Dr George Baker and Others

[London, 20 January 1767]

Dr George Baker (bap. 1723, d. 1809), physician, was elected a fellow of the College of Physicians in 1757. He settled in London in 1761, where his patients included George III, Queen Charlotte and Joshua Reynolds. He had charge of the king's health during his period of mental illness from 1788. He was well known for his literary talents, particularly his Latin prose and epigrams, and one tradition identifies him as the dedicatee of Thomas Gray's 'Elegy Written in a Country Churchyard' (1751). He caused significant controversy with his *Essay Concerning the Cause of the Endemical Colic of Devonshire* (1767), which linked colic to the use of lead in the processing of cider; although there was much scepticism, he was eventually proved right. He continued his research into lead poisoning and corresponded with Benjamin Franklin on the topic. He retired in 1798.

We date the letter 20 January 1767: this is conjectural and based on the internal evidence of the letter-poem. Balderston conjectures that the date was May 1769 but she relied on Forster. He claimed that the complimentary lines on Reynolds and painting sensation Angelica Kauffman (1741–1807) in the *Public Advertiser*, referred to in the final line, appeared in the newspaper the same day as the advertisement for Goldsmith's *Roman History* (18 May 1769). However, as noted by Wardle and others, the lines composed by '*An* ADMIRER *of* MERIT' were actually published in the *Public Advertiser* on 20 January 1767.[1] The eulogium was prompted by Kauffman's celebrated portrait of Reynolds, begun in October 1766 and completed in early 1767, and compares it to her portraits of Anne Seymour Conway (1749–1828) and probably Anne Hussey, Lady Stanhope (1737–1812). The poem's reference to Charles Horneck's intention to enlist also supports this earlier date (see n11 below).

The copy-text is the manuscript owned by Loren R. Rothschild, Los Angeles (reproduced in his *Verses in Reply to an Invitation to Dinner at Dr. George Baker's* (Los Angeles: Rasselas Press, 1994)). A version of the poem was first published in Prior's *Miscellaneous Works of Goldsmith* (London: John Murray, 1837), IV: 132–3. This version, used by all editors of Goldsmith's works until now, is based upon the copy given to Prior by Major General Sir Henry Bunbury, son of Catherine Bunbury *née* Horneck, and diverges in several instances from the original given here.[2]

To
The Devonshires.
to the care of Doctor Baker.[3]

This is a poem.) (This is a Copy of verses![4]

Your mandate I got.
You may all go to pot.
Had your senses been right
You'd have sent before night; ~~written in five~~
As I hope to be sav'd, ~~minutes upon~~
I put off being shavd

For I could not make bold
While the weather was cold
To meddle in Suds
Or to put on my duds
So tell Horneck and Nesbitt[5]
And Baker that he's bit.[6]
And Kauffman beside[7]
And the Jessamy bride[8]
With the rest of the crew
The Reynoldses two[9]
Little Comedy's face[10]
And the Captain in lace[11]
(By the bye you may tell him
I have something to sell him
Of use I insist,
When he comes to enlist
Your worships must know
That a few days ago
An order went out
For the foot guards so stout
To wear tails in high taste[12]
Twelve inches at least
Now I've got him a scale
To measure each tail,
To lengthen a shorttail
And a long one to curtail

Yet how can I when vext
Thus stray from my text.
Tell each other to rue
You Devonshire crew
For sending so late
To one of my state
But 'tis Reynoldses way
From wisdom to stray
And Angelica's whim
To be foolish like him

But Alass your good Worships how could they be wiser
They both have been spoild in to day's Advertiser.
OLIVER Goldsmith.[13]

[1] While fair Angelica, with matchless Grace,
Paints Conway's lovely Form, and Stanhope's Face,
Our Hearts to Beauty willing Homage pay,
We praise, admire, and gaze our Souls away.
But when the Likeness she has done for thee,
O, Reynolds, with Astonishment we see;
Forc'd to submit with all our Pride, we own
Such Strength, such Harmony, excell'd by none,
And thou are rivall'd by Thyself alone.

See *W*, 174, 312n16; and Horace Walpole, *Anecdotes of Painting in England*, ed. Frederick W. Hilles and Philip B. Daghlian, 5 vols. (New Haven: Yale University Press, 1937), V: 46n.

[2] Rothschild gives a history of the manuscript in his 'Introduction', *Verses in Reply*, 7–10.

[3] Dr Baker, Joshua Reynolds and the Hornecks were all from Devonshire.

[4] Goldsmith's jocular mood was perhaps a response to some light-hearted ribbing from the addressees related to his anthology *Poems for Young Ladies. In Three Parts. Devotional, Moral, and Entertaining*, just published in December 1766. Wardle comments on the 'wry occasional verse' that Goldsmith produced in early 1767 (*W*, 175).

[5] Hannah Horneck (1727–1803), known as 'The Plymouth Beauty' and mother of Mary and Catherine Horneck.
Arnold Nesbitt (bap. 1721, d. 1779) came from an Irish merchant and banking family of significance which benefited from the patronage of the Pelhams. Nesbitt married Susanna, sister of his friend Henry Thrale, the brewer, in 1758 and consequently became part of the Johnson–Thrale circle at Streatham Place from the mid-1760s. The reference could be to either Susanna or Arnold.

[6] Dr George Baker, the host. The reference to his 'bit' is maybe a play on his well-known interest in horse-riding, as well as suggesting that he has been caught out.

[7] Angelica Kauffmann (1741–1807), the most celebrated female artist of the eighteenth century, renowned for her history paintings and portraits. Born in Switzerland, she came to London in 1766, and achieved instant popularity, not least due to the portrait of Reynolds referenced in Goldsmith's lines. She was one of only two women among the thirty-six founding members of the Royal Academy in 1768 (Mary Moser (1744–1819), known for her paintings of flowers, was the other). Paintings exhibited at the Royal Academy included *Cleopatra Adorning the Tomb of Mark Anthony* (1770), *Vortigern, King of Britain Enamoured of Rowena at the Banquet of Hengist* (1770) and *Tender Eleanora Sucking the Venom out of the Wound of Edward I* (1776), but portrait painting generated much of her income. She left England in 1781 with the considerable sum of £14,000.

[8] Mary Horneck (1752?–1840). Jessamy: of jasmine, scented or coloured (light yellow). The nickname perhaps stuck: Reynolds's portrait of Mary Horneck (exh. RA 1770–5; Cliveden Estate, National Trust) has her kneeling, dressed in pale yellow Oriental garb 'as if in a Turkish mosque' (*London Evening Post*, 4–6 May 1775). The perception that Goldsmith had romantic feelings for her is probably accurate. She married Colonel F. E. Gwyn in 1779, some five years after Goldsmith's death.

[9] Joshua Reynolds and his sister, Frances.

[10] Catherine Horneck (1754–99), Mary's younger sister and nicknamed 'Little Comedy' by Goldsmith. She married the artist and caricaturist Henry William Bunbury (1750–1811). Joshua Reynolds was godfather to their second son, Henry.

11 Charles Horneck (d. 1804), Mary and Catherine's older brother, who would go on to purchase an ensignship in the third regiment of Footguards on 26 March 1768. He married Sarah Keppel, niece of Admiral Augustus Keppel, in 1773.

12 Rothschild suggests that 'tails' here may be a reference to the fashionable long queues worn by macaronis – men of fashion with Continental affectations who tended towards gender-neutral mannerisms – at the time, and refers to Matthew Darly's 1771 etching depicting Charles Horneck sporting 'a prodigiously long queue attached to the back of his head' (*Verses in Reply*, 16n39). See M. Dorothy George and Frederick Stevens (eds.), *A Catalogue of Political and Personal Satires Preserved in the Department of Prints and Drawings in the British Museum*, 12 vols. (London: British Museum, 1870–1954), IV: no. 4711. Above the figure is written 'Pray S[rs]. do You Laugh at me'. Added in a contemporary hand to the bottom right is an identification of the figure as 'Ensign Horneck'.

13 Under his own name, there is a series of crudely inked symbols or letters of which little sense can be made. To the left of Goldsmith's signature a pair of faces is sketched, possibly by Goldsmith himself.

23

To George Colman

London, 19 July [1767]

George Colman the Elder (bap. 1732, d. 1794), playwright and theatre manager, had his greatest success with *The Clandestine Marriage* (Drury Lane, 1766), which he co-wrote with David Garrick. Colman then became part of Covent Garden's management team, along with Thomas Harris, John Rutherford and William Powell, in 1767. He committed £15,000 for his share of the royal patent and seems to have taken primary responsibility for managing the theatre's day-to-day affairs. Goldsmith had initially courted David Garrick of Drury Lane to represent his first play *The Good Natur'd Man* which he completed in spring 1767. Garrick's reluctance and objections had inflamed Goldsmith and so he sent the manuscript to Colman: his acceptance of the piece without his partners' acquiescence may have been a cause of dispute between them, settled in a lawsuit in Colman's favour in 1769. The letter's expression of appreciation to Colman is heartfelt, as are the bitter references to Garrick's previous equivocation. Balderston notes that Goldsmith's finances were in a parlous state as is evidenced by the fact that he had borrowed £10 from Newbery on a promissory note on 7 July, even though he still had a note of £48, dating from 11 October 1763, still unpaid. Goldsmith had refused to subjugate himself to Garrick's wish for flattery in order to get his play accepted and he also rejected the Drury Lane manager's suggestions for improvements to the manuscript. His willingness in this letter to accede to any amendments that Colman might request betrays his eagerness to have the play performed, or might indicate a desire to spite Garrick, whatever the cost.

The copy-text is the manuscript in the Victoria and Albert Museum, London. It was first published by Forster in 1848. It is addressed 'To | George Colman Esqr. | Richmond.' It is possibly postmarked 20 July although the '2' is not clearly visible. The folio is also marked, in a different hand, 'Dr Goldsmith to Colman'. Balderston notes that it was found among the papers of David Morris (1770?–1842) who gradually took over the management of the Haymarket from his brother-in-law George Colman the Younger (1762–1836) during the 1810s.

Temple, Garden Court, July 19th[1]

Dear Sir,

I am very much obliged to you, both for your kind partiality in my favour, and your tenderness in shortening the interval of my expectation. That the play is liable to many objections I well know, but I am happy that it is in hands the most capable in the world of removing them.[2] If then Dear Sir, you will complete your favours by putting the piece into such a state as it may be acted, or of directing me how to do it I shall ever retain a sense of your goodness to me. And indeed tho' most probably this be the last I shall ever write yet I can't help feeling a secret satisfaction that poets for the future are likely to have a protector who declines taking advantage of their dependent situation, and scorns that importance which may be acquir'd by triffling with their anxieties.

I am Dear Sir with the greatest esteem
your most obedient humble servant.

Oliver Goldsmith.

[1] Goldsmith lived here briefly before moving to his permanent home at nearby 2 Brick Court, also in Temple Bar, at the end of 1767.

[2] The play was first performed on 29 January 1768 at Covent Garden and had modest success with ten performances that season. The author benefit nights earned Goldsmith around £400. A 'low' bailiff scene aggravated the audience but the successful performance of comic actor Edward Shuter (1728?–76) as Croaker helped to ensure its run. William Griffin published the play on 5 February 1768, for which Goldsmith received an additional £50. It is possible that Colman was admitted to the Club on 15 February 1767 because of his agreement to stage the comedy. The play did not maintain a place in the repertory: it was performed only three times in Goldsmith's lifetime after the first season (twice in 1771 and again in 1773). It experienced something of an afterlife in the 1780s in the controversy over Denis O'Bryen's *A Friend in Need is a Friend Indeed* (Haymarket, 1783) in which O'Bryen and Colman (now Haymarket manager) clashed over the terms of their original agreement in an extensive newspaper war. O'Bryen's play is largely based on *The Good Natur'd Man* and Colman provided its epilogue. In an ironic echo of Goldsmith's capitulation in accepting Colman's changes, many of O'Bryen's

complaints were around the fact that he had acceded to every change Colman had demanded. See Lucyle Werkmeister, *The London Daily Press 1772–1792* (Lincoln: University of Nebraska Press, 1963), 72–8, and David O'Shaughnessy, 'Making a Play for Patronage: Dennis O'Bryen's *A Friend in Need is a Friend Indeed* (1783)', *Eighteenth-Century Life* 39.1 (2015), 183–211.

24

To David Garrick

London, 20 July 1767

David Garrick (1717–79), actor and playwright, was also manager of Drury Lane which he ran for almost thirty years (1747–76). His London debut as Richard III in 1741 was a sensational success: his naturalistic style of acting was exuberant and energetic, and supplanted the more classical style of older actors such as James Quin. Goldsmith's earlier writings on theatre in the *Enquiry into the Present State of Polite Learning* and the *Bee* applaud him as an actor but are more critical of his managerial practices. Garrick, in turn, had refused to support Goldsmith for the position of secretary to the Society of Arts and Sciences so their relationship was always awkward. Garrick would continue to be associated with Shakespearean roles throughout his career and was instrumental in the Shakespeare Jubilee in 1769. He collaborated successfully with George Colman when the pair wrote *The Clandestine Marriage* (1766), the comedy for which he is best remembered as a playwright. He retired from acting in 1776 after a series of farewell performances and he sold his share of Drury Lane to a consortium led by Richard Brinsley Sheridan.

Garrick had turned more to management and writing at the date of this letter's composition. Goldsmith had submitted the manuscript of *The Good Natur'd Man* for his consideration despite their lukewarm relations, perhaps because the management situation at Covent Garden was uncertain following the retirement of John Rich. Garrick vacillated for a period before agreeing to meet with Goldsmith to discuss changes to the play, but the nascent dramatist refused to submit to Garrick's requested amendments. When Colman agreed to stage the comedy, Goldsmith wrote this politic letter to smooth things over with Garrick, whose friendly response seems to indicate that he held no grievance.

The copy-text is the manuscript in the New York Public Library. It was first published by Prior in 1837. It is addressed 'To | David Garrick Esqr. at | Litchfield'. There are two postmarks dated 20 and 21 July respectively. It is marked by Garrick on the front, perpendicular to the address: 'Dr Goldsmith's | Letter wth. my | Answer'. On the verso of the sheet is written 'My Answer', and on the recto of that sheet appears a draft of Garrick's reply, in his own hand:

My answer Lichfield July 25 1767.

S^{r}. I was at Birmingham when y^{r}. letter came to this place, or I sh^{d}, have ~~answd~~ thank'd you for it immediately—I was indeed much hurt that yr warmth at our last meeting mistook my sincere & friendly Attention to y^{r}. Play for y^{e}. remains of a former misunderstanding, wch. I had as much forgot as if it never had existed—what I said to you at my own house, I now repeat, that I felt more pain in giving my Sentiments than you possibly could in receiving them. it has been ye business & ambition of my Life to live upon ye best terms wth. Men of Genius, & as I know that D^{r}. Goldsmith will have no reason to change his present friendly disposition towards me, so I shall be glad of any future opportunity to convince him how much

I am his Obed^{t}. Serv & well wisher

.D. Garrick.

Sir London July 20th 1767

A few days ago Mr. Beard renewd his claim to the piece which I had written for his stage, and had as a friend submitted to your perusal.[1] As I found you had very great difficulties about that piece I complied with his desire, thinking it wrong to take up the attention of my friends with such petty concerns as mine or to load your good nature by a compliance rather with their requests than my merits.[2] I am extremely sorry that you should think me warm at our last meeting, your judgement certainly ought to be free especially in a matter which must in some measure concern your own credit and interest.[3] I assure you Sir I have no disposition to differ with you on this or any other account, but am with an high opinion of your abilities and with a very real esteem Sir

your most obedient humble serv^{t}

Oliver Goldsmith.

[1] John Beard (1716/17–91), singer, was John Rich's son-in-law, and acting manager of Covent Garden since Rich's death in 1761. Beard had resigned his managership to Colman on 14 May and Goldsmith's reason for using his name here is not clear. Forster speculates that Goldsmith

wished to spare Garrick's feelings with regard to Colman's defection from Drury Lane earlier that year; however, it seems more probable that Goldsmith was claiming that his putative commitment to Covent Garden was long-standing.

2 Balderston suggests that Goldsmith is referring to Johnson and Reynolds. Prior refers to a letter 'still in existence' (*CW*, II: 151) from Reynolds to Garrick, bringing him and Goldsmith together, and states further, on unnamed authority, that Johnson and Reynolds were told by Garrick that the play would not succeed on presentation. Reynolds's letter has not been located.

3 It seems clear that strong words were exchanged when Garrick and Goldsmith met to discuss the play manuscript. Thomas Davies suggests that Goldsmith was too intransigent to take well-meaning advice from Garrick; however, his account is likely biased in Garrick's favour: Davies, *Memoirs of the Life of David Garrick*, 2 vols. (Boston: Wells and Lilly, 1818), II: 146. On the other hand, contemporaries generally and readily acknowledged Goldsmith's lack of social diplomacy.

25
To the *St. James's Chronicle*
London, 25 July 1767

Goldsmith's letter to the *St. James's Chronicle; Or, the British Evening-Post* was prompted by two separate letters the newspaper had recently printed.[1] The first was an almost apologetic correction from 'D. H.' in a letter printed in the issue for 12–14 May. Goldsmith had endorsed the recent publication of Blainville's *Travels through Holland, Germany, Switzerland and Italy*, 3 vols. (London: J. Johnson, B. Davenport and T. Cadell, 1767). The various advertisements for this work claimed that it had never been published, a claim that was exposed as spurious by the letter-writer.[2] 'D. H.' had 'too much Respect for Dr. Goldsmith to suffer him to authorise so pitiful an Artifice'. The various advertisements for Blainville's *Travels* in the *St. James's Chronicle* and other newspapers do not, however, contain any reference to Goldsmith so it is not clear how his endorsement was publicized.[3] In any event, Goldsmith owns up to his error in his letter and is happy to concede his mistake.

The second, more serious accusation, was an anonymous letter, often attributed to William Kenrick, in its issue for 18–21 July 1767.[4] Kenrick had replaced Goldsmith as chief reviewer for the *Monthly Review* and had written a caustic review of Goldsmith's *An Enquiry into the Present State of Polite Learning* (1759), probably at the instigation of Ralph Griffiths, the proprietor.[5] 'DETECTOR' accuses Goldsmith of plagiarism: the substance of his claim is that Goldsmith's poem 'Edwin and Angelina' was inappropriately derived from a ballad in Percy's *Reliques of Ancient English Poetry* (1765). The letter is reproduced here:

To the Printer of the ST. J. CHRONICLE.

SIR,

IN the Reliques of antient Poetry published about two Years ago, is a very beautiful little Ballad called "A Frier of Orders Grey." The ingenious Editor Mr. Piercy supposes that the Stanzas sung by Ophelia in the Play of Hamlet, were Parts of some Ballad well known in Shakespeare's Time, and from these Stanzas, with the Addition of one or two of his own to connect them, he has formed the above-mentioned Ballad; the Subject of which is, a Lady comes to a Convent to enquire for her Love–, who had been driven there by her Disdain. She is answered by a Frier that he is dead.

No, no, he is dead, gone to his Death's Bed,
He will never come again.

The Lady weeps and laments her Cruelty, the Frier endeavours to comfort her with Morality and Religion; but all in vain: She expresses the deepest Grief, and the most tender Sentiments of Love; till at last the Frier discovers himself,

And, lo! beneath this Gown of Grey.
Thy own true Love appears.

This Catastrophe is very fine, and the Whole, joined with the greatest Tenderness, has the utmost Simplicity: yet, though this Ballad was so recently published in the ancient Reliques, Dr. Goldsmith has been hardy enough to publish a Poem, called The Hermit, where the Circumstances and Catastrophe are exactly the same, only with this Difference, that the natural Simplicity and Tenderness of the Original is almost entirely lost in the languid Smoothness, and tedious Paraphrase of the Copy, which is as short of the Merit of Mr. Piercy's Ballad as the Insipidity of Negus is to the genuine Flavour of Champaigne.[6]

I am, Sir, your's, &c.

DETECTOR.

In his response Goldsmith claims that, insofar as the question of influence goes, the reverse is true as he had read his poem to Percy before the publication of *Reliques.* Percy gives qualified support to Goldsmith's account of the history of the poem in the third edition of his *Reliques of Ancient English Poetry*, 3 vols., 3rd edn. (1775), I: 250, and also in his '*Life*' (74–5). Percy agrees that Goldsmith's poem predates his but also insists that both of them owe a considerable debt to 'Gentle Herdsman, Tell to Me', also from *Reliques*, which Goldsmith 'had seen and admired long before it was printed' ('*Life*', 75).

The copy-text is the *St. James's Chronicle*, 23–25 July 1767, where it was first published.

To the Printer of the S. J. CHRONICLE.

SIR,

As there is nothing I dislike so much as a News Paper Controversy, particularly upon Trifles, permit me to be as concise as possible, in informing a Correspondent of yours, that I recommended Blainville's Travels, because I thought the Book was a good one, and I think so still. I said, I was told by the Bookseller, that it was then first published; but in that it seems I was misinformed, and my Reading was not extensive enough to set me right.

Another Correspondent of yours accuses me of having taken a Ballad, I published some Time ago, from one by the ingenious Mr. Percy. I do not think there is any great Resemblance between the two Pieces in Question. If there be any, his Ballad is taken from mine. I read it to Mr. Percy some Years ago, and he (as we both considered these Things as Trifles at best) told me, with his usual Good Humour, the next Time I saw him, that he had taken my Plan to form the Fragments of Shakespeare into a Ballad of his own. He then read me his little Cento, if I may so call it, and I highly approved it. Such petty Anecdotes as these are scarcely worth printing, and were it not for the busy Disposition of some of your Correspondents, the Publick should never have known that he owes me the Hint of his Ballad, or that I am obliged to his Friendship and Learning for Communications of a much more important Nature.

I am, Sir, your's, &c.

OLIVER GOLDSMITH.

[1] The *St. James's Chronicle; Or, the British Evening-Post* began publication on 12 March 1761 and appeared on Tuesdays, Thursdays and Saturdays. It was the successor to the *St. James's Evening Post*. George Colman and David Garrick were among the earliest proprietors of the newspaper, which may have contributed to Goldsmith's decision to respond to the accusations that were made against him. Its editorial line was anti-government and its editor, Henry Baldwin, was prosecuted when the newspaper reprinted the *Public Advertiser*'s letter from Junius of 19 December 1769 criticizing King George III.

[2] A further letter from John Turnbull, one of the translators, published in the *St. James's Chronicle* for 7–9 July 1767 sheds more light on the issue. See also John Lockman's corroborating letter to the *St. James's Chronicle*, 9–11 July 1767.

[3] Prior wrote to John Bowyer Nichols, in a letter of 23 September 1834: 'I have not met with the opinion on Blainville's Travels notwithstanding a search for it': British Library, Add. MS 43377C, fo. 6.

[4] The attribution to Kenrick is not absolutely certain, but it is probable, and is generally accredited or suggested. See *P*, II: 85; *W*, 179.

[5] See Introduction, xxxvi–xxxvii, and *CW*, I: 246–8.

[6] Negus is a drink composed of hot water, sugar, and port or wine, attributed to soldier Francis Negus (bap. 1670, d. 1732).

26

To Anne Percy

London, [4 October 1768]

Anne Percy, *née* Gutterridge (d. 1806), was from Desborough, Northamptonshire. She married Thomas Percy in 1758. She was appointed wet-nurse to Queen Charlotte's baby son Edward (the future father of Queen Victoria) in 1767, a post she held for eighteenth months. She knew Goldsmith through her husband; he had met Goldsmith in 1759 and became a close friend.

Goldsmith asks Anne Percy for tickets for two ladies so they can attend a forthcoming masquerade ball. Although these two ladies cannot be identified categorically, we can be almost certain that he is referring to Catherine and Mary Horneck, daughters of the widowed Hannah Horneck and wards of Joshua Reynolds. Goldsmith was very fond of the girls. He accompanied them to Paris in 1770 (see Letters 32 and 33 below). We might also note here that Goldsmith was strongly associated with the London masquerade scene: his frequent attendance drew the satiric ire of William Kenrick (*P*, II: 350–3).

The date of this letter is conjectural. Balderston suggests early January 1768 but on thin circumstantial evidence. There are a number of factors which suggest our later proposed date: Anne Percy's connection to Queen Charlotte and to her lady of the bedchamber Elizabeth Percy (1716–76); the reference to meeting Percy in winter; the cultural context of masquerades in 1768; and the date of the two possibilities for the event referred to in the letter. A full discussion is in the Introduction, xlv–xlvii.

The copy-text is the manuscript in the British Library. It was first published by Alice C. C. Gaussen in *Percy, Prelate and Poet* (London: Smith, Elder, & Co., 1908). It is addressed 'For | Mrs. Percy | at the Queen's Palace'.[1]

Doctor Goldsmith's best respects to Mrs. Percy he requests the favour of two tickets for two young Ladies for the Masquerade which is to be on Friday night. If she can procure them for him it will be a singular obligation, and make two young Ladies extremely happy. I have not seen Mr. Percy for some time, but hope this winter we shall frequently have the happiness of being together.[2]

Teusday. Temple. Brick court.

1 Goldsmith's nomenclature was a little ahead of events as Buckingham House was not formally settled on Queen Charlotte until 1775.

2 Percy was elected to Johnson's Literary Club on 15 February 1768. Goldsmith may be gently reminding Anne Percy of their 'clubbable' relationship in the interests of procuring tickets. Percy's journal has little information on the winter of 1768–9, but an entry for 18 January 1769 states 'I took [the children] to dine at Dr Goldsmith's': British Library, Add. MS 32336, fo. 129v.

27

To Thomas Percy

[London, October 1768]

Thomas Percy (1729–1811), a Church of Ireland minister and later bishop of Dromore. Percy was also a writer, best known for his anthology *The Reliques of Ancient English Poetry* (1765), which he had dedicated to Elizabeth Seymour, Duchess of Northumberland, a decision which served his wife, Anne, and himself well. He was friendly with many in London cultural circles including Burke, Johnson and David Garrick; he became a member of the Literary Club in 1768. He had a close friendship with Goldsmith who asked him to write his biography. Their first meeting on 21 February 1759 at Dr Grainger's house is recorded in Percy's journal, an important source for evidence of their friendship, and indeed Goldsmith's sociability more broadly.[1] His memoir of Goldsmith was published in 1801.

The extent of their friendship can be seen in this frank series of questions that Goldsmith posed in response to an invitation to Percy's rectory at Easton Maudit in Northamptonshire. Clearly, he appreciated the offer but is anxious to avoid being disturbed as he was trying to write up his *Roman History*, which would be published by Thomas Davies in May 1769. In the end, Goldsmith did not take up the invitation.

The date of the letter is conjectural but, as Balderston observes, it is highly likely that this letter followed closely on the previous one to Anne Percy: the letters appear identical. They are written on the same size paper with the same watermark ('VI'), folded and sealed the same way and have the address written in the corner in a manner not done elsewhere in his correspondence with the exception of Letter 28 (to Boswell, 1769). The letter indicates that both Thomas and Anne Percy were away from Northamptonshire, which also indicates that this was the period when she was working as a wet-nurse.

The copy-text is the manuscript in the British Library. It was first published by Gaussen in *Percy, Prelate and Poet* in 1908. The letter is addressed 'To | The Rev^{d}. Mr. Percy | Northumberland-house'.

Dear Percy
I have been thinking of your Northampton-shire offer. I beg you'l send me an answer to the
following Queries.
1 In the first place are there any prying troublesome neighbours?
2 Can I have a chamber to myself where I can buy coals &c?
3 Will I not cumber the house and take up the room of others?
4 How long can you spare me the appartment?
5 Is there a stage? The price. And can my books be carried down.
6 Can I have milk, meat, &c tea, in the place?
And lastly will it be any way inconvenient to you or Mrs. Percy?
And when will you want to be down yourselves?

I am your faithful freind

Oliver Goldsmith.

[1] British Library, Add. MS 32336, fo. 19v.

28

To James Boswell

London, [*c.* 21 September 1769]

James Boswell (1740–95), lawyer and diarist, was a well-known man of letters in London. He came from a noble Scottish family, and on his father's death in

1782 became the ninth laird of Auchinleck. He is best known as the biographer of Samuel Johnson, and his *Life of Johnson* is a rich source of information on Goldsmith, albeit one with an often hostile tone. He met Goldsmith in 1762 at Thomas Davies's house, with publisher Robert Dodsley also present. Boswell's *London Journal 1762–1763* is an evocative account of his early years in London, during which he won the friendship of Johnson, Garrick and Thomas Sheridan. After a tour of Europe, where he met Voltaire, Rousseau and Corsican freedom fighter Pasquale Paoli, he returned to London where he met Joshua Reynolds, to whom he would later dedicate his *Life of Johnson*.

Goldsmith and Boswell had met at bookseller Thomas Davies's house on Thursday 21 September: it was their first encounter for almost three years, according to Boswell. The meeting was genial with Goldsmith telling Boswell that George Colman had praised Boswell's character the night before over dinner. Goldsmith had just received an advance of 500 guineas from William Griffin for his natural history, doubtless a factor that helped to prompt his invitation to Boswell and the others. Boswell's journal records the presence of writer Giuseppe Baretti, architect William Chambers (Letters 51 and 52) and Colman at the dinner and that the conversation centred on the theatre.[1]

The copy-text is the manuscript in the Beinecke Rare Book and Manuscript Room, Yale University. It was first published, in facsimile, along with the printed transcription, in the *Private Papers of James Boswell from Malahide Castle: In the Collection of Lt. Colonel Ralph Hayward Isham*, ed. Geoffrey Scott and Frederick A. Pottle, vol. IX: *1772–1774* (Mount Vernon, NY: William Edwin Rudge, 1930). It is addressed 'To | Boswell Esqr. | Carey St.'

To Boswell Esqr.
Carey Street.

Mr Goldsmiths best respects to Mr Boswell and begs the favour of his company to dinner next tuesday at four o clock to meet Sr J. Reynolds, Mr. Colman &c.

Temple Brick Court No 2.

[1] Giuseppe Marc'Antonio Baretti (1719–89) was a writer who came to England first in 1751. He became tutor to Charlotte Lennox and, through her networks, he made the acquaintance of Reynolds, Garrick and Johnson, among others. He would later tutor Hester Thrale's daughter. His *Dictionary of the English and Italian Languages* (1760) was a critical and commercial success. A stint in Italy in the early 1760s was unsuccessful and he returned to England in 1766. He became a member of the Club, a fact which stood him in good stead when tried for murder in 1769. His *Discours sur Shakespeare et M. Voltaire*, published in 1777, was an important defence of Shakespeare.

29

To Maurice Goldsmith

[London, *c.* 10 January 1770]

Maurice Goldsmith (1736?–94?) was Goldsmith's younger brother. Maurice lived with his cousin Jane Lawder, and her husband James, for a period in Kilmore, Co. Roscommon, as this letter indicates. He appears to have lacked a fixed direction in life and Goldsmith declined to take him on a planned trip to India in 1758. Instead, he offered to find him some employment in London, provided he 'would accustom himself to write and spell' (Letter 11). The situation does not seem to have ameliorated between then and the date of this letter. However, Percy reveals that Maurice followed Goldsmith's advice to find a trade and apprenticed himself to a cabinet-maker. He eventually opened a shop in Dublin where the Duke of Rutland appointed him inspector of licences during his tenure as lord lieutenant of Ireland in 1784–7.[1] This was apparently done at the suggestion of his chief secretary Thomas Orde Powlett, later Lord Bolton, 'out of regard to his brother's memory' (Percy, 'Life', 87). He was also appointed mace-bearer to the Royal Irish Academy. When Goldsmith died, Maurice travelled to London but to no material benefit, although he wrote a courteous letter of thanks to William Hawes who had attended his brother on his deathbed.

In this letter below, Goldsmith informs his brother that, although he has been appointed to the Royal Academy and maintains an illustrious London acquaintance, he is not in a position to offer much by way of direct financial support. Insofar as a small legacy is concerned, however, Goldsmith happily waives any claim. It appears that Maurice was not slow to act on his brother's decision: his receipt for this transferred legacy is written on the back of the address page, the money thus hastily secured:

> Received from Jams. Lawder Esqr fifteen pounds Sterl. ye which sum is in full of a Legacy bequeathed to my Brother Oliver Goldsmith by ye last will and Testament of ye Revd Mr Thos Contrine I say received ye same by Virtue of ye within power given to me by my sd. Brother Oliver Goldsmith. Wittness my hand this twenty fourth day of February 1770 seventy. | Maurice Goldsmith. | Wittness prsent. | Will: Hodson. | 13 Gue … 14.15.9 | change … 4.3 | |15.0.02

The copy-text is the manuscript in the British Library. It was first published by Percy in 1801.

The letter is addressed 'To Mr. Maurice Goldsmith at Mr. James | Lawder's at Kilmore near | Carrick on Shannon. | Ireland.' It is postmarked 10 January.

TO MAURICE GOLDSMITH, [LONDON, C. 10 JANUARY 1770]

Dear Brother,

I should have answered your letter sooner, but in truth I am not very fond of thinking of the necessities of those I love when it is so very little in my power to help them. I am sorry to find you are still every way unprovided for, and what adds to my uneasiness is that I received a letter from My Sister Johnson by which I learn that she is pretty much in the same circumstances.[3] As to myself I believe I might get both you and my poor brother in law something like that which you desire, but I am determined never to ask for little things or exhaust any little interest I may have untill I can serve you him and myself more effectually. As yet no opportunity has offered, but I believe you are pretty well convinc'd? that I will not be remiss when it arrives. The King has been lately pleasd to make me Professor of ancient history in a Royal Accademy of Painting which he has just establishd, but there is no sallary anex'd and I took it rather as a compliment to the institution than any benefit to myself.[4] Honours to one in my situation are something like ruffles to a man that wants a shirt.[5] You tell me that there are fourteen or fifteen pound left me in the hands of my Cousin Lawder, and you ask me what I would have done with ~~them~~ it? My dear Brother I would by no means give any directions to my dear worthy relations at Kilmore how to dispose of money that is more properly speaking theirs than mine. All that I can say is that I entirely, and this letter will serve to witness give up any right or title to it, and I am sure they will dispose of it to the best advantage. To them I entirely leave it, whether they or you may think the whole necessary to fit you out, or whether our poor sister Johnson may not want the half I leave entirely to their and your discretion. The kindness of that good couple to our poor shattered family demands our sincerest gratitude, and tho' they have almost forgot me yet If good things at last arrive I hope one day to return and encrease their good humour by adding to my own. I have sent my cousin Jenny a miniature picture of myself, as I believe it is the most acceptable present I can offer.[6] I have ordered it to be left for her at George Faulkener's folded in a letter.[7] The face you well know is ugly enough but it is finely painted, I will shortly also send my friends near the Shannon some Metzotinto prints of myself, and some more of my friends here such as Burke, Johnson, Reynolds and Coleman.[8] I believe I have written an hundred letters to different friends in your country and never received an answer from any of them. I dont know how to account for this, or why they are unwilling to keep up for me those regards which I must ever retain for them. If then you have a mind to oblige me you will write often whether I answer you or not. Let me particularly have the news of our family and old acquaintances. For instance you may begin by telling me about the family where you reside how they spend their time and whether they ever make mention of me. Tell me about my mother. My Brother Hodson, and his son, my brother Harry's son and daughter, My Sister Johnson, The family of Bally Oughter what is become of them where they live and how they do.[9] You talked of being my only Brother. I dont understand you. Where is Charles?[10] A sheet of paper occasionally filld with news of this kind would make me very happy, and would keep you nearer my mind. As it is my dear Brother believe me to be yours most affectionately

Oliver Goldsmith.

1 *Critical Review* 4.112 (October 1813), 367.

2 The full points noted here are manuscript full points, rather than ellipses.

3 Jane Johnson (*c.* 1725–?), Goldsmith's older sister, who married poorly – in his view, at least.

4 The Royal Academy, established on 10 December 1768, emerged from a decade of dispute within the Society of Artists, the previously dominant artistic organization. Members had to be 'men of fair moral characters, of high reputation', as well as a painter, sculptor or architect. Joshua Reynolds was the founding president and this helps to explain why Johnson and Goldsmith were both appointed honorary professors, respectively in ancient literature and ancient history. The position carried no duties but entitled the post-holder to attend the annual dinner.

5 Cf. *The Haunch of Venison* (*CW*, 1: 314): 'It's like sending them Ruffles, when wanting a Shirt.' Forster points out that this is borrowed from Tom Brown's *Laconics: or, New Maxims of State and Conversation* (1701): 'If your Friend is in want, don't carry him to the Tavern, where you treat your Self as well as him, and entail a Thirst and Headach upon him next Morning. To treat a poor Wretch with a Bottle of *Burgundy*, or fill his Snuff-box, is like giving a pair of Lace-Ruffles to a Man, that has ne'er a Shirt on his Back. Put something in his Pocket' (Part III, LXVI).

6 No trace of this portrait can be found. There has been some speculation that it might be the original portrait engraved by Thomas Cook for Thomas Evans's (not to be confused with the Thomas Evans of Letter 53) edition of the *Poetical and Dramatic Works* (1780). Another possibility is that it is the painting owned by Goldsmith's friend and founder of the Literary Fund, Reverend David Williams, engraved by William Ridley. See Austin Dobson, *The Complete Poetical Works of Oliver Goldsmith* (London: H. Froude, 1906), 261.

7 George Faulkner (1703?–75) was a Dublin bookseller. He is best known for his publishing relationship with Swift, whose *Works* he published in four volumes in 1735. He was a regular visitor to London, sufficiently well known to be targeted by Samuel Foote in his satire

The Orators (Haymarket Theatre, 1762). As Letter 15 illustrates, Goldsmith may have had a longstanding acquaintance with him, and possibly availed of his assistance in having items delivered to, and collected in, Dublin. Faulkner was also a correspondent of Samuel Derrick, another London Irishman of letters, also known to Johnson, Boswell and Goldsmith.

8 Mezzotint prints, Balderston observes, were particularly in vogue in this year (*BL*, 86n2). She cites Horace Walpole, writing to Sir Horace Mann on 6 May 1770: 'Another rage is for prints of English portraits; I have been collecting them above thirty years, and originally never gave for a mezzotinto above one or two shillings. The lowest are now a crown, most from half a guinea to a guinea': *The Yale Edition of Horace Walpole's Correspondence*, XXIII: 211. The level of interest can be largely attributed to the Royal Academy's series of public exhibitions dating from 1769. Of the portraits listed here, those of Goldsmith, Johnson and Colman were displayed at a Royal Academy exhibit in April 1771.
Reynolds's portrait of Goldsmith (National Portrait Gallery) was engraved in 1770 by Giuseppe Filippo Liberati Marchi (1735?–1808), Reynolds's Italian protégé, and his 1769 portrait of Burke was engraved in 1770 by James Watson (1739/40?–90), principal engraver to Reynolds. Watson was also responsible for engraving one of the four self-portraits which Reynolds made in 1769, a half-length, showing him with a cloak thrown over his shoulder, and his right hand in a portfolio. No 1770 print of Colman is known; Goldsmith may be anticipating one or simply name-dropping. Reynolds's portrait of Colman, exhibited at the Royal Academy in this year, was not engraved until 1773, when it was done by Marchi.

9 Goldsmith is looking for news of Henry and Catherine Goldsmith. The family based in Ballyoughter, near Elphin in Co. Roscommon, is that of his uncle, John Goldsmith, with whom Goldsmith had stayed in the 1730s while attending the Diocesan School at Elphin.

10 Charles Goldsmith (b. 1737?), younger brother, had arrived in London somewhat unexpectedly in 1757 hoping in vain that Oliver could help establish him there. He appears to have returned to Ireland soon after, where he became a cabinet-maker before emigrating to Jamaica. See Letter 31.

30

To William Hunter

[London, *c.* June 1770]

Dr William Hunter (1718–83), physician, anatomist and male-midwife, was born in Lanarkshire in Scotland, educated at the University of Glasgow where he was taught by, among others, the moral philosopher Francis Hutcheson. Without graduating, Hunter was apprenticed to William Cullen in the latter's Hamilton medical practice. Hunter attended Alexander Monro's lectures on anatomy in 1739, after which point he emigrated to London in 1740 to study midwifery with William Smellie. In Paris in September 1743, Hunter attended the anatomy lectures of Antoine Ferrein, the recently appointed Professor of Medicine and Surgery with whom Goldsmith intended to study when he travelled to Paris in 1754 (see Letter 4 above). Hunter returned to London by the summer of 1744, where he regularly lectured for the rest of his life. In 1754, Hunter became a member of the Society of London Physicians. In 1761, he became midwife to Queen Charlotte for the birth of her son in August 1762, after which point he became physician extraordinary to the Queen, attending upon all her pregnancies. He was elected Professor of Anatomy at the Royal Academy of Arts upon its foundation by the King in December 1768. Hunter was a Whig in politics, and a friend to Horace Walpole, who viewed his association with the royal family with some scepticism. Polite and socially capable, Hunter was friendly also with Henry Fielding, Hester Thrale, David Hume and, it would seem from this correspondence, with Goldsmith. Goldsmith cites Hunter's writing on bones found near the River Ohio in America in his *History of the Earth, and Animated Nature* (1774).

In this letter, Goldsmith writes in support of his nephew William, son of Daniel Hodson and Goldsmith's sister Catherine. In the letter following, Goldsmith writes to Hodson – a rare familial letter by this point in his life – to report William's safe arrival in London. That letter to Hodson also provides the conjectural date for this one.

The copy-text is the manuscript in the Royal College of Surgeons in England. It was first published by Balderston in 1928.

Dear Sir,

The young gentleman who carries this is my nephew. He has been liberally bred and has read something of physic and surgery, but desires to take the shortest and best method of being made more perfect in those studies. I beg sir you will put him in the way of improvement, and while he will take care to satisfy his instructors, I shall think my self laid under a particular obligation by your services or advice.[1]

I am
Dear Sir
Your very humble servt
Oliver Goldsmith.

[1] Hunter was very much involved in the Society of Collegiate Physicians, formed in 1767 in response to the refusal to admit many licentiates of the Royal College of Physicians who lacked an Oxbridge degree – including himself – to fellowship. Goldsmith identified Hunter as a key person within a medical network that could advance the career of his non-graduate nephew. In eighteenth-century medicine, serving an apprenticeship with someone of reputation served, in the patient's view, as almost a guarantee of reliability. William Hodson is not recorded as having attended Trinity College Dublin as his uncle did.

31

To Daniel Hodson

[London, *c.* June 1770]

Goldsmith writes to Hodson to confirm the safe arrival of his son, William, in London. As Hodson, alongside Oliver's beloved brother Henry, had given him financial support in his earlier life, notably in Edinburgh, Goldsmith was pleased to reciprocate.

The letter is also noteworthy for the expression of Goldsmith's ambiguity towards the stage. Although it is clear from Boswell's records that theatre was of great interest not only to Goldsmith but to his circle more broadly, Goldsmith also 'recounted all the disagreeable circumstances attending a dramatic author'.[1] The difficulties attending getting *The Good Natur'd Man* performed and its modest success seem to be preying on his mind. On the other hand, dismissing the stage in this letter to a worried father would also have helped to assuage Daniel's fears. As to where William might have 'contracted so beggarly an affection', Goldsmith is surely being disingenuous, perhaps even writing with his tongue firmly in his cheek.

The date is conjectural. Following Balderston, we agree that it must fall approximately a year before Letter 36, and must allow sufficient time after Letter 29 to Maurice for a second exchange of letters between Maurice and Oliver, and for Maurice's visit.

The copy-text is the manuscript in the Houghton Library, Harvard University. It was first published in Austin Dobson's *Life of Goldsmith* (1888). It was addressed to 'Danl: Hodson Esqr'.

My dear Brother

I have the pleasure of informing you that your son William is arrived in London in Safety and joins with me in his kindest love and duty to you. Nothing gives me greater pleasure than the prospect I have of his behaving in the best and most dutiful manner both to you and the rest of the family. Sincerly I am charmd with his disposition and I am sure he feels all the good nature he expresses every moment for his friends at home. He had when he came here some thoughts of going upon the stage; I dont know where he could have contracted so beggarly an affection, but I have turned him from it and he is now sincerely bent on pursuing the study of physic and surgery in which he has already made a considerable progress and to which I have very warmly exhorted him. He will in less than a year be a very good ~~phy~~ Surgeon and he will understand a competent share of physic also, when he is fit for any business or any practice I shall use all my little interest in his favour.[2] As for the stage it was every way [a] wild scheme and he is beside utterly unfit to succeed upon it. But while he is fitting himself for other business my dear Brother it is not proper that he should be utterly neglected. I have endeavoured to answer for you and my sister that some little thing should be done for him either here or at Edinburgh, and for my own part I am willing to contribute something towards his education myself. I believe an hundred pounds for a year or two would very completely do the business, when once he has got a profession he then may be thrown into any place with a prospect of succeeding. My Dear Dan think of this for a little, something must be done. I will give him twenty pounds a year, he has already about twenty more, the rest must be got. and your own good sense will suggest the means. I have often told you and tell you again that we have all good prospects before us, so that a little perseverance will bring things at last to bear. My brother Maurice was with me in London but it was not in my power to serve him effectually then; Indeed in a letter I wrote him I desired him by no means to come up but he was probably fond of the journey. I have already written to Doctor Hunter in William's favour and have got him cloaths &c, I only wait your answer in what manner further to proceed and with the sincerest affection to you and my sister I am Dear Dan your most affectionate

Brother
Oliver Goldsmith

I had a letter from Charles who is as he tells me possessed of a competency and settled in Jamaica.

[1] James Boswell, *Boswell in Search of a Wife 1766–1769*, ed. Frank Brady and Frederick A. Pottle (London: William Heinemann, 1957), 318.

[2] In the mid eighteenth century, apprentices proceeded to a period of medical instruction which could involve a year at a provincial hospital under the tutelage of an established surgeon and another year of attending lectures in London and doing ward rounds in hospitals. There was no official syllabus and there were no examinations. While the Company of Surgeons did issue a diploma, they were rarely acquired. Students received instead large ornate certificates of attendance for display. See Irvine Loudon, *Medical Care and the General Practitioner 1750–1850* (Oxford: Clarendon Press, 1986), 35.

32

To Sir Joshua Reynolds

[Lille, 27 July 1770]

Joshua Reynolds (1723–92) was an artist and art theorist who was the founding president of the Royal Academy. He also established the Club and this is where his intimacy with Goldsmith developed, the pair having first met in 1761 through their mutual friend Johnson. Reynolds, also a bachelor, was a great champion of Goldsmith throughout his career, encouraging him to practise medicine again in 1765, advocating on behalf of *The Good Natur'd Man*, and even making Goldsmith Professor of Ancient History at the Royal Academy, much to his friend's delight, as we can see in Letter 29 above. This faith in Goldsmith's abilities was warmly acknowledged in *The Deserted Village*'s dedication to Reynolds, which imagined him as a surrogate brother. Reynolds also featured in *Retaliation*, one of Goldsmith's final poems.

This letter and the one following describe a trip to Paris taken by Goldsmith and the Horneck sisters and their mother, probably at the behest of Reynolds. They travelled to the French capital via Lille before returning to England. The trip, according to Prior, lasted six weeks in total and, despite the reasonably energetic tone of the first letter, appears to have been a failure. Money, as often, seems to have been at the heart of the difficulty. At a dinner with John Ridge, an Irish lawyer (the 'anchovy' of *Retaliation*), Goldsmith was asked for his views on such trips. He replied, more than a little bitterly, 'I recommend it by all means to the rich if they are without the sense of *smelling*, and to the poor if they are without the sense of *feeling*' (*P*, II: 297). As the following letter reveals, this letter was never sent.

The copy-text is Balderston's; her transcription was taken from the original in the possession of Constance Meade (Percy's great-granddaughter) which was inserted in her album and not deposited at the British Library with the rest of her Goldsmith letters. Its current location is unknown. It was first published by Percy in 1801. It has no address. The letter was given by Reynolds to Boswell and then on to Thomas Percy, confirmed by a marginal note 'Original letter of Dr. Goldsmith to Sir Joshua Reynolds, who gave it to me. James Boswell'.

My dear Friend,

We had a very quick passage from Dover to Calais which we performed in three hours and twenty minutes, all of us extremely sea-sick, which must necessarily have happened as my machine to prevent sea-sickness was not completed.[1] We were glad to leave Dover, because we hated to be imposed upon, so were in high spirits at coming to Calais where we were told that a little money would go a great way. Upon landing two little trunks, which was all we carried with us We were surprised to see fourteen or fifteen fellows all running down to the ship to lay their hands upon them, four got under each trunk, the rest surrounded and held the hasps, and in this manner our little baggage was conducted with a kind of funeral solemnity till it was safely lodged at the custom house. We were well enough pleased with the peoples civility till they came to be paid; every creature that had the happiness of but touching our trunks with their finger expected six-pence, and they had so pretty civil a manner of demanding it that there was no refusing them. When we had done with the porters, we had next, to speak with the custom house officers, who had their pretty civil way too. We were directed to the Hotel d'Angleterre where a valet de place came to offer his service and spoke to me ten minutes before I once found out that he was speaking English.[2] We had no occasion for his service so we gave him a little money because he spoke English and because he wanted it. I can't help mentioning another circumstance, [ ][3] bought a new ribbon for my wig at Canterbury, and the barber at Calais broke it in order to gain six-pence by buying me a new one.

[1] The travellers' passage indeed appears to have been startlingly quick: a contemporary travel guide states that 'the passage is commonly made in sixteen, or twenty hours': Philip Playstowe, *The Gentleman's Guide in his Tour Through France* (Bristol, [1766]), 15. No trace of Goldsmith's intriguing machine to prevent seasickness has been found.

[2] The hotel made famous by Sterne in *A Sentimental Journey* in 1768. Sterne had stayed there in October 1765.

[3] A name is blotted out in the manuscript at this point, which Balderston proposed was 'Mary'. We have assumed that her rationale was based on her assessment of the manuscript rather than any biographical supposition.

33
To Sir Joshua Reynolds
Paris, 29 July [1770]

Some days into the trip with the Hornecks, this letter suggests the expedition to France was not as harmonious as anticipated. In a later letter to their mutual friend Bennet Langton, Johnson confirms that the trip had not gone well: 'Dr

Goldsmith has been at Paris with the Hornecks not very delightfully to either side.'[1] In addition to financial pressures, the presence of Joseph Hickey, lawyer to Burke and Reynolds and who had much more up-to-date knowledge of Paris than he, appears to have irked Goldsmith, cast somewhat into the shadows.[2] As later correspondence shows (see Letters 35 and 64), Goldsmith and the Hornecks repaired their friendship. This letter, with its litany of complaints about the diurnal aggravations of Continental travel, provides a humorous counterpoint to the cosmopolitan Goldsmith evoked by his poem *The Traveller.* The overarching sense of the letter is of a man who is missing the metropolitan whirl of London and its literary homosociality.

The copy-text is the manuscript in the Free Library of Philadelphia. It was first published by Prior in 1837. It is addressed: 'To | Sir Joshua Reynolds | Leicester Fields | London'. The postmark is incomplete at the edge of the sheet but most likely records 4 August.

Paris July 29th

My Dear Friend.

I began a long letter to you from Lisle giving a description of all that we had done and seen but finding it very dull and knowing that you would shew it again I threw it aside and it was lost.[3] You see by the top of this letter that we are at Paris, and (as I have often heard you say) we have brought our own amusement with us for the Ladies do not seem to be very fond of what we have yet seen. With regard to myself I find that travelling at twenty and at forty are very different things, I set out with all my confirmd habits about me and can find nothing on the continent so good as when I formerly left it. One of our chief amusements here is scolding at every thing we meet with and praising every thing and every person we left at home. You may judge therefore whether your name is not frequently bandied at table among us. To tell you the truth I never thought I could regret your absence so much as our various mortifications on the road have often taught me to do. I could tell you of disasters and adventures without number, of our lying in barns, and of my being half poisoned with a dish of green peas, of our quarelling with postillions and being cheated by Landladies but I reserve all this for an happy hour which I expect to share with you upon my return.[4] I have very little to tell you more but that we are at present all well and expect returning when we have staid out our month, which I did not care tho it were over this very day. I long to hear from you all, how you yourself do, how Johnson, Burke, Dyer, Chamier, Colman, and every one of the club do.[5] I wish I could send you some amusement in this letter but I protest I am so stupefied by the air of this country (for I am sure it can never be natural) that I have not a word to say. I have been thinking of the plot of a comedy which shall be entituled a journey to Paris, in which a family shall be introduced with a full intention of going to France to save money. You know there is not a place in the world more promising for that purpose. As for the meat of this country I can scarce eat it, and tho we pay two good shillings an head for our dinner I find it all so tough that I have spent less time with my knife than my pick tooth. I said this as a good thing at table but it was not understood. I believe it to be a good thing. As for our intended journey to Devonshire I find it out of my power to perform it, for as soon as I arrive at Dover I intend to let the ladies go on, and I will take a country lodging for a couple of months somewhere near that place in order to do some business.[6] I have so out run the Constable that I must mortify a little to bring it up again.[7] For Godsake the night you receive this take your pen in your hand, and tell me some thing about yourself, and my self if you know of any thing that has happened. About Miss Reynolds, about Mr Bickerstaff, my Nephew, or any body that you regard.[8] I beg you will send to Griffin the Book seller to know if there be any letters left for me and be so good as to send them to me at Paris.[9] They may perhaps be left for me at the Porters Lodge opposite the Pump in Temple lane. The same messenger will do. I expect one from Lord Clare from Ireland.[10] As for others I am not much uneasy about.[11] Is there any thing I can do for you at Paris, I wish you would tell me. The whole of my own purchases here is one silk coat which I have put on, and which makes me look like a fool. But no more of that. I find that Colman has gaind his law suit.[12] I am glad of it. I suppose you often meet. I will soon be among you, better pleasd with my situation at home than I ever was before. And yet I must say that if any thing could make France pleasant the very good women with whom I am at present would certainly do it. I could say more about that but I intend shewing them this letter before I send it away. What signifies teizing you longer with moral observations when the business of my writing is over, I have one thing only more to say, and of that I think every hour in the day namely that I am your most

sincere and most affectionate
friend

Oliver Goldsmith

Direct to me at the Hotel de Denemarcs
Rue Jacob. Fauxbourg St Germains.

1 Letter from Johnson to Langton, 24 October 1770: Redford, ed., *Letters of Samuel Johnson*, I: 352.

2 *P*, II: 296.

3 The usual route to Paris was through Boulogne, Abbeville and Amiens rather than Lille: *The Gentleman's Guide*, 17–18.

4 Balderston notes that mutual visiting after the completion of a journey was a staple of their friendship.

5 Samuel Dyer (*c.* 1721–72) was a translator and became the first elected member of the Club in 1764; he had previously been elected to the Royal Society in 1760. Well respected and liked by Johnson and Burke, Dyer's publications were limited. Some contemporaries believed him to be Junius but this identification is not given much credence today. His connection to Goldsmith may have been strengthened by his studies in Leiden, where Goldsmith was also in part educated.
Anthony Chamier (1725–80) was an important and influential financier for the governments of Newcastle and Bute. Lord Barrington, then treasurer of the navy, appointed him as secretary to the war office in 1763, where he rose through the ranks until he became an MP for Tamworth in 1778. He was one of the original members of the Club.

6 Goldsmith never took this trip to Devonshire with Reynolds who travelled alone in early September. The 'business' probably refers to *Animated Nature*, for the first five volumes of which William Griffin had paid him the previous September, and *The History of England from the Earliest Times to the Death of George II*, which he had contracted to finish for Davies by June 1771.

7 'A man who has lived above his means, or income is said to have outrun the constable': Francis Grose, *A Classical Dictionary of the Vulgar Tongue*, 3rd edn (London: Hooper and Co., 1796), n.p.

8 Frances Reynolds (1729–1807), painter, poet and writer on art, moved to London in order to be housekeeper to Joshua Reynolds, her brother, on his return from Italy in 1752. Despite a distinct lack of encouragement on the part of her brother, she had paintings exhibited at the Royal Academy in 1774 and 1775. She published an aesthetic treatise *Enquiry Concerning the Principles of Taste and the Origins of our Ideas on Beauty &c* (1789), dedicated to Elizabeth Montagu. She knew and was admired by Johnson, Frances Burney and Cornelia Knight.
Isaac Bickerstaff (1733–*c.* 1808), Irish playwright, had a military background but resigned his commission to pursue a literary career in London from 1755. He achieved great success with pieces such as *Love in a Village* (1762), *The Maid of the Mill* (1765) – based on Samuel Richardson's 1740 novel *Pamela* – and *The Padlock* (1768). He was forced to flee the country after accusations about his homosexuality were publicized in the newspapers in April 1772.

9 William Griffin (d. 1803), bookseller in Catherine Street in the Strand. He was an Irishman himself and patron of many Irish men of letters in London as evidenced by 'The Poetical Triumvirate', Kenrick's parody of Dryden: 'Step into G--ff-n's shop, he'll tell ye / Of G--ds--th, B--k-rs--ff, and K-ll-', *Poems; Ludicrous, Satirical and Moral* (London: Printed for J. Fletcher, [1768]), 269. Griffin was publishing Goldsmith's *The Deserted Village* at this time; it went into a fifth edition in August.

10 Robert Nugent, Earl Clare (1709–88), came from a landed Irish background but, through marriage, gained wealth and political influence in England. He was a friend of Alexander Pope's and his first literary composition, *An Ode to William Pulteney* (1739), a reflection on his conversion from Catholicism, gained him considerable applause. He became an MP in 1741 and had a successful political career through deft and opportunistic manouevring. He was elevated to the Irish peerage in 1767 as Viscount Clare, and became an earl in 1776. He had always retained his interest in literature and sought Goldsmith's acquaintance after publication of *The Traveller*. He became a firm supporter of Goldsmith and was rewarded with his immortalization in *The Haunch of Venison, a Poetical Epistle to Lord Clare* (1776).

11 Balderston speculates that the news of Goldsmith's mother's death was contained in this packet of letters, and that for this reason he came directly back to London, abandoning his intended retreat near Dover.

12 George Colman and his partners Thomas Harris, John Rutherford and William Powell had purchased the patent for Covent Garden in 1767 for £60,000. The agreement soon collapsed into rancour over whether Colman had assumed excessive control over the theatre's management. The case went to law and reached chancery in July 1770; the ruling went in Colman's favour. Balderston writes that Colman's acceptance of *The Good Natur'd Man* without his partners' consent was cited as evidence against him in the case (*BL*, 97n1). This implication that the play was a failure would have rankled with Goldsmith. Moreover, his countryman and fellow playwright Arthur Murphy was one of the prosecuting lawyers, although this did not prevent them collaborating later (see Letter 49, n2). However, newspaper accounts of the chancery case do not list Goldsmith's comedy among the grievances aired in the court by the plaintiffs' counsel. Nor does Friedman mention this. The newspaper trial reports indicate that Colman's rather egregious errors were in allowing Charles Dibdin, Charles Macklin and Isaac Bickerstaff to leave Covent Garden: *Lloyd's Evening Post*, 18–20 July 1770; *Whitehall Evening Post*, 17–19 July 1770.

34
To Colin Mackenzie
[London, 1771–1772]

Colin Mackenzie (1697/8–1775) was a physician and midwife. Like Goldsmith, Mackenzie received some of his training at Leiden (albeit earlier, in the 1720s). He was a student of the renowned obstetrician William Smellie, mentioned favourably in his *Treatise on Midwifery* (1764), and he was responsible for some startling advances in obstetric knowledge relating to maternal and foetal blood supplies. Mackenzie's discoveries were claimed by William Hunter, however, and he did not receive due credit until 1780. He ran midwifery courses from the 1750s and also maintained a private lying-in establishment in Southwark until his death in 1775.

Goldsmith may be meeting him in order to advocate on behalf of his nephew William Hodson, recently arrived in London (see Letter 31), perhaps with a view to expanding William's portfolio of medical skills before a departure to India. It is also possible that Mackenzie may have been the 'friend in Town' referred to in Letter 36 with the medical and commercial connections to get William a surgeon's place in India. However, these suppositions are speculative – not least because the extant evidence points towards Mackenzie initiating the contact: his communication to Goldsmith is in the British Library and reads 'Monday 10 [month illegible] Dr. Mackenzie presents his compliments to Dr. Goldsmith. Begs he will let him know when he can have the pleasure of seeing him.'

The copy-text is the manuscript in the British Library. The date is conjectural and based on the watermark, 'SP': the manuscript sheets of Goldsmith's *History of the Earth, and Animated Nature*, written c. 1772 and also in the British Library, bear the same watermark.

Doctor Goldsmith presents his compliments to Doctor Mackenzie, he will be at home this day till three, or at any other time the Doctor shall appoint. Or he will wait upon him, at Southwark. He is engaged to dinner every day for this six or seven days.

35

To George Augustus Selwyn

[London], 15 April 1771

George Selwyn (1719–91) was a politician and wit, better known in the latter capacity as he did not speak once in House of Commons debates during his 44-year parliamentary career. He was an enthusiastic participant in London club culture, a noted conversationalist, gambler and member of White's Club. A much-discussed peculiarity of his was his interest in executions; he even travelled to Paris in 1757 to watch the brutal execution of would-be royal assassin Damiens. His friends and associates included Thomas Gray, Horace Walpole and Charles James Fox.

Although Goldsmith's trip to Paris does not appear to have gone well, it does not seem to have diminished his enthusiasm for assisting the social ambitions of the Horneck sisters, the 'finer people' referred to in the letter. The masquerade took place on the Thursday following the letter, 18 April, at the Theatre Royal, Haymarket. An approving report on the masque, whose '*magnificence*, *splendor*, *elegance*, *brilliancy*, and *taste*, beggars all description!', indicates that Goldsmith's entreaty was probably successful: the report notes the presence of 'the two sisters (*tout charmant*) the Miss Hor—ks, alike in *dress*; *grace*; and *beauty!*' (*General Evening Post*, 20–23 April 1771).

The copy-text is the manuscript in the Society of Antiquaries, London. It was first published by Balderston in 1928. It is addressed 'To | George Augustus Selwyn Esqr. | Newmarket | Cambridge shire' and postmarked 15 April. The letter is also stamped 'Free', which suggests that Goldsmith took the liberty of using Selwyn's member of parliament franking privilege to cover the cost of postage to Newmarket when he found him away from home.

Monday, April 15th. 1771.

Sir

I did my self the honour of calling at your house in Chesterfield street to deliver the enclosed, but not finding you at home and not knowing when you intend to return I take leave to inform you that Colonel Nugent entreats you will remember your promise of putting Lord Marsh in mind of sending the tickets for the next Masquerade to me, or sending what they call checque tickets which will answer the same purpose.[1] I entreat Sir you will not impute this to my own impatience but that of some finer people who if disappointed on this occasion will be quite unhappy. Be pleased to direct to Oliver Goldsmith at his chambers in the Temple Brick Court No. 2. I am Sir your

most obedient humble Servant
Oliver Goldsmith

[1] Lieutenant-Colonel Edmund Craggs Nugent of the 1st Regiment of Foot Guards and Groom of the Bedchamber to his Majesty, who would shortly die on 26 April (see Letter 36) as recorded in the *Public Advertiser*, 30 April 1771.
William Douglas (1725–1810), third Earl of March and, later, fourth Duke of Queensberry, was a close friend of Selwyn's, also a member of White's, and a committed pleasure-seeker with a pronounced interest in women and gambling.

36

To Daniel Hodson

[London, *c.* June 1771]

Goldsmith pleads with Hodson to allow his son travel to India as a surgeon; he makes it clear that this is an excellent opportunity, not least in financial terms. He is at pains to describe the efforts he has made on behalf of William since his arrival to London, in terms both of networking and financial support.

The copy text is the manuscript in the Houghton Library, Harvard University. It was first published in Dobson's *Life of Goldsmith* (1888). It was addressed 'To Daniel Hodson Esqr.' The address page is also marked 'Doctor Goldsmith letter' in another near-contemporary hand. The dating is conjectural. Lieutenant-Colonel Nugent died on 26 April. As this letter shows, there was a subsequent exchange of letters between William Hodson and his father: June then seems a reasonable estimate for this letter's composition.

My Dear Brother

It gave me great concern to find that you were uneasy at your son's going abroad. I will beg leave to state my part in the affair and I hope you will not condemn me for what I have endeavourd to do for his benefit. When he came here first I learned that his circumstances were very indifferent, and that something was to be done to retrieve them. The stage was an abominable resource which neither became a man of honour, nor a man of sense. I therefore dissuaded him from that design and turned him to physic in which he had before made a very great progress, and since that he has for this last twelve month applied himself to surgery, so that I am thoroughly convinced that there is not a better surgeon in the kingdom of Ireland than he. I was obliged to go down to Bath with a friend that was dying when my nephew sent me down your letter to him in which you inform him that he can no longer have any expectations from you and that therefore he must think of providing for himself.[1] With this letter he sent me one of his own where he asserted his fixed intentions of going surgeon's mate to India. Upon reading the two letters I own I thought something was to be done. I therefore wrote to a friend in Town who procured him the assurance of a place [a]s full Surgeon to India.[2] This with supplying him with about five and forty pounds is what I did in my endeavours to serve him. I thought him helpless and unprovided for, and I was ardent in my endeavours to remove his perplexities. Whatever his friends at home may think of a Surgeon's place to the East Indies it is not so contemptible a thing, and those who go seldom fail of making a moderate fortune in two or three voyages. But be this as it may William is now prevaild upon to return home to take your further advice and instructions upon the matter. he has labour'd very hard since he left you, and is capable of living like a gentleman in any part of the world. He has answered his examination as a Surgeon and has been found sufficiently qualified.[3] I entreat therefore you will receive him as becomes him and you, and that you will endeavour to serve the young man effectually not by foolish fond caresses but by either advancing him in his business or setlling him in life. I could my Dear Brother say a great deal more, but am obliged to hasten this letter as I am again just setting out for Bath, and I honestly say I had much rather it had been for Ireland with my nephew. but that pleasure I hope to have before I die.

I am Dear Dan
Your most affectionate
Brother Oliver Goldsmith.

[1] The Hon. Lieutenant-Colonel Nugent MP was the only son of Lord Clare. Goldsmith's particular intimacy with Lord Clare flowered in the spring and summer of 1771, during Clare's mourning for his son. The trip to Bath occurred after 23 April, when Goldsmith was present at the first annual dinner of the Royal Academy, on which occasion he informed Horace Walpole of the death of Thomas Chatterton. Present at the dinner was Lord Hardwicke who subsequently wrote Goldsmith a letter advising him to visit Bristol on his projected trip to Bath and to recover any available Chatterton manuscripts. Balderston notes that this must have been the occasion of Goldsmith's unsuccessful attempt to purchase the Rowley manuscripts from George Catcott, a merchant and son of poet and Church of England clergyman Alexander Stopford Catcott (1692–1749): *European Magazine* 21 (1792), 88.

[2] Balderston speculates that this may be Joshua Reynolds, who was a substantial stock-holder in the East India Company, as well as a friend of William Hodson.

[3] See Letter 31, in which Goldsmith seeks to reassure his brother-in-law of the veracity of William's professional accomplishments.

37

To Bennet Langton

London, 4 September 1771

Bennet Langton (bap. 1736–1801) became friendly with Johnson due to his great admiration for the *Rambler*. He was also a close friend of Topham Beauclerk. Langton was an original member of the Club and also rose to the rank of major in the Lincolnshire militia. In 1770 he married Mary Lloyd (1743–1820), the widow of John Leslie, Earl of Rothes (1698?–1767) and the Lady Rothes referred to in the letter. A well-regarded Greek scholar despite an acute lack of publications, he succeeded Johnson as Professor of Ancient Literature at the Royal Academy in 1788. In this letter Goldsmith declined an invitation to visit Langton and his wife at their home in Lincolnshire. It is also the first time Goldsmith alludes to his comic masterpiece, *She Stoops to Conquer*. Langton's letter of invitation (also in the British Library) is given in full here:

My dear Sir,

You was so kind, when I had the Pleasure of seeing you in Town, as to speak of having Thoughts of giving me your Company here. I wish very much you would put your kind intention in Execution, in which Lady Rothes, who desires Her best Compliments, very sincerely concurs with me—it was, if you remember, at Joshua Reynolds's that we talked of this, who gave me Hopes too of Letting us see Him. I would have wrote to Him likewise to request that Favour, but in the Papers it was said that he went to France some time ago, and I do not know whether he is yet returned; if He is, and You have an opportunity of seeing Him, will You be so kind as to mention what I have said, and how much we wish for the Pleasure of His Company—I have sent for the History of England, but have not yet receivd it—some short extracts y^{t}. I have already seen have entertained me much.[1] Let me have the Pleasure of hearing from you, Dear Sir, as soon as you conveniently can after you receive this, and then, if you are so good as to say you are coming, I will immediately write you word of the particulars of the Road to this place and Means of conveyance &c—Will you give me Leave to ask in what Forwardness is the Natural History, or whether you are about any other Work that you chuse as yet to

speak of?[2] I hope Poetry takes up some of Your attention—tout
I will intrude upon you no longer than to say that I am, Dear Sir,
with great Respect and Regard

Your obedient humble Servant
Bennet Langton.

My Direction is Langton near Spilsby Lincolnshire.

The copy-text is the manuscript in the British Library. It was first published by Percy (who was given it by Langton) in 1801. It is addressed, 'To | Bennet Langton Esqr at Langton | near Spilsby | Lincoln shire'. It is postmarked 10 September.

Sepr. 4th 1771

My Dear Sir

Since I had the pleasure of seeing you last I have been almost wholly in the country at a farmer's house quite alone trying to write a Comedy.[3] It is now finished but when or how it will be acted, or whether it will be acted at all are questions I cannot resolve. I am therefore so much employd upon that that I am under a necessity of putting off my intended visit to Lincolnshire for this season. Reynolds is just returned from Paris and finds himself now in the case of a truant that must make up for his idle time by diligence. We have therefore agreed to postpone the affair till next summer when we hope to have the honour of waiting upon her Ladyship and you and staying double the time of our late intended visit. We often meet and never without remembering you. I see Mr Beauclerc very often both in town and country. He is now going directly forward to become a second Boyle. Deep in Chymistry and Physics.[4] Johnson has been down upon a visit to a country parson Doctor Taylor's and is returned to his old haunts at Mrs. Thrale's.[5] Burke is a farmer en attendant a better place, but visiting about too.[6] Every soul is visiting about and merry but myself. And that is hard too as I have been trying these three months to do something to make people laugh. There have I been strolling about the hedges studying jests with a most tragical countenance. The natural History is about half finished and I will shortly finish the rest. God knows Im tired of this kind of finishing, which is but bungling work, and that not so much my fault as the fault of my scurvy circumstances. They begin to talk in town of the opposition's gaining ground, the cry of Liberty is still as loud as ever.[7] I have published or Davis has published for me an Abridgement of the History of England for which I have been a good deal abused in the newspapers for betraying the liberties of the people.[8] God knows I had no thoughts for or against liberty in my head. My whole aim being to make up a book of a decent size that as Squire Richard says would do no harm to nobody.[9] However they set me down as an arrant Tory and consequently no honest man. When you come to look at any part of it you'l say that I am a soure Whig.[10] God bless you, and with my most respectful compliments to her Ladyship I remain dear Sir

Your most affectionate
humble Servant,
Oliver Goldsmith.

Temple Brick Court
Sep[r]. 7th 1771.

1 Goldsmith's *History of England from the Earliest Times to the Death of George II* was published by Thomas Davies on 6 August 1771 in four volumes.

2 Goldsmith signed an agreement with Ralph Griffiths in February 1769 for an eight-volume 'Natural History of Animals, &c.' for 800 guineas.

3 Goldsmith was staying at a farm on Edgeware Road where he was working on *She Stoops to Conquer*. Despite Goldsmith's claim that it was finished, the play underwent considerable revision and it was not performed until 15 March 1773 at Covent Garden Theatre. See *CW*, V: 87–9.

4 Topham Beauclerk (1739–80) was a book collector who was said to have accumulated over 30,000 volumes. A great-grandson of Charles II, Beauclerk was wealthy, aristocratic and a close friend of Bennet Langton and Johnson. He was one of the founding members of the Club. He also maintained a private laboratory to indulge his keen interest in chemistry and was Johnson's choice for a chair in natural philosophy when he considered setting up a college in St Andrews. The sale of his substantial library took place over fifty days and raised £5,011. Robert Boyle (1627–91) was an Irish natural philosopher who was at the centre of a vibrant academic network at Oxford in the 1650s. The son of the Earl of Cork, Boyle published prodigiously on a wide range of philosophical, scientific and theological subjects and was present at the inaugural meeting of the Royal Society. He was known for his piety and demanding moral standards as well as his intellect.

5 John Taylor (bap. 1711, d. 1788) was a lifelong friend of Johnson's, with whom he attended Lichfield grammar school. A Whig in politics, Taylor benefited from the patronage of the Duke of Devonshire, notably in obtaining a prebendary stall at Westminster. He held a number of other lucrative ecclesiastical appointments which brought him a rumoured annual income of £7,000. He spent much of his time at his family seat in Ashbourne (40 miles north of Lichfield), where Johnson often visited him.

Hester Thrale *née* Salusbury (1741–1821) was a writer and close confidante of Johnson's. See headnote to Letter 55.
Johnson had started on a six-week trip to Staffordshire and Derbyshire on 20 June. After his return he wrote to Langton on 29 August, excusing himself for having failed to visit him at Langton, near Spilsby, where it seems he was expected with Goldsmith and Reynolds: Redford, ed., *Letters of Samuel Johnson*, II: 142.

6 Burke had purchased Gregories, an estate near Beaconsfield, once the home of the poet Edmund Waller, for £20,000 in 1768, where he was carrying out experiments in agricultural improvement.

7 Goldsmith is referring to the Junius affair which was at its height at this time. Junius was the anonymous author of a series of letters published in the *Public Advertiser* in 1769–72. The letters were collectively a vituperative attack on Tory policies, and an endorsement of John Wilkes and his championing of 'liberty'. The letters drew the ire and horror of Burke and Johnson, among others. Goldsmith's suspicion of champions of liberty found expression in the drunk servant Jeremy in *She Stoops to Conquer*: 'Please your honour, liberty and Fleet-street for ever! Tho' I'm but a servant, I'm as good as another man' – IV.i.13–14 (*CW*, V: 181). See also the voicing of Wilkesite opinion through the character of Mr. Arnold's duplicitous butler 'Wilkinson' in chapter 19 of *The Vicar of Wakefield* (*CW*, IV: 98–106).

8 In the preface to *The History of England from the Earliest Times to the Death of George II* (1771), Goldsmith made clear that he saw this work as an abridgement of Hume, Carte, Rapin and Smollett: 'They have each their peculiar admirers, in proportion as the reader is studious of historical antiquities, fond of minute anecdote, a warm partizan, or a deliberate reasoner. Of these I have particularly taken Hume for my guide, as far as he goes; and it is but justice to say, that wherever I was obliged to abridge his work I did it with reluctance, as I scarce cut out a line that did not contain a beauty' (*CW*, V: 338–9). Goldsmith can be accused of being somewhat disingenuous here as the preface makes clear where his sympathies lay: 'For my own part, from seeing the bad effects of the tyranny of the great in those republican states that pretend to be free, I cannot help wishing that our monarchs may still be allowed to enjoy the power of controlling the encroachments of the great at home' (*CW*, V: 339). The passage which aroused especial censure was the account of the trial of Jacobite conspirator Sir John Friend (d. 1696), in which Lord Chief Justice Holt is accused of influencing the jury to pronounce Friend guilty (*P*, II: 327–8). The *Gazetteer and New Daily Advertiser* and the *Middlesex Journal or Chronicle of Liberty* both printed a lengthy attack by '*An* HISTORIOGRAPHER' which argued that Goldsmith had 'prostituted the sacred character of an historian' (5 September 1771), while a further extensive attack can also be found in the *Middlesex Journal* for 10–12 September. Brief extracts from the work, which disparaged the characters of Charles II and James II, appeared earlier (*Middlesex Journal*, 17–20 August 1771).

9 Unidentified. Balderston suggests Richard Burke, brother of Edmund. It may also be a playful nickname for a mutual acquaintance, inspired by the dimwitted and uncouth Squire Richard, a character in Colley Cibber's *The Provok'd Husband* (1728).

10 History-writing was a notoriously difficult literary medium to negotiate successfully. Goldsmith anticipates David Hume's famous complaint about the reception of his *History of England* in 'My Own Life', published in 1777: 'I thought that I was the only historian, that had at once neglected present power, interest, and authority, and the cry of popular prejudices; and as the subject was suited to every capacity, I expected proportional applause. But miserable was my disappointment: I was assailed by one cry of reproach, disapprobation, and even detestation; English, Scotch, and Irish, Whig and Tory, churchman and sectary, freethinker and religionist, patriot and courtier, united in their rage against the man, who had presumed to shed a generous tear for the fate of Charles I. and the Earl of Strafford': David Hume, 'My Own Life', *The History of England*, 8 vols. (London: printed for T. Cadell, 1778), I: xi.

38
To Joseph Cradock
[London, December 1771]

Joseph Cradock (1742–1826) was a writer from Leicester. Upon moving to London, he became friendly with David Garrick and was well known to the literary set as an avid theatregoer. He was elected a fellow of the Society of Antiquaries in 1768 and assisted Garrick in the preparations for the Shakespeare Jubilee in 1769. He wrote a tragedy called *Zobeide* based on Voltaire's *Les Scythes* which was first performed on 11 December 1771 at Covent Garden. It had a further ten performances that season, ensuring that Cradock benefited from three author nights.

As the letter below shows, Goldsmith supplied the prologue to *Zobeide*, probably at the behest of one or both of the actors Richard and Mary Ann Yates. Cradock gave Mary Ann Yates, who played the eponymous heroine, the profit from the ninth night (£59 16s), presumably for her success in the role but perhaps also acknowledging her part in securing Goldsmith's prologue, which added to the new play's metropolitan appeal, as the reviews testify. The *Middlesex Journal* (12–14 December 1771) reported: 'Upon the whole, there is merit in the Prologue, and the town was too just to withhold the tribute of approbation', and the *Critical Review* (December 1771) went as far as to say that the Prologue and Epilogue (the latter supplied by Arthur Murphy) were 'not excelled by many on the English stage'.

Cradock's literary output was not prodigious but there are some efforts of note. A pamphlet, *The Life of John Wilkes, Esq., in the Manner of Plutarch* (1773), inspired a Wilkesite mob to smash his windows. He later published another play and a novel but is best remembered for his four-volume *Literary and Miscellaneous Memoirs* (1826–8), which holds a wealth of anecdotal information about London's literary life.

The copy-text is Cradock's *Literary and Miscellaneous Memoirs*, where it was first published in 1826. It was addressed 'For the Rt. Hon. Lord Clare, (Mr Cradock,) Gosfield, Essex'.

Mr. Goldsmith presents his best respects to Mr. Cradock, has sent him the Prologue, such as it is. He cannot take time to make it better. He begs he will give Mr. Yates the proper instructions; and so, even so, he commits him to fortune and the public.[1]

[1] The prologue was actually spoken by the comic actor John Quick (1748–1831). Cradock explains 'a comic Prologue, by the husband, in the character of a Sailor, would have ill-suited with the lofty dignity of the first tragic actress' (*Memoirs*, I: 224). See also the headnote to Letter 49.

39
To Joseph Cradock
[London, 16 February 1772]

In Cradock's *Memoirs*, he did not remember to what performance the letter below referred, but noted that it 'seems to refer to one of his earlier productions' (I: 224). The production can be identified as *Threnodia Augustalis*, written to be performed in commemoration of Augusta, the Princess Dowager of Wales and mother of George III, who died on 8 February 1772. The identification is possible from a letter from William Woodfall to Goldsmith: Woodfall was acting on behalf of Teresa Cornelys (1723?–97) who put on various entertainments at Carlisle House, and he commissioned Goldsmith to write the piece on behalf of Cornelys and Goldsmith had agreed, provided his anonymity was preserved. Woodfall wanted Goldsmith to collaborate with an Italian composer, Matthias Vento (1735–76), and wrote on 16 February to remind him of his appointment with Vento. This letter provoked this hastily written note to Cradock, postponing their engagement. Goldsmith's authorship of the *Threnodia Augustalis*'s libretto, a piece of which he was not proud, was not known until it appeared in Chalmers's 1810 edition of his works. Goldsmith's apologetic advertisement refers to it as a 'Compilation' rather than a poem and makes clear it was written in haste. A printed version was advertised for sale at the door of the performance for 1s (*Public Advertiser*, 20 February 1772).

We can be reasonably certain of the date offered here. The Princess Dowager died on Saturday 8 February. Goldsmith could not have written this letter the day after so it must have been written on Sunday 16 February before the performance of the *Threnodia Augustalis*, on Thursday 20 February.

The copy-text is a facsimile of the manuscript in the Rosenbach of the Free Library of Philadelphia. The location of the original manuscript is unknown. It was first published in Cradock's *Literary and Miscellaneous Memoirs* in 1826. Balderston records, based on access to the original owned by A. S. W. Rosenbach, that it was addressed 'To J. Craddock Esqr at the Hotel in Pall Mall'. There is no address visible on the facsimile.

Mr. Goldsmith's best respects to Mr. Craddock when he ask'd him to day he quite forgot an engagement of above[1] a weeks standing

which has been made purposely for him, he feels himself quite uneasy at not being permitted to have his instructions upon those parts where he must necessarily be defective. He will have a rehearsal on monday; when if Mr. Craddock would come, and afterwards take a bit of mutton chop it would add to his other obligations.
Sunday morning.

1 Balderston mistranscribed 'above' as 'about' but there is no ambiguity that the former is correct.

40

[To John Lee]

[London, *c.* February 1772]

John Lee (1725–81), actor and theatre manager, began his career in Goodman's Field Theatre, London, in 1745. As was typical of the time, his career fluctuated between theatres, and he had periods at Drury Lane and Covent Garden. These changes in allegiance were not without problems and in 1750 David Garrick sued him for breach of articles after he left Drury Lane rather abruptly the year before. Forced to return, Lee acted at Drury Lane until 1752, when he left to follow his wife to Dublin. However, he only performed once at Thomas Sheridan's Smock Alley before he left for Edinburgh. Here he began his management career and introduced a number of innovations before his tenure at Edinburgh also collapsed into ignominy and legal wrangling. The remainder of his career saw him continue his itinerant ways and he had periods back in Dublin, Bath, Bristol and London. Lee also adapted a number of established plays but, it appears, without success. He was the father of the literary sisters, Sophia and Harriet Lee.

The date of the letter is conjectural. John Lee played one of the speaking parts in *Threnodia Augustalis* and it is likely their contact was motivated by this piece. Lee may have wished to speak to Goldsmith in advance of the performance, or perhaps to discuss it afterwards.

The copy-text is the manuscript in Somerville College, Oxford. It is published here for the first time. The letter is only partial with the manuscript cut away to the right side, where begins what remains of the letter. The sheet is marked, in a different hand in pencil 'To Mr. Lee'.

I am oblig[ed] to be out this evening otherwise should do my self the pleasure to meet you. I am Dear Sir your aff[t] humble Serv[t].

Oliver Goldsmith

41

To Richard Penneck

[Edgeware Road, *c.* 16 March 1772]

The Reverend Richard Penneck (1728–1803)[1] was rector of Abinger in Surrey, and of St John, Southwark, courtesy of his patron the second Earl of Godolphin. A nephew of antiquary William Borlase (1696–1772), Penneck became the second keeper of the reading room of the British Museum in 1761 when the first holder, Peter Templeman, was sacked. He remained in this office until his death. He was also a chaplain of Trinity College, Cambridge (1757–1802), where he took his BA and MA degrees.

In 1771, Goldsmith took up residence at the cottage of a farmer named Selby who lived outside the village of Hyde, about 6 miles outside of London on the Edgeware Road. He would stay here for the summer, go back to the city in the winter, before returning again in the spring of 1772.

This letter throws additional light upon Goldsmith's and Percy's dependence on each other's interest in early English poetry. Goldsmith's ballad 'Edwin and Angelina' had been privately printed in 1765 to complement Percy's *Reliques of Ancient English Poetry* before its appearance in *The Vicar of Wakefield* a year later. This letter shows that this mutual interest was sustained into the 1770s.

The date can be determined from the letter following which acknowledges receipt of the poem requested here so we can be confident they were written in close proximity.

The copy-text is the manuscript in the Library of the Historical Society of Pennsylvania, Philadelphia. It was first published in S. H. Harlowe, 'Original Letters of Dr. Johnson and Oliver Goldsmith', *Notes and Queries* 5.7.163 (1877), 101–2. The letter was endorsed by Penneck '([NB] I sent Dr G. the M.S.)' in the top right-hand side of the folio. Below this 'No. 50' was written, first in pencil and then in ink, in a different hand.

Dear Sir,

I know not what appology to make for troubling you with this letter, but the consciousness of your readiness to oblige when it lies in your power. Without more preface, I was some time ago, when in London looking over the Catalogue of the Harleian manuscripts, and in the middle or about the middle of that large book the title and the beginning of an old Saxon poem struck me very much.[2] I soon after desired our friend Doctor Percy to look out for it and get it transcribed for me but he tells me he can find no such poem as that I mentioned. However the poem I am sure is there, and there is nothing I so much desire, here, in a little country retirement where I now am, as to have that poem transcribed by one of the servants of the Museum, and I don't know any body who can get that done for me except yourself. The poem is in Saxon before the time of Chaucer and is I think about the middle of the volume among the names of several other poems. The subject is a consolation against repining at distress in this life, or some such title. The poem begins with these words which are expressed in the Catalogue,

"Lollai, Lollai, littel Childe, why weppest tou so sore?"[3]

If you would find it out and order it to be transcribed for me, I will consider it as a singular favour, and will take care that the clerk shall be paid his demand. I once more ask pardon for giving you this trouble, and am, Dear Sir, your very humble serv^{t}.

Oliver Goldsmith

P.S. A letter directed to me at the Temple will be receiv'd.

[1] Balderston's edition has 'Pennick' as per Goldsmith's spelling in the following letter. We defer to the *Oxford Dictionary of National Biography*.

[2] Goldsmith's medieval scholarship was a little off. The poem is known as the 'Lollai lullaby', a child's lullaby found in an early fourteenth-century Irish Franciscan friar's commonplace book: British Library, MS Harley 913. It is one of a group of lyrics formerly known as the 'Kildare Poems'. The poem has attracted considerable interest from scholars as arguably the earliest example of the Christian genre of the Virgin Mary singing to the child Christ; however, Angela M. Lucas has argued that it is rather an ordinary mother singing to her child: *Anglo-Irish Poems of the Middle Ages* (Dublin: Columbia Press, 1995). Wilhelm Heuser's commentary, *Die Kildare-Gedichte* (Bonn, 1904), is still considered authoritative.

[3] It is listed as 'A Poem upon the Sorrows, & deceitfulness of this World. Incip. "Lollai, lollai, litil Child, whi wepistou so sore"', in *A Catalogue of the Harleian Manuscripts in the British Museum*, 2 vols. (London, 1808), I: 473.

42

To Richard Penneck

Edgeware Road, [16 March 1772]

Goldsmith was working on *An History of the Earth, and Animated Nature* at his writer's retreat in Farmer Selby's. Nonetheless, much as when he went to Paris with the Hornecks, the letter suggests that he was anxious to keep in touch with his social circles and the news from London.

The date of the letter can be determined from a number of circumstances. Goldsmith did not take up his residence at Edgeware until the summer of 1771 when Percy was at Alnwick, and Percy, for his part, did not return to London until October, after Goldsmith had returned to town. We can be confident then that the exchanges with Penneck occurred the following spring, after Goldsmith had returned to Edgeware. As Isaac Bickerstaff, whose invitation to dinner is mentioned in this letter, had fled London in mid-May, the dinner must have occurred before then. Finally, Sir Joshua Reynolds's pocket book for 1772 helpfully records an engagement with Goldsmith on Sunday 22 March.[1]

The copy-text is the manuscript in the library of Haverford College, Philadelphia. It was first published in S. H. Harlowe, 'Original Letters of Dr. Johnson and Oliver Goldsmith', 101–2. It is addressed 'To | the Rev^d. Mr. Pennick | at the | Museum', and above, in a different hand, is written, 'Doctor Goldsmith No. 49'. There are two postmarks, one of which has a 'W' (Wednesday?) visible but the rest is smudged; the other reads 'Penny Post Paid WTU'.

Monday

Dear Sir

I thank you heartily for your kind attention, for the poem, for your letter, and every thing. You were so kind as to say would not think it troublesome to step out of town to see me. Sir Joshua Reynolds Mr. Bickerstaff and a friend or two more will dine with me next Sunday at the place where I am which is a little Farmer's house about six miles from town, the Edgeware road.[2] If you come either in their company or alone I will consider it as an additional obligation.

I am dear Sir,

Your's most aff^tly

Oliver Goldsmith.

An Answer would be kind.
The place I am in is at Farmer Selby's at the six mile Stone Edgeware road.

[1] Royal Academy of Arts Archives, REY/1/15.

[2] The identity of the others present is unknown although Prior records that 'Sir Joshua Reynolds, Sir William Chambers, and other eminent men whose names are now indistinctly remembered, occasionally visited him here; once or twice it is believed Dr. Johnson was in company with the former. Among others who frequently spent an evening with him was Hugh Boyd, one of the supposed writers of the Letters of Junius, who resided for some time at the neighbouring village of Kenton above two miles distant' (*P*, II: 334).

Hugh Macaulay Boyd (1746–94) was an Irish political writer who edited Chatham's speeches and wrote as 'The Whig' for the *London Courant* (1779–80) before travelling to India in 1781 with the East India Company. Modern scholarship has dismissed his claim to be Junius.

43
To John Eyles
[Edgeware Road, late March 1772]

John Eyles is identified by Prior as Goldsmith's occasional 'man-servant' (II: 511). Nothing more is known of him. As Goldsmith was busy at this time writing *An History of the Earth, and Animated Nature*, it seems probable that he is asking Percy to bring the book referred to in the letter on his next visit.

The verso of the manuscript shows the date of the letter from which it was torn, 'March 21, 1772'. Percy's journal has the following entry for 31 March 1772: 'Mrs. Percy and I went to see Dr. Goldsmith and dined with him, came home in the evening'.[1] If Percy did indeed retrieve the book from Eyles, this may be when he brought it to Goldsmith.

The copy-text is the manuscript in the British Library. It was first published in Gaussen's *Percy, Prelate and Poet* in 1908. In addition to the date noted above, the verso of the manuscript also includes a list of fish, notes for the passages on 'cartigilanous fish' in his *Animated Nature*: 'Lamprey. Pike | skate or flat fish. | Shark. | Sturgeon | The sun fish | The lump fish | And the fishing frog. | And the sea snail.'[2]

Honest John.

Give Doctor Percy, My History of Animals.[3] Which you will find among my books.

[1] British Library, Add. MS 32336, fo. 162v.

[2] See *An History of the Earth, and Animated Nature*, 8 vols. (London: Printed for John Nourse, 1774), VI: 234–89.

[3] It is not possible to identify this book with certainty but Goldsmith's prefaces to Richard Brookes's *A New and Accurate System of Natural History* (1763–4) make the first volume of this work ('The History of QUADRUPEDS, including Amphibious Animals, Frogs, and Lizards') a strong candidate. Another possibility is that it is a volume of Buffon's *Histoire Naturelle* (1749–), a major source for *An History of the Earth, and Animated Nature*.

44
To Hugh Percy, Duke of Northumberland
London, 22 May 1772

Hugh Percy, Duke of Northumberland (bap. 1712, d. 1786) began life as Hugh Smithson. He was elected MP for Middlesex in 1740 and, in the same year, he made an advantageous marriage to Elizabeth Seymour (1716–76), who shortly after became heir to the Percy estates in Middlesex and Northumberland. Smithson succeeded to the title in 1750 and took the Percy name by an Act of Parliament. A number of honours followed and, after astutely exploiting the coal resources of his lands, he became extremely wealthy. The 1760s saw him hold a number of other offices including – of particular relevance to Goldsmith – the lord lieutenancy of Ireland (1763–5). Percy's wealth meant that he was not consumed by politics and the acquisition of high office and he pursued other interests. He was Fellow of the Royal Society as well as a trustee of the British Museum. A patron of the arts, he was acquainted with Johnson, Goldsmith and his namesake Thomas Percy, who stayed with him at Alnwick Castle regularly in his capacity as chaplain and secretary, as well as tutor to his son. He died at Sion House in 1786 and was buried at Westminster Abbey.

The copy-text is the manuscript in the British Library. It was first published by Balderston in 1928 which suggests that Thomas Percy secured this note from the duke for his *Memoir* but ultimately decided to omit it.

Mr. Goldsmith presents his most respectful compliments to the Duke of Northumberland, and as his Grace was pleased to allow him the liberty, he begs permission for a few friends some day next week to see his Grac[e's cast]le at Sion.[1]

Temple. May 22^{d}. 1772.

[1] Sion House, in west London, was acquired by Henry Percy, 9th Earl of Northumberland, in 1594. Hugh Percy commissioned Lancelot 'Capability' Brown to carry out improvements, which took place between 1762 and 1769. It is possible that Goldsmith was taking advantage of his connection to show some friends around the improved building. There is some irony at play here given Goldsmith's hostility to the 'improvement' so closely associated with Brown in the mid eighteenth century, evident in *The Deserted Village*.

45
To Thomas Bond
London, 16 December 1772

Thomas Bond was a lawyer who operated from Mountrath Street, Dublin, behind the Four Courts. Balderston identifies Bond as probably the 'connection of the family by marriage', mentioned by Prior (I: 17), who purchased the estate of Lissoy from Goldsmith's nephew Henry in 1802. Here we can see continued evidence of Goldsmith's concern for his nephew, William Hodson.

The copy-text is the manuscript in the Houghton Library, Harvard University. It was first published in Dobson's *Life of Goldsmith* (1888). It was addressed to 'Mr. Thos. Bond Attorney in | Montrath-Street | Dublin', and postmarked 21 December.

Temple. Brick Court. December 16 1772.

Dear Sir,

I received your letter, inclosing a draft upon Kerr and Company which when due shall be applied to the discharge of a part of my Nephew's debts He has written to me from Bristol for ten pound which I have sent him in a bank note enclosed he has also drawn upon me by one Mr. Odonogh for ten pound more, the balance therefore having paid his servant maid, as likewise one or two trifles more remains with me.[1] As he will certainly have immediate and pressing occasion for the rest when he arrives I beg youl remit the rest to me and I will take care to see it applied in the most proper manner. He has talk'd to me of a matrimonial Scheme.[2] If that could take place all would soon be well. I am Dear Sir your affectionate Kinsman

and humble Servant.

Oliver Goldsmith.

Be pleas'd to answer this directly.

[1] William Hodson kept a separate establishment at 41 Newman Street (*P*, II: 145).

[2] According to Prior, Hodson's first wife was a Miss Longworth, of Westmeath (II: 145).

46

To Thomas Percy

[London, 1772–1773]

Goldsmith was preparing an edition of the *Spectator* for an Irish publisher, William Wilson (*c.* 1745–1801), who was once described by Charlemont, the first president of the Royal Irish Academy, as 'the most spirited printer in this spiritless City'.[1] Wilson published Dublin editions of popular novels such as *The Expedition of Humphry Clinker* (1771) and *Robinson Crusoe* (1781) and supplied books in bulk to Marsh's Library in Dublin, Ireland's first public library. He edited the *Dublin Directory* 1772–1801, an important overview of Dublin's commercial activity initiated by his father, Peter, in 1751. A letter from Wilson to Goldsmith sounded him out on the idea of an Irish edition of the *Spectator* and asked him for his terms.[2] Wilson did eventually publish an eight-volume edition in 1778. Prior's list of Goldsmith's books (II: 583) also includes an eight-volume edition of the *Spectator* (1729).

The copy-text is the manuscript in the British Library. It was first published by Balderston in 1928. It is addressed, 'To | The Rev[d] Doctor Percy.' 'Sent' is inserted with a caret, in a different hand and in pencil after 'I have' in the final sentence.

[London, 1772 or 1773][3]

Dear Sir

I wish you would write for me the names of such persons as have written papers in the Spectator, at the end of every paper belonging to Addison and Steel &c there are letters. There are some however which are without marks. Those names I wish to have. I have you a little book where the numbers are mark'd, to which I beg you'l add the names.

Yours ever.
Oliver Goldsmith.

Ill call or send on Sunday morning, being constrain'd for time.

[1] Pollard, *A Dictionary of Members of the Dublin Book Trade*, 629.

[2] *A Catalogue of Autographs Letters, Original Documents Being Composed of James R. Osgood's Collection and Other Valuable and Desirable Specimens Recently Purchased, Forming in All One of the Finest Assortments Ever Offered for Sale in America March 4, 1886* (New York: William Evarts Benjamin, 1886), 21. According to Balderston, the letter formed part of a group of letters which became detached from Percy's collection and were offered for sale together in this catalogue.

[3] Balderston conjectured the date from the water-mark of the paper – 'LVG' – familiar in Goldsmith's correspondence during 1772 and 1773, and unknown before September 1771. The later period is made more probable by the fact that the letter of the publisher Wilson was included in the packet given to Percy by Goldsmith in 1773.

47

To George Colman

[London, January 1773]

In this letter Goldsmith betrays his anxieties about the fate of the comedy that would eventually be titled *She Stoops to Conquer*, a complete draft of which he had completed by September 1771 (see Letter 37). Evidently, Goldsmith was under some financial pressures at this time but the precise nature of his troubles is not known.

Prior states that Goldsmith was actively trying to secure the play's representation from the start of the 1772–3 season (i.e. September 1772), hence the somewhat frantic tone. Colman, manager of the Covent Garden Theatre, had many objections to the piece, even writing them out on the manuscript for Goldsmith's consideration (possibly by way of response to this letter) although Goldsmith apparently ignored them (*CW*, V: 87). The precise nature of these objections is not known although Colman may have read the scenes with Tony Lumpkin in The Three Jolly Pigeons and remembered uneasily the audience reaction to the similarly 'low' bailiff scene in *The Good Natur'd Man*. In any case, Colman would regret his disapproval as it made him an object of public ridicule in the press after the success of the piece. One ditty began:

Come, Coley, doff those mourning weeds,
Nor thus with jokes be flamm'd;
Tho' Goldsmith's present play succeeds,
His next may still be damn'd.

Colman was eventually compelled to write to Goldsmith and ask him to intercede with the vituperative press on his behalf.

The copy-text is taken from *Posthumous Letters, from Various Celebrated Men: Addressed to Francis Colman, and George Colman, the elder....* (1820), where the letter was first published. The location of the original manuscript is unknown.

Dear Sir

I entreat you'l relieve me from that state of suspense in which I have been kept for a long time. Whatever objections you have made or shall make to my play I will endeavour to remove and not argue about them. To bring in any new judges either of its merit or faults I can never submit to. Upon a former occasion when my other play was before M^{r}. Garrick he offered to bring me before M^{r}. Whitehead's tribunal but I refused the proposal with indignation: I hope I shall not experience as hard treatment from you as from him.[1] I have as you know a large sum of money to make up shortly; by accepting my play I can readily satisfy my Creditor that way, at any rate I must look about to some certainty to be prepared. For God sake take the play and let us make the best of it, and let me have the same measure at least which you have given as bad plays as mine.

I am your friend
and servant

Oliver Goldsmith

[1] William Whitehead (bap. 1715, d. 1785), poet and playwright, had his first dramatic success with his tragedy *The Roman Father* (Drury Lane, 1750). This began an association with Garrick, who played the lead, that continued over the next twenty years. In the wake of other literary productions, he was appointed poet laureate in 1757 after Thomas Gray declined the position. Whitehead's work tended towards the derivative and he had no great dramatic success in the 1760s, which might explain Goldsmith's indignation.

[2] After the success of his play, Goldsmith paid off a debt to the physician William Hawes of £9 1s. Wardle also reports that he paid William Filby, his tailor, £50 towards his bill and that he also paid off 'a large sum of money' owed to Francis Newbery with the copyright (241). See also *P*, II: 417.

48

To David Garrick

[London, early February 1773]

Exasperated at Colman's dithering over his comedy, Goldsmith sent a copy to David Garrick, manager of the rival patent theatre, Drury Lane. After discussing this move with the 'sensible friend' noted in the letter, he soon repented this fit of pique and requested the return of the manuscript. The identity of the 'sensible friend' is unknown, although Johnson must be a very likely candidate; Joseph Cradock and Arthur Murphy, both of whom contributed epilogues, are also possibilities.

The copy-text is the manuscript in the Beinecke Rare Book and Manuscript Library, Yale University. It was first published in James Boaden, *The Private Correspondence of David Garrick with the Most Celebrated Persons of his Time*, 2 vols. (London: Henry Colburn, 1835), I: 527. It is addressed, 'To | David Garrick

Esqr. | Adelphi.' and is endorsed in Garrick's hand 'Dr. Goldsmith's about his play'. The letter is dated 6 February by Boaden but nothing on the manuscript corroborates the date.

Dear Sir

I ask you many pardons for the trouble I gave you of yesterday. Upon more mature deliberation and the advice of a sensible friend I begin to think it indelicate in me to throw upon you the odium of confirming Mr. Colman's sentence. I therefore request you will send my play by my servant back, for having been assured of having it acted at the other house, tho' I confess yours in every respect more to my wish, yet it would be folly in me to forego an advantage which lies in my power of appealing from Mr. Colman's opinion to the judgement of the town.[1] I entreat, if not too late, you will keep the affair a secret for some time. I am Dear Sir

Your very humble servant
Oliver Goldsmith.

[1] Cf. *An Enquiry into the Present State of Polite Learning in Europe*, 'Upon Criticism': 'And this may be the reason why so many writers at present are apt to appeal from the tribunal of criticism to that of the people' (*CW*, I: 318).

49

To Joseph Cradock

[London, *c.* 17–18 March 1773]

The opening night of *She Stoops to Conquer* saw Goldsmith, sick with nerves, go for a walk in St James's Park rather than attend Covent Garden Theatre. His apprehension – and indeed that of George Colman – proved unfounded as both audiences and critics expressed their approbation on the first few performances of the play. Reviews in the London newspapers were generally very positive and some noted that, unlike many contemporary authors, Goldsmith had not relied on the biased support of his friends who attended the opening night (Johnson, Reynolds, Burke and Richard Cumberland) to carry the play. In this letter, Goldsmith is anxious to assuage any imagined offence he had given Cradock by not using his epilogue but, typically, he also slides into melancholy even at this moment of great success. The letter must have been written after the first performance on 15 March but before the first benefit night of 18 March.

The copy-text is the manuscript in the Bibliotheca Bodmeriana, Switzerland. It was first published in Cradock's *Literary and Miscellaneous Memoirs* (1826). It is addressed 'To | J. Cradock Esqr. at Gumbley | near Harbro' | Leicester-Shire'. It is postmarked 20 March. Balderston dated the letter 16 March. We suggest a slightly later date because of the postmark and also because the newspapers' attacks on Colman appear first in an evening paper of 16 March.

Balderston relied on the version published in Cradock's *Memoirs.* There are many minor differences in our transcription, related to capitalized letters and punctuation in the main. There are also three significant omissions in Cradock which are restored here. Firstly, the post scriptum text 'I beg you'd send me an answer' indicates an unusual level of concern for Goldsmith about the reply. Secondly, we have reversed Cradock's judicious deletion of Goldsmith's second sentence: 'The news papers are now abusing Colman to some purpose.' It is possible that Cradock, impecunious when publishing his *Memoirs* and who had dramatic ambitions himself, was hesitant about irritating George Colman the Younger, then Examiner of Plays, but it may simply have been common courtesy. Goldsmith's dismissive reference to the then retired actor John Quick ('for nobody would think of letting Quick speak the Epilogue') is also restored here for the first time.

My dear Sir,

The play has met with a success much beyond your expectations or mine. The news papers are now abusing Colman to some purpose.[1] I thank you sincerely for your Epilogue which however could not be used, but with your permission shall be printed. The story in short is this; Murphy sent me rather the outline of an Epilogue than an Epilogue, which was to be sung by Mrs. Catley, and which she approved.[2] Mrs. Bulkley hearing this insisted on throwing up her part unless according to the custom of the theatre she were permitted to speak the Epilogue.[3] In this embarrassment I thought of making a quarelling Epilogue between Catley and her debating who should speak the Epilogue, but then Mrs. Catley refused after I had taken the trouble of drawing it out. I was then at a loss indeed, an Epilogue was to be made and for none but Mrs. Bulkley. I made one, and Colman thought it too bad to be spoken, I was obliged therefore to try a fourth time, for nobody would think of letting Quick speak the Epilogue, and I made a very mawkish thing as you'l shortly see. Such is the history of my stage adventures, and which I have at last done with. I cannot help saying that I am very sick of the stage, and tho I believe I shall get three tolerable benefits yet I shal[l] upon the whole be a loser, even in a pecuniary light. My ease and comfort I certainly lost while it was in agitation.[4]

I am, my Dear Craddock,
your obliged and obedient humble servant,

Oliver Goldsmith.

P.S. Present my most humble respects to Mrs. Craddock
I beg you'd send me an answer.

1 See *Middlesex Journal: Or, Universal Evening-Post* (16–18 March 1773) and the *Morning Chronicle* (18 March 1773).

2 Arthur Murphy (1727–1805), a playwright and political journalist, was a compatriot and old friend of Goldsmith's, as well as a friend of Cradock's and Johnson's. His most successful and well-known tragedy *The Grecian Daughter* had been performed at Drury Lane the year previously. His many publications include *Essay on the Life and Genius of Samuel Johnson* (1792) and his *Life of Garrick* (1801).
Anne Catley (1745–89), a singer, made her debut at Vauxhall Gardens and Covent Garden in 1762. She was subsequently engaged at Smock Alley Theatre in Dublin after a recommendation from Charles Macklin. She was enormously successful in Dublin before returning to the London stage in 1770. The part of Miss Neville, for which she was cast, was actually taken in the performance by Mrs Kniveton, for unexplained reasons.

3 Mary Bulkley (1747/8?–92), dancer and actress, was a niece of John Rich, proprietor of Covent Garden Theatre. She made her first appearance on the stage as a dancer in 1758 and remained with them (becoming an actress in 1765) until 1780. As well as playing Kate Hardcastle, she also played Miss Richland in *The Good Natur'd Man* and Julia in Sheridan's *The School for Scandal* before her career went into a steep downward spiral.

4 The author benefit system in operation at this time stipulated that a playwright would receive the door receipts less the theatre's costs ('charge of the house') on the third, sixth and ninth nights of performance. Goldsmith's profits from his three nights were £183 10s (from receipts of £247 15s on 18 March), £171 17s (receipts £236 2s; 12 April), and £147 11s 6d (receipts £211 16s 6d; 29 April), totalling £502 18s 6d (*Covent Garden Ledger, July 1772–June 1773*, British Library, Egerton MS 2277, fols. 99v, 110v, 120v).

50

To the Duke of Northumberland

[London], 18 March [1773]

The letter appears to be an acknowledgement for Northumberland's support for *She Stoops to Conquer*. His presence at a performance – perhaps the benefit performance of 18 March – would have helped the play at a time when the presence of persons of fashion contributed to the success of a piece. Moreover, Goldsmith, through providing 'orders' – suggested by his promise to 'take care for his Graces reception' – would also have been pleased by the opportunity to do an elevated friend a favour. 'Orders' were the means by which a theatre gave free admission to selected patrons: on this, Goldsmith's first benefit night, he would have borne the cost of the tickets.

The copy-text is the manuscript in the British Library. It was first published by Balderston in 1928. The verso is marked 'Goldsmith' in red ink by Percy. 'Duke of North' is also inserted in pencil with a caret, not by Goldsmith, after 'Grace'.

Temple. Thursday March 18.

Doctor Goldsmith presents his most humble respects to his Grace with his sincere thanks for his kind countenance and protection upon the present occasion. He will take care for his Graces reception.

51

To William Chambers

[London, *c.* 19 March 1773]

Sir William Chambers (1722–96), architect, was born in Sweden and, after being educated largely in England, returned there to work for the Swedish East India Company. He acquired great wealth as well as knowledge of Chinese architectural styles through two voyages to China in the 1740s. He later studied architecture in Paris and Rome before setting up practice in London in 1755. Initially, he lived above Tom's Coffee House and it was here that he most likely first met Goldsmith and Johnson. Chambers produced some notable publications such as 'Of the art of laying out gardens' (1757) (much admired by Edmund Burke and Thomas Percy), *Treatise on Civil Architecture* (1759), and his provocative *Dissertation on Oriental Gardening* (1772), which brought him into conflict with Capability Brown. The argument with Brown, as this letter shows, coincided with the appearance of *She Stoops to Conquer*. His career was considerably progressed by his appointment as architect to Princess Augusta at Kew, and as architectural tutor to Prince George. A number of high-profile and lucrative commissions followed, culminating in the redesign and rebuilding of Somerset House, which he began in 1775 and which kept him occupied until his death in 1796.

The letter which provoked Goldsmith's response is extant and we have reproduced it in full below. Chambers's delight in the play is evident as are his reservations about John Quick (Tony Lumpkin) and Charles Lewes (Marlow).[1] Chambers was also keen to solicit Goldsmith's views on the second edition of the controversial *Dissertation on Oriental Gardening*, to which he had annexed what he purported to be an explanatory discourse by Chitqua (or Tan-Che-Qua, as the *Oxford Dictionary of National Biography* also offers). Chitqua (*c.* 1728–96) was a Chinese artist who visited England between 1769 and 1772 and who moved in socially elite circles. The addition was supposed to assuage the controversy that the first edition had caused through its attack on Capability Brown. Chambers wished to recruit Goldsmith's pen to his cause, and to sound out Burke's stance in the debate, which, as the reference to the disparaging poem in the final paragraph suggests, had established itself in the public mind.

Dr Sir

We had taken a box for your benefit some time ago so thank you for your offer of tickets but cannot accept of them we were all exceedingly delighted with your play which is indeed remarkably entertaining from the number of Incidents and the Vein of humour which runs through the whole piece but certainly they might have afforded you better performers I think in particular the part of the Young Squire suffers considerably by bad acting and that more might be made of the bashful gentleman in better hands but in spight of all that your performance is generally liked which is the Strongest proof of its intrinsich merit.

herewith I take the liberty of Sending you a copy of my Second Edition with Chetqueu Discourse Annexed and if a Successful poet can Step down from the Clouds for half an hour to read forty pages of Sublunary nonsense I should be very glad to hear his Opinion of the thing now it is in print[2]

I am Glad to hear that the Virtuosi divide between Monsieur Brown and me at first the cry was all for Monsieur Brown if they once begin to doubt there is hopes of a reformation, and if you can find leisure to draw your pen in defence of the new System there is no doubt but it will have a great effect I wish you would take Mr Burks advice, but apropos are you Sure it was not a Sneer for I have always Considered Mr Burke as no favourer of my System not owing to any thing he has Said, but rather to what he has not Said, pray tell me if you think he was Sincere for he is a man of Judgement and his opinion counts

With regard to the Poem ascribed to Ansty he is a damned Brownite to be Sure but his poem I do not admire though it has sold all the remainder of my first edition if I took in hand to laugh at my self I could do it much better than Mr Ansty has done.[3]
I am, D^r^ S^r^

Yours most Sincerely

Wm Chambers

March 19th 1773.[4]

The copy-text is Chambers's transcription in his letter-book in the British Library. The letter was first published in R. W. Seitz, 'Goldsmith to Sir William Chambers', *Times Literary Supplement*, 1808 (26 September 1936), 772.

My dear Sir

this is the first time I had one moment to Spare to sit down and thank you for your kind Sollicitude for the fate of my play which has turned out beyond my expectation. when will your book come out. you have read no doubt a poem with some share of humour supposed to be written by Mr Ansty against you. whoever the Author is he is I perceive a steady Brownist. no matter, it will all in the end contribute to do you honour. most of the Companies that I now go into divide themselves into two parties the Chamberists and ye Brownists, but depend upon it you'l in the end have the Victory, because you have truth and Nature on your side.[5] Mr Burke was advising me about four days ago to draw my pen in a poem in defence of your System, and sincerely I am very much warmed in the Cause. if I write I will print my name to it boldly. I wonder you have not excited much more envy than you do? I am

Dear Sir

Your sincere freind and Admirer

Oliver Goldsmith.

PS if Lady Chambers and the ladys desire to see my play I beg they may send to me.

1 These are reservations that were not shared by the reviewer for the *Morning Chronicle* (16 March 1773), who gave the most detailed account of the opening night. He reported that while Quick had 'rather too much grimace', he was generally 'exceedingly well', while Lewes 'gave the most perfect satisfaction to the audience'. Goldsmith himself must have been pleased with their efforts as testified by his penning an epilogue for Lewes's benefit night (Drury Lane, 7 May 1773) and his adaptation of *The Grumbler*, a two-act farce translated from the French by Charles Sedley, for Quick's benefit night (Covent Garden, 8 May 1773).

2 William Chambers, *A Dissertation on Oriental Gardening; by Sr William Chambers, Comptroller-General of His Majesty's Works, &c. The Second Edition, with Additions. To which is Annexed, an Explanatory Discourse, by Tan Chet-qua, of Quang-chew-fu, Gent* (London: Printed for W. Griffin, T. Davies, J. Dodsley; Wilson and Nicoll; J. Walter, and P. Elmsley, 1773).

3 Christopher Anstey (1724–1805), poet, was well known for his satirical *The New Bath Guide* (1766), which was extremely popular over the rest of the century for its gently mocking account of life in the spa town. The poem referenced here, as we can surmise from its description in the following letter, is probably William Mason's *An Heroic Epistle to Sir William Chambers, Knight, Comptroller General of his Majesty's Work And Author of a late Dissertation on Oriental Gardening* (London: Printed for J. Almon, 1773).

4 British Library, Add. MS 42515, fols. 118, 119.

5 Goldsmith's approval of Chambers is evident in *The Citizen of the World* (*CW*, II: 134–7).

52

To William Chambers

[London, late March 1773]

See headnote to previous letter.

This letter continues the exchange with Chambers from Letter 51. As was the case with the previous missive, we have the letter to which Goldsmith responded, itself a response to Goldsmith, and have reproduced it in full below.

To Doctor Oliver Goldsmith
Dear Doctor

My Wife and Daughters thank you for your kind Invitation, but they have already seen your play twice and laughed so immoderately both times that they dare not venture upon a third, for fear of the Hystericks.

What you tell me of Burke Surprises me for I imagined him upon the whole rather averse to my System, not indeed from anything he had said, but from what he had not Said. if you take his advice, the Publick will gain by the acquisition of another good poem, and I shall be honoured by having so eminent a defender, but for my book I shall not quarel about it myself, nor do I wish any friend of mine should take that trouble. the poem you mention as written by Ansty! though I have heard it father'd on H Walpole, has a great deal of humour, and will no doubt carry the laugh against me; but it is a kind of humour that cannot last, being like that of some plays, when you must see the actors before you can find the jokes.[1] for the rest; the author whoever he is, has put me in excellent Company; and though his poem is addressed to me, yet he has, like a man of true breeding, taken most notice of my betters; the K___, Lord Talbot, Lord Sandwich, and several other worthy Lords and learned Doctors figure much more in the piece than Sir William.[2] the thing is written by a Masterly hand; and so artfully seasoned with politicks and abuse, that it cannot fail to have a great run; yet, in point of real criticism, it appears to me a Very trifle in short; not worth an answer; I shall give myself no trouble about it, nor would I have you.[3]—employ your pen my dear Doctor on better subjects; and leave my little book to fall or stand by its own strength.[4] I am ever yours most sincerely

Wm Chambers[5]

The copy-text is Chambers's transcription in his letter-book in the British Library. The letter was first published in R. W. Seitz, 'Goldsmith to Sir William Chambers', *Times Literary Supplement*, 1808 (26 September 1936), 772.

Mr Burke You may say upon my Authority, as also on that of S^ir^ Joshua Reynolds is a profest Chamberist. he always speaks of your system with respect I am

Dear Sir

Yours Affectionately

Oliver Goldsmith

[1] Horace Walpole (1717–97), fourth Earl of Orford, was the author of *The Castle of Otranto* (1764) and a number of other literary works. He had an extensive correspondence with William Mason, with whom he discussed the authenticity of Chatterton's Rowley poems. On the basis of their discussions, Walpole disavowed Chatterton. Goldsmith told Walpole of Chatterton's death and later tried to purchase the Rowley manuscripts (see Letter 36, n2).

[2] King George III (1738–1820); William Talbot (1710–82), first Earl of Talbot; and John Montagu (1718–92), fourth Earl of Sandwich. Mason, *An Heroic Epistle to Sir William Chambers*.

[3] The *Eighteenth-Century Collections Online* database records eleven editions up to 1773.

[4] Goldsmith appears to have taken this advice to heart; there is no evidence that he wrote a poem in support of Chambers.

[5] British Library, Add. MS 41134, fo. 21b.

53

To the *Daily Advertiser*

London, 31 March 1773

Goldsmith attempted to draw a dignified line under an unfortunate public incident with a letter to this newspaper. The *London Packet* had printed a damning indictment of his talents and appearance by William Kenrick (see Letter 25) on 24 March 1773. Goldsmith was described in the article as having a 'grotesque Oranhotan's figure'; *The Deserted Village* was dismissed as 'a *pretty* poem, of easy numbers, without fancy, dignity, genius or fire', while the recent *She Stoops to Conquer* was jeered as a '*speaking pantomime* [...] an incoherent piece of stuff'. The article also scoffed at Goldsmith's unsuitability as a companion for the Jessamy Bride, Mary Horneck, to whom Goldsmith was very attached and of whom he was, like many of his peers, genuinely admiring. The offending piece can be found in full in Percy's biography; Percy also felt obliged to relegate the attack from the main text: 'We would not defile our page with this scurrilous production, so shall insert it in the margin.'[1] As a result of the article, Goldsmith had tried to administer a beating to Thomas Evans (1738/9–1803), a Welsh bookseller in Paternoster Row and the publisher of the *London Packet*. Evans feigned ignorance of the matter but Goldsmith sought to give him a beating anyway, though Evans was, by all accounts, more than his physical match. According to one account, Evans defended himself 'in a true pugilistic style', and soon Goldsmith 'was disarmed, and extended on the floor, to the no small diversion of the by-standers'.[2] Kenrick himself, in a neighbouring room at the time, intervened to put an end to the skirmish which his own writing had brought about. Goldsmith left the scene, well beaten, and would eventually pay £50 to a Welsh charity to settle with Evans, who threatened a suit.

The copy-text is the *Daily Advertiser* (31 March 1773), where it was first published. It also appeared in the *London Chronicle* (1–3 April 1773).

To the PUBLIC

Lest it should be supposed that I have been willing to correct in others an Abuse of which I have been guilty myself, I beg Leave to declare, that in all my Life I never wrote, or dictated, a single Paragraph, Letter, or Essay, in a News-Paper, except a few moral Essays, under the Character of a Chinese, about ten Years ago, in the Ledger; and a Letter, to which I signed my Name, in the St.

James's Chronicle.[3] If the Liberty of the Press therefore has been abused, I have had no Hand in it.

I have always considered the Press as the Protector of our Freedom, as a watchful Guardian, capable of uniting the Weak against the Encroachments of Power. What concerns the Public most properly admits of a public Discussion. But of late, the Press has turned from defending public Interest, to making Inroads upon private Life: From combating the Strong, to overwhelming the Feeble. No Condition is now too obscure for its Abuse, and the Protector is become the Tyrant of the People. In this Manner the Freedom of the Press is now beginning to sow the Seeds of its own Dissolution; the Great must oppose it from Principle, and the Weak from Fear; till at last every Rank of Mankind shall be found to give up its Benefits, content with Security from its Insults.

How to put a Stop to this Licentiousness, by which all are indiscriminately abused, and by which Vice consequently escapes in the general Censure, I am unable to tell; all I could wish is, that, as the Law gives us no Protection against the Inquiry, so it should give Calumniators no Shelter after having provoked Correction. The Insults which we receive before the Publick, by being more open are the more distressing; by treating them with silent Contempt, we do not pay a sufficient Deference to the Opinion of the World. By recurring to legal Redress, we too often expose the Weakness of the Law, which only serves to increase our Mortification by failing to relieve us. In short, every Man should singly consider himself as a Guardian of the Liberty of the Press, and as far as his Influence can extend, should endeavour to prevent its Licentiousness becoming at last the Grave of its Freedom.

OLIVER GOLDSMITH.

[1] Percy, 'Life', 103–5.
[2] *Gentleman's Magazine* 1st ser., 73 (1803), 696.
[3] Letter 25 above.

54
To James Boswell
London, 4 April 1773

James Boswell wrote to Goldsmith congratulating him on the success of *She Stoops to Conquer*, and asking that Goldsmith should congratulate him on the birth of his daughter Veronica. The letter is dated 29 March, but we know from his *Journal* that Boswell was on his way to London the next day, and so, as Balderston speculates, he may have been deliberately misleading Goldsmith about his location so as to elicit a proper letter from the most famous playwright of the hour:

Dear Sir, – I sincerely wish you joy on the great success of your new comedy, She Stoops to Conquer, or The Mistakes of a Night. The English nation was just falling into a lethargy. Their blood was thickened and their minds creamed and mantled like a standing pool; and no wonder—when their comedies which should enliven them, like sparkling champagne, were become mere syrup of poppies, gentle soporific draughts.[1] Had there been no interruption to this, our audiences must have gone to the theatres with their nightcaps. In the opera houses abroad, the boxes are fitted up for tea-drinking. Those at Drury Lane and Covent Garden must have been furnished with settees and commodiously adjusted for repose. I am happy to hear that you have waked the spirit of mirth which has so long lain dormant, and revived natural humour and hearty laughter.[2] It gives me pleasure that our friend Garrick has written the prologue for you. It is at least lending you a postilion, since you have not his coach; and I think it is a very good one, admirably adapted both to the subject and to the author of the comedy.

You must know my wife was safely delivered of a daughter, the very evening that She Stoops to Conquer first appeared. I am fond of the coincidence. My little daughter is a fine, healthy, lively child and, I flatter myself, shall be blessed with the cheerfulness of your comic muse. She has nothing of that wretched whining and crying which we see children so often have; nothing of the comédie larmoyante. I hope she shall live to be an agreeable companion and to diffuse gaiety over the days of her father, which are sometimes a little cloudy.[3]

I intend being in London this spring and promise myself great satisfaction in sharing your social hours. In the meantime, I beg the favour of hearing from you. I am sure you have not a warmer friend or a steadier admirer. While you are in the full glow of theatrical splendour, while all the great and the gay in the British metropolis are literally hanging upon your smiles, let me see that you can stoop to write to me. I ever am with great regard, dear Sir, your affectionate humble servant,

James Boswell

Goldsmith might not have written if he had known that Boswell was already on his way to London. So, when Goldsmith wrote his letter, Boswell had already been in London two days. Boswell would not, therefore, receive the letter until five weeks later, when he returned to Scotland. Boswell, it seems, definitely wrote on 29 March, and the fact that Goldsmith responded on 4 April means that just enough time had elapsed for the letter to have been delivered and for Goldsmith to pen a response on that same day. That the letter was a ploy to prompt a celebrity collectible is further evidenced by the words on the wrapper: 'Pray write directly. Write as if in repartee. My address is James's Court, Edinburgh'.

Boswell's letter catches Goldsmith in a strange mood, likely a mixture of anxious defiance and embarrassment over the incident with Thomas Evans (see Letter 53).

The copy-text is the manuscript in the Beinecke Rare Book and Manuscript Library, Yale University. It was first published, in facsimile, along with the printed transcription, in the *Private Papers of James Boswell*. It is addressed 'To | The Honourable James Boswell | James's Court | Edinburgh.' It is postmarked 5 April. Balderston notes that this letter was not available for publication in 1928 (*BL*, 121).

To the Honourable James Boswell,
James's Court
Edinburgh

London, Temple, April 4th, 1773

My Dear Sir

I thank you for your kind remembrance of me, for your most agreeable letter, and for your congratulation. I believe I always told you that success upon the stage was great cry and little wool. It has kept me in hot water these three months, and in about five weeks hence I suppose I shall get my three benefits.[4] I promise you, my Dear Sir, that the stage earning is the dirtiest money that ever a poor poet put in his pocket; and if my mind does not very much alter I have done with the stage.

It gives me pleasure to hear that you have encreasd your family, and I make no doubt the little stranger will one day or other, as you hint, become a Conqueror. when I see you in town, and I shall take care to let Johnson Garrick and Reynolds know of the expected happiness I will then tell you long stories about my struggles and escapes, for as all of you are safely retired from the shock of criticism to enjoy much better comforts in a domestic life, I am still left the only Poet militant here, and in truth I am very likely to be militant till I die, nor have I even the prospect of an hospital to retire to.[5]

I have been three days ago most horridly abused in a news paper, so like a fool as I was I went and thrashd the Editor. I could not help it. He is going to take the law of me. However, the press is now so scandalously abusive that I believe he will scarcely get damages. I don't care how it is, come up to town and we shall laugh it off whether it goes for or against me.

I am Dear Sir,
Your most affectionate
humble Serv[t].

Oliver Goldsmith.

P.S. Present my most
humble respects
to Mrs Boswell.

1 'There are a sort of men whose visages / Do cream and mantle like a standing pond': William Shakespeare, *The Merchant of Venice*, I.i.88–9.

2 This suggests that Boswell had read, or at least was aware of the argument of, Goldsmith's 'An Essay on the Theatre' published on 1 January 1773 in the *Westminster Magazine* (*CW*, III: 209–13).

3 Veronica (1773–95) was Boswell's first surviving child.
4 Goldsmith had already had one benefit night by the time of this letter's composition.
5 Alexander Pope to John Gay, 21 July [1730]: 'Mrs. *Howard* is so concern'd about you, and so angry at me for not writing to you, and at Mrs. *Blount* for not doing the same, that I am piqu'd with Jealousy and Envy at you, and hate you as much as if you had a great Place at Court; which you will confess a proper Cause of Envy and Hatred, in any Poet-militant or unpension'd': George Sherburn, ed., *The Correspondence of Alexander Pope*, 5 vols. (Oxford: Clarendon Press, 1956), III: 121.

55
To Hester Thrale
[London, *c.* 12 April 1773]

Hester Thrale (1741–1821), writer, was introduced to Dr Johnson through their mutual friend the playwright Arthur Murphy in 1765. Stuck in a loveless marriage and burdened by a state of almost constant pregnancy in the late 1760s and 1770s, Thrale took great pleasure and inspiration from Johnson's friendship, while he derived equal enjoyment and gain from her conversation and literary prowess. Thrale undertook some significant translation tasks as well as making an important contribution to Johnson's *Journey to the Western Isles* and his *Lives of the Poets*. She also provided Johnson with a safe refuge when his mental and emotional health deteriorated. Thrale, with Johnson's assistance, was soon hosting a vibrant salon at her home in Streatham where guests included members of the Club, including Goldsmith; she was largely unimpressed by his 'anomalous Character'.[1] The death of her ne'er-do-well brewer husband liberated her financially as well as personally. She later married a Catholic Italian singer, Gabriel Piozzi, and her most serious period of literary activity ensued, including *Anecdotes of the Late Samuel Johnson* (1786), *Letters to and from the Late Samuel Johnson* (1788) and *Retrospection* (1801), before her death from gangrene.

The copy-text is a facsimile of the letter in a sales catalogue cutting in the New York Public Library. It was first published in A. M. Broadley, *Doctor Johnson and Mrs. Thrale* (1910). According to Balderston, it is addressed 'To Mrs. Thrale'. It is endorsed by her 'a Letter from Dr. Goldsmith'. Balderston established the date of the letter from the sale catalogue of William Evarts Benjamin, March 1886: 'Hester L. Thrale (Mrs. Piozzi). 12th April 1773. A.L.S. 1 p., 4to. To Doctor Goldsmith, urging him to let her have the fourth and fifth volumes of his book (she does not say which one), and couched in terms of much stately courtesy' (*BL*, 121).

Madam

I ask a thousand pardons. I did not know what were the volumes I sent, but sent what I had. Nor did I know the volumes you wanted, for I knew you had read some. I beg youl not impute it to any thing but the strange dissipation of one who hates to think of any thing like his duty. I will take care tomorrow of the volumes in question, and am Madam with the utmost respect and

esteem your humble serv[t].
Oliver Goldsmith.

1 Cited in *W*, I.

56

To Thomas Percy

[London, 1773]

The enigmatic tone of this brief message suggests that a matter of reasonable import was afoot, possibly the meeting between the two men at Northumberland House on 28 April 1773 in which Percy took from Goldsmith's dictation a memorandum of biography which would form the basis for his 1801 memoir. St James's Palace in the Mall area of London was not far from Northumberland House, and it may be that the two men met at the former before repairing to the latter.

The copy-text is the manuscript in the Beinecke Library, Yale University. It was first published as a 'Doubtful Letter' by Balderston, who had the text from the November 1895 sale catalogue of William Evarts Benjamin, noting that 'The provenance of the letter is unknown, and the MS., although it has been traced to a sale in March, 1925, has not been available for examination' (*BL*, 147n1). There is a facsimile image of the letter excerpted from an American Art Association sale catalogue of 18 March 1925 in the New York Public Library; however, it is unclear whether Balderston was able to view this image in order to assess the handwriting. The original note, now at Yale, can more safely be confirmed as Goldsmith's. In the top right-hand corner in a near-contemporary hand is written '73 ~~G~~', which may indicate that the note is from 1773. Underneath the signature is written, in light red ink and a different hand, 'the Poet'. Further down the page there is a biographical note, in another near-contemporary hand: 'Oliver Goldsmith was born at Roscommon in Ireland, in A.D. 1729, ob. Ap. 1774 at 45'.

Dear Percy

I thank you for your trouble and advice, which shall be follow[d]. I will wait at the palace at two.

Goldsmith

57

To John Nourse

[London, 26 April 1773]

John Nourse (bap. 1705, d. 1780), bookseller, specialized in language books, contemporary foreign literature, and scientific books. Based at the Lamb without Temple Bar, near the Strand, he would become bookseller to the Society for the Encouragement of Learning and then bookseller to the king, 1762–80. Not only was Nourse's shop an important venue for scientific discussion in London, it was an important node in the Enlightenment republic of letters; he had trade connections in Paris, The Hague and Leiden. Nourse disseminated key English texts abroad and published translations of significant European authors for British audiences – notably Voltaire. William Griffin had been forced to sell his interest in Goldsmith's *History of Earth, and Animated Nature* (for which he had already given £500 to Goldsmith by way of advance) to Nourse, who eventually published the eight-volume work on 1 July 1774.

Here Goldsmith is providing an aspiring author with a letter of introduction, an indication of Goldsmith's status – or, at the very least, his perceived status – among London booksellers. John Andrews (1736–1809), historian, would become best known for his *History of the War with America, France, Spain, and Holland*, 4 vols. (London: Printed for John Fielding and John Jarvis, 1785–6). The *History of the Revolutions of Denmark*, the text referred to here by Goldsmith and which Nourse published in April 1774, was his first publication. The introductory note 'To the Reader' observes: 'Denmark having by the remarkable Events which happened in that Kingdom, during the Course of the last Year, attracted the Attention of all Europe, and particularly of the British Nation, from the Family Connexion subsisting between the two Crowns' (1) makes clear that Andrews was exploiting interest in the shocking events surrounding the divorce and expulsion from Denmark of Queen Caroline Matilda – sister to George III – in 1772, events which captivated the British public. Goldsmith's interest in Andrews's book may also have been piqued by his personal recollection of King Christian VII's visit in 1768 and the masquerade for which he sought tickets for the Hornecks (see Letter 26).

Andrews's file in the Royal Literary Fund archive (British Library, RLF/26/1) contains a list of his extensive publications between 1773 and 1808, and they include a number of surveys and analyses of European countries. If these cosmopolitan tendencies were evident when Goldsmith met him, this might also account for his interest. The file's many plaintive letters from Andrews and his daughter also indicate that, despite this helpful start given by Goldsmith, his career had petered out by the 1790s.

The copy-text is the manuscript in the Library of the Historical Society of Pennsylvania. It was first published by Prior in 1837. It is addressed, 'To | Mr. Nourse', and is endorsed, in another hand, 'Dr. Goldsmith. | April 26, 1773', providing the basis for our dating.

Sir

The bearer is Dr. Andrews who has just finish'd a work relative to Denmark which I have seen, and read with great pleasure. He is of opinion that a short letter of this kind expressing my approbation will be a proper introduction of it to you; I therefore once more recommend it in the warmest manner, and unless I am mistaken, it will be a great credit to him, as well as of benefit to the purchaser of the copy.

I am Sir

Your most obedient Serv[t]

Oliver Goldsmith.

58

To David Garrick

London, 10 June 1773

This letter refers to Goldsmith's planned (but later abandoned) dictionary of the arts and sciences 'on the model of the French Encyclopedia' (Frances Burney, *Memoirs of Doctor Burney*, 3 vols. (London: Edward Moxon, 1832), I: 271). He had secured commitments from a number of friends to write various articles: Johnson on ethics; Burke on the sublime and on Berkeley; Reynolds on painting; and Garrick on acting (*P*, II: 428–9; *Memoirs of Doctor Burney*, I: 271–2). He had further solicited Garrick's assistance in signing up Charles Burney (1726–1814), composer and renowned music teacher, to write the article on music. Garrick sent the letter to Burney on 11 June with the following note: 'My dear Doctor, I have sent you a letter from Dr. Goldsmith. He is proud to have your name among the elect.

Love to all your fair ones. Ever yours, D. Garrick'. Frances Burney was sufficiently impressed by Goldsmith's letter to copy it from memory into her diary.[1]

The copy-text is from Prior (II: 429). It was first published by Frances Burney (then Frances D'Arblay) in her *Memoirs of Doctor Burney* in 1832. Following Balderston, we prefer Prior's transcription, which was secured from Burney on a visit to her in August 1831, as it seems likely she introduced additional punctuation by way of correction in her published version.

Temple, 10 June 1773[2]

Dear Sir,

To be thought of by you obliges me; to be served by you is still more. It makes me very happy to find that Dr. Burney thinks my scheme of a dictionary useful; still more that he will be so kind as to adorn it with any thing of his own. I beg you will also accept my gratitude for procuring me so valuable an acquisition.

I am, dear Sir,

Your most affectionate servant,

Oliver Goldsmith.

[1] *The Early Journals and Letters of Fanny Burney*, ed. Lars E. Troide, 3 vols. (Oxford: Clarendon Press, 1988), I: 271–2.

[2] Burney had the date as 10 January, presumably a misreading.

59

To Charles Burney

London, 5 November [1773]

Charles Burney (1726–1814), Shrewsbury-born musician and historian, was apprenticed in 1744 to Thomas Arne as the latter commenced in his post as composer to Drury Lane Theatre in London. Burney made the acquaintance of David Garrick in 1745 at the home of Arne's sister, the famous actress Susannah Cibber. In the 1760s Burney would compose music for Drury Lane. The University of Oxford awarded Burney the degrees of Bachelor and Doctor of Music in 1769. In 1770 he left London to tour the continent with a view to collecting materials for his most cherished project, *A General History of Music*, the first volume of which would be published in 1776. The previous letter indicates that in June 1773 Goldsmith was not yet personally acquainted with Burney. Though acquainted with Samuel Johnson from the mid-1760s, Burney would not become a member of the Club until 1784, which may explain the relative lateness of his acquaintance with Goldsmith. The informality of tone in this communication, and the reference to the passing between them of a map, suggests that they had become friendly in the intervening months as Goldsmith engaged in preparatory work for his proposed *Universal Dictionary of the Arts and Sciences*.

The copy-text is the manuscript fragment, unsigned, now in the possession of Loren R. Rothschild of Los Angeles, California, and never before published. It was addressed 'To D^{r}. Burney. S^{t}. Martin's Street | Leicester Fields | London' and postmarked 5 November. We date it 1773 for the reasons given above.

> [...] plain dress, for an ordinary man or woman, implies at least Modesty, & always procures kind quarter from the Censorious — Who will ridicule a personal Imperfection in one ~~Who~~ that seems conscious that it is an imperfection? Who ever said an Anchoret[1] was? poor? But who w^{d}. spare so very absurd a Wronghead, as sh^{d} bestow Tinsel to make his deformity the more Conspicuous?
>
> I have just Parted with an <u>immense</u> beau one Mr Thomspson — the ugliest man I think I ever saw.[2] I know but little of him, or of his Character & Am in doubt whether I sh'd ~~to~~ put him down for a Great fool or a smatterer in Wit — Something, methinks, I saw wrong in him by his dress: If this fellow delights not so much in <u>ridicule</u> that he will not spare <u>himself</u>, he must be plaguy silly to take such pains to make his ugliness more conspicuous that it w^{d}. otherwise be — XX
>
> Thanks, ten thousand thanks for Your kindly remembering the[3] Map—It will do I' well as I could wish it —At first I was afraid you would have ~~refused~~ denyed me — if You had —I could have said nothing — for I have often censured the boldness of those, who, applying for a favour, which it is in a Person's option to grant, or to refuse, take the liberty of being offended if they are not gratified; as if the Petitioned had not as much right to refuse, as the Petioner to ask.

1 A recluse or a hermit.

2 Mr Thomspson is unidentified.

3 This may be 'my': Goldsmith corrects himself but it is not clear whether 'my' or 'the' is the final version. We have preferred 'the' as it is marked in heavier ink, suggesting this was the correction.

60

To Thomas Cadell

[London, 1773–1774]

Thomas Cadell (1742–1802), bookseller, was apprenticed to London bookseller Andrew Millar before becoming his partner in 1765. After Millar retired in 1767, Cadell took over and operated out of 141 The Strand until his death. He was noted for generous payments to authors which enabled him to publish some of the most significant volumes of his day, including many of Johnson's important works, Gibbon's *Decline and Fall of the Roman Empire* (1776–88), and Hester Thrale Piozzi's *Anecdotes of the Late Samuel Johnson* (1786) and her *Letters to and from the late Samuel Johnson* (1788). He was the founding member of a booksellers' dining club which met on The Strand each month. After his retirement, his son, Thomas, and assistant, William Davies, took over the business. Cadell remained prominent in London's public life, taking on a number of civic and charitable roles, including governor of the Foundling Hospital and treasurer of the Asylum. Goldsmith's *History of England* was published by Thomas Davies in August 1771. Cadell brought out the second edition in 1774, having purchased the copyright from Davies.

The date of the letter is uncertain. Goldsmith was preparing the second edition of his *History of England* but its publication was first announced in the *London Chronicle* on 15 December 1774, more than eight months after Goldsmith's death.

The copy-text is the manuscript in the Bodleian Library, Oxford. It was first published by Prior in 1837. The name 'Cadell' has been covered in the manuscript by a mount on which 'Nourse' was written erroneously by William Upcott (1779–1845), the antiquary and autograph collector, to whom the manuscript formerly belonged. The end of the note is also cut away.

Doctor Goldsmiths compliments to Mr. [Cadell], and desires a set of the history of England for correction if interleaved the better.

61

To Thomas Cadell

[London, 1773–1774]

William Cooke, Goldsmith's friend and chronicler, made the following observation on Goldsmith's methodological approach to history writing:

> His manner of compiling this History was as follows: - he first read in a morning, from Hume, Rapin, and sometimes Kennet, as much as he designed for one letter, marking down the passages referred to on a sheet of paper, with remarks, he then ... spent the day generally convivially ... and when he went up to bed took up his books and paper with him, where he generally wrote the chapter, or the best part of it, before he went to rest. This latter exercise cost him very little trouble, he said; for having all his materials ready for him, he wrote it with as much facility as a common letter.[1]

Goldsmith, working on the second edition of his *History of England*, indicates in this letter that he read widely and was assiduous in consulting the latest available sources. Frances Brooke (bap. 1724, d. 1789), writer and playwright, was the author of *Elements of the History of England from the Invasion of the Romans to the Reign of St George*, 4 vols. (London: 1771). This was a translation of Claude-François-Xavier Millot's original publication, *Élémens de L'Histoire d'Angleterre depuis son Origine sous les Romains jusqu'au Règne de George II* (Paris, 1769). It is possible that Goldsmith knew Brooke: she was acquainted with Johnson, and Garrick had rejected a tragedy of hers. Another plausible connection may be through Arthur Murphy and John Boyle, Earl of Cork and Orrery, who contributed to her periodical *Old Maid* (1755–6).

The copy-text is the manuscript in the Rosenbach of the Free Library of Philadelphia. It was first published by Prior in 1837. It is addressed to 'Mr. Cadell. | Strand.' The letter must follow the preceding letter very closely.

Mr. Goldsmith's compliments to Mr. Cadell, begs for an hour or two the use of Millot's History by Mrs. Brooke.

[1] *European Magazine* 24 (1793), 93.

62

To David Garrick

[London, *c.* 24 December 1773]

Despite his success with *She Stoops to Conquer*, money, as ever, remained a problem for Goldsmith. This letter, opening with an appropriate touch of flattery, shows Goldsmith looking to wheedle an additional loan from Garrick, guaranteed by Newbery. Garrick, as Letter 63 shows, agreed to the loan but the endorsement 'Goldsmith's parlaver' (on both letters) suggests that he was a little exasperated. The date is determined by the date of Letter 63, which it immediately precedes.

The copy-text is the manuscript in the Houghton Library, Harvard University. It was first published by Forster in 1848. It was addressed 'To David Garrick Esqr.| Adelphi'.

My Dear Sir,

Your saying you would play my Good natured man makes me wish it.[1] The money you advanced me upon Newbery's note I have the mortification to find is not yet paid, but he says he will in two or three days.[2] What I mean by this letter is to lend me sixty pound for which I will give you Newbery's note, so that the whole of my debt will be an hundred for which you shall have Newbery's note as a security. This may be paid either from my alteration if my benefit should come to so much, but at any rate I will take care you shall not be a loser.[3] I will give you a new Character in my comedy and knock out Lofty which does not do, and will make such other alterations as you direct.[4]

I am yours
Oliver Goldsmith.

I beg an answer.

[1] The latest performance of the play was on 3 May 1773 at Covent Garden. Garrick never acted in this play nor was it acted at Drury Lane in his lifetime. Balderston speculates that this was due to ill health. It may also be because the play was part of the Covent Garden repertory or that he simply did not wish to deepen his connection with Goldsmith.

[2] Forster believed it was unpaid because of 'disputed claims on behalf of the elder Newbery's estate' (589). As Balderston points out, Newbery had accepted the copyright of *She Stoops to Conquer* in satisfaction of all his claims on Goldsmith, whose irritation in the letter regarding the non-payment of this note was justified.

[3] It is unclear as to what benefit Goldsmith is referring. There was a benefit night performance of *She Stoops to Conquer* on 30 December 1773; however, the funds were for the benefit of

the anonymous author of the afterpiece, *Achilles in Petticoats*. There was another benefit performance of the play on 28 April 1774 for Lee Lewes, possibly in partial (and canny) tribute to the recently deceased Goldsmith. There is no evidence of any additional benefit night for Goldsmith before his death (*Covent Garden Ledger June 1773–June 1774*, British Library, Egerton MS 2278).

4 Lofty is a character in *The Good Natur'd Man*. It may be that Garrick expressed his dislike of the character as contemporary reviews of the play do not seem to object to him.

63

To David Garrick

[London, 25 December 1773]

See headnote to previous letter.

Goldsmith gratefully acknowledges Garrick's willingness to accept Newbery's note as per his request in the preceding letter. Balderston includes a brief note, in the form of a bill of exchange, which accompanied the letter. The current location of the note is unknown. It reads:

> 'Sir, 28 Jany. £60 0 0 December 25th, 1773.
> One month after date pay the bearer the sum of sixty pounds and place it to the account of Sir your humble servant
> Oliver Goldsmith.
>
> To David Garrick Esq[r] |Adelphi.'

The bill is signed 'Dec. 25, 1773 Accepted—D. Garrick'. Goldsmith's signature is on the back, along with those of Charles Ekerobh Mall, and Josiah Shaw, for B. St. Moyen Esqr. The date, '28 Jany.' is likely to have been the date of payment.

Our copy-text is the manuscript in the Houghton Library, Harvard University. The date is determined by the date of Goldsmith's note accompanying the letter.

My Dear Friend

I thank you! I wish I could do something to serve you. I shall have a comedy for you in a season or two at farthest that I believe will be worth your acceptance, for I fancy I will make it a fine thing.[1] You shall have the refusal. I wish you would not take up Newbery's note, but let Waller teize him, without however coming to extremities, let him haggle after him and he will get it.[2] He owes it and will pay it. Im sorry you are ill. I will draw upon you one month after date for sixty pound, and your acceptance will be ready money part of which I want to go down to Barton with.[3] May God preserve my honest little man for he has my heart.

ever Oliver Goldsmith.

[1] There is no further evidence that Goldsmith was planning another comedy, although the success of *She Stoops to Conquer* must have made it an attractive proposition.
[2] Forster suggests that Goldsmith meant Albany Wallis, Garrick's solicitor.
[3] Barton Hall in Suffolk, residence of the Bunbury family. See the following letter.

64

To Catherine Bunbury *née* Horneck

[London, *c.* 25 December 1773]

Catherine Horneck, 'Little Comedy' as Goldsmith called her (see Letter 22, n8), married Henry Bunbury in 1771. They resided at Barton Hall, Great Barton, Suffolk. Goldsmith here responds to an invitation to visit. Her verse letter of invitation is preserved in a contemporary copy, in a hand resembling Edmund Burke's, and is held at the Free Library of Philadelphia. It is reproduced here in full:

I hope my good Doctor you soon will be here
And your Spring velvet coat very smart will appear
To open our Ball the first day of the year
And bring with you a wig that is modish & Gay
To dance with the Girls that are makers of Hay
Tho of Hay we dont often hear talk in these times
Yet it serves very well towards making of rhimes
My Sister will laugh at my rhimes about Hay
Yet this I am sure I may venture to say
That we all here do wish and intreat & desire
You will Straightway come hither & sit by our fire
And if you will like in the Evening to game
We'll all play at Loo where you'll surely get fame
by winning our Money away in a trice
As my Sister & I will give you Advice
Or if you would Shoot Sir we'll lend you a gun
And Druid t'oblige will after Birds run
But if you like better to hunt o'er the Ground[s]

Mr. B----y'll lend you so[me] v[ery] [g]ood Hound[s]
But these simple Sports to a fine London Beaux
Who doubtless is thinking of fashion & show
And whose int'rested friends all wish to detain
As they know very well what pleasure they gain
By keeping one with them they so much admire
And whose chearful Company always desire
Yet to leave these pleasures if he condescends
He will greatly oblige his very Good friends

The copy-text is the manuscript in the Morgan Library, New York. It was first published in Prior's edition of Goldsmith's *Miscellaneous Works* in 1837. A copy of this letter, in the hand of Bennet Langton, is in the Free Library of Philadelphia. Goldsmith's visit was dependent on Garrick's loan so the letter could not predate his acquiescence. It could not have been written before the acceptance of the loan on 25 December and it is improbable that it could have been written later than 26 December, since Goldsmith refers to his proposed New Year's visit as 'some day next week' (26 December was a Saturday).

Madam.

I read your letter with all that allowance which critical candour would require, but after all find so much to object to, and so much to raise my indignation, that I cannot help giving it a serious reply. I am not so ignorant madam as not to see there are many sarcasms contain'd in it, and solœcisms also (solœcism is a word that comes from the town of Soleis in Attica among the Greeks, built by Solon, and applied as we use the word kidderminster for curtains from [a] town also of that name, but this is learning you have no taste for) I say madam there are sarcasms in it and solecisms also.[1] But not to seem an ill natured critic Ill take leave to quote your own words and give you my remarks upon them as they occur. You begin as follows.

I hope my good Doctor you soon will be here
And your spring velvet coat very smart will appear
To open our ball the first day in the year.[2]

Pray madam where did you ever find the Epithet good applied to the title of Doctor? Had you calld me learned Doctor, or grave Doctor or Noble Doctor it might be allowable because these belong to the profession. But not to cavil at triffles; you talk of my spring velvet coat and advise me to wear it the first day in the year, that is in the middle of winter. A spring velvet in the middle of winter?!! That would be a solœcism indeed. And yet to encrease the inconsistence, in another part of your letter you call me a beau. Now on one side or other you must be wrong. If Im a beau I can never think of wearing a spring velvet in winter, and if I be not a beau – why – then – that explains itself. But let me go on to your next two strange lines

And bring with you a wig that is modish and gay
To dance with the girls that are makers of hay.

The absurdity of making hay at Christmass you yourself seem sensible of. You say your sister will laugh, and so indeed she well may—the lattins have an expression for a contemptuous kind of laughter, <u>naso contemnere adunco</u> that is to laugh with a crooked nose, she may laugh at you in the manner of the ancients if she thinks fit.[3] But now I come to the most extraordinary of all extraordinary propositions which is to take your and your sister's advice in playing at Loo.[4] The presumption of the offer raises my indignation beyond the bounds of prose it inspires me at once with verse and resentment. I take advice! And from who? You shall hear.

First let me suppose what may shortly be true
The company set, and the word to be Loo.
All smirking, and pleasant, and big with adventure
And ogling the stake which is fixd in the center.
Round and round go the cards while I inwardly damn
At never once finding a visit from Pam.[5]
~~I lay down my stake, [to] double that too,~~
~~While some harpy beside me picks up the whole~~
I lay down my stake, apparently cool,
While the harpies about me all pocket the pool.
I fret in my gizzard, yet cautious and sly
I wish all my friends may be bolder than I.
Yet still they sit snugg, not a creature will aim
By losing their money to venture at fame.
Tis in vain that at niggardly caution I scold
Tis in vain that I flatter the brave and the bold

All play in their own way, and think me an ass.
What does Mrs. Bunbury? I sir? I pass.
Pray what does Miss Horneck?[6] Take courage. Come do.
Who I! Let me see sir. Why I must pass too.
Mr. Bunbury[7] frets, and I fret like the devil
To see them so cowardly lucky and civil.
Yet still I sit snugg and continue to sigh on
Till made by my losses as bold as a lion
I venture at all, while my avarice regards
The whole pool as my own. Come give me five cards.
Well done cry the ladies. Ah Doctor that's good.
The pool's very rich. Ah. The Doctor is lood.[8]
Thus foild in my courage, on all sides perplext,
I ask for advice from the lady that's next
Pray mam be so good as to give your advice
Dont you think the best way is to venture fort twice.
I advise cries the lady to try it I own.
Ah! The Doctor is lood. Come Doctor, put down.
Thus playing and playing I still grow more eager
And so bold and so bold, Im at last a bold beggar.
Now ladies I ask if law matters youre skilld in
Whether crimes such as yours should not come before Fielding[9]
For giving advice that is not worth a straw
May well be call'd picking of pockets in law
And picking of pockets with which I now charge ye
Is by Quinto Elizabeth death without Clergy.[10]
What justice when both to the Old Baily brought
By the gods Ill enjoy it, tho''tis but in thought.
Both are placed at the bar with all proper decorum.
With bunches of Fennel and nosegays before em.[11]
Both cover their faces with mobbs[12] and all that
But the judge bids them angrily take of their hat.
When uncovered a buzz of enquiry runs round
Pray what are their crimes? They've been pilfering found.
But pray who have they pilfered? A Doctor I hear.
~~Yon handsome fac'd [sm]all~~ What, yon solemn fac'd odd looking man that stands near,

The same. What a pitty. How does it surprize one
Two handsomer culprits I never set eyes on.
Then their friends all come round me with cringing and leering
To melt me to pitty, and soften my swearing.
First Sir Charles[13] advances, with phrases well strung
Consider Dear Doctor the girls are but young.
The younger the worse I return him again.
It shews that their habits are all dy'd in grain.
But then theyre so handsome, one's bosom it grieves.
What signifies handsome when people are thieves.
But where is your justice; their cases are hard.
What signifies justice; I want the reward.-------- Theres the parish of Edmonton offers forty pound; there's the parish of St Leonard Shoreditch offers forty pound; there's the parish of Tyburn from the hog in the pound to St Giles's watch-house offers forty pound, I shall have all that if I convict them.

But consider their case, It may yet be your own
And see how they kneel; is your heart made of stone?
This moves, so at last I agree to relent
For ten pounds in hand, and ten pound to be spent.
The judge takes the hint, having seen what we drive at
And lets them both off with correction in private.[14]

I chalenge you all to answer this. I tell you you cannot. It cuts deep. But now for the rest of the letter, and next—but I want room—so I believe I shall battle the rest out at Barton some day next week. I dont value you all.

1 The word's origins can be traced to the Greek city of Soloi, located in what is today southern Turkey, home to a corrupted Greek dialect: *A New Dictionary of Eponyms* (Oxford University Press, 1997), 237.
Kidderminster, a town near Birmingham in Worcestershire, famous for patterned weaves, in clothing and carpeting.

2 This is the first of four verse sections in the letter. Goldsmith clearly indented the first two sections and the last to distinguish them from the prose commentary. He also indented much of the third lengthy section, only omitting to do so when he began a new folio and filled it entirely with verse. For ease of legibility, we have indented all the verse.

3 Dobson quotes Horace, *Satires* i.6.5: '*naso suspendis adunco / Ignotos ...*' : *Poetical Works of Oliver Goldsmith*, 253. The Loeb translation refers to Maecenas being unlike other men as he does not 'curl up [his] nose at men of unknown birth': Horace, *Satires, Epistles and Ars Poetica*, ed. H. Rushton Fairclough (London: William Heinemann; New York: G. P. Putnam, 1926), 77.

Dobson also cites Martial, *Epigram* i.4.6: '*Et Pueri nasum Rhinocerotis habent*' (he turns his nose up like a Rhinoceros's horn).

4 Balderston writes: 'A round game played on the principle of whist, with trumps, in which any number could participate, the object being to take the pool by winning the largest number of tricks. There were two kinds, three-card and five-card Loo, the latter being evidently in favour at Barton' (*BL*, 131n2).

5 The Jack of Clubs, the highest card in the five-card version of the game.

6 Mary Horneck, Catherine's sister.

7 Henry Bunbury, Catherine Horneck's husband.

8 The player who won no tricks was 'looed', and as a penalty had to forfeit the pool and contribute to the next pool.

9 Sir John Fielding (1721–80), magistrate, was half-brother to Henry Fielding and succeeded him as justice of the peace for Westminster, on the latter's death in 1754. He initiated a major crime prevention plan in 1772, which is probably why he came to Goldsmith's mind. Measures included advertising crimes in newspapers and keeping detailed records at his office at Bow Street.

10 The Act referred to, as Dobson points out, is really Octavo Elizabeth, an act against 'Cutpurses or Pyckpurses', condemning them to 'suffer Death in suche maner and fourme as they shoulde if they were no Clarkes' (*Complete Poetical Works*, 253). See *The Statutes of the Realm*, 11 vols. (London: Record Commission, 1819), IV: 488. Balderston suggests that Goldsmith's familiarity with the law, the mistake notwithstanding, lends plausibility to the tradition that Goldsmith was at one time interested in competing for the Gresham lectureship in civil law (*BL*, 133n3). See also *P*, II: 156–7.

11 'A practice dating from the gaol-fever of 1750' (Dobson's *Life of Goldsmith*, 168n). Fennels and nosegays were thought to ward against infection.

12 An informal women's morning head-dress fashionable in the eighteenth century.

13 Sir Charles Bunbury (1740–1812), horse-racing administrator and politician, was Henry's elder brother. He became MP for Suffolk in 1761 and was briefly secretary to the lord lieutenant of Ireland, Lord Weymouth, in 1765.

14 Balderston observes that Prior's and Bunbury's transcription of this letter omits the couplet 'The judge takes the hint [...] correction in private' (*BL*, 135n1). That the lines appear in Langton's transcription and were carefully scored out suggests a deliberate omission on Bunbury's part for reasons that are unclear.

65
To John Nourse
[London, 20 February 1774]

Although John Nourse published Goldsmith's *History of the Earth, and Animated Nature*, Goldsmith originally signed a contract with William Griffin for the work in 1769. He paid Goldsmith 500 guineas on 26 September 1769 for the first five volumes; however, at this point he had sold half the copyright to Nourse, probably, as Prior speculates, to raise the cash for Goldsmith. Nourse would go on to acquire the entire copyright on 30 June 1772 but, before this happened, he insisted that Goldsmith transfer the copy legally to Griffin and acknowledge receipt of £840 in full payment. This agreement was then made over to Nourse. Nourse did not accept Goldsmith's suggestion in this letter that Griffin be permitted to buy back part of the property in the work. The *St. James's Chronicle* advertised *An History of the Earth, and Animated Nature* on 5 February 1774, 'to be published next month', but the work was not, in fact, published until 30 June, after Goldsmith's death.

The copy-text is the manuscript in the Taylor Library at Princeton University. It was first published by Prior in 1837. The letter is endorsed 'Dr Goldsmith | received — Febry 20 1774', which supplies our date.

Sir

As the work for which we engaged is now near coming out, and for the over payment of which I return you my thanks I would consider myself still more obliged to you if you would let my friend Mr. Griffin have a part of it. He is ready to pay you for any part you will think proper to give him, and as I have thoughts of extending the work into the vegetable and Fossil kingdoms you shall share with him in any such engagement as may happen to ensue.

I am Sir
Your very humble serv^{t}.
Oliver Goldsmith.

66

To Isaac Jackman

[London, *c.* March 1774]

Isaac Jackman (1752?–1831), Irish journalist and playwright, moved from Dublin to London for a financially advantageous marriage. After his wife died – and her annuity stopped – Jackman began to write for the stage. He had a poorly received comic opera *The Milesian* staged at Drury Lane in 1777 before going on to moderate success with *All the World's a Stage* (1777), *The Divorce* (1781) and a two-act burletta *Hero and Leander* (1787). He edited the *Morning Post* for a period between 1791 and 1795. Jackman may have had radical tendencies: John Thelwall sent him 'some Songs and other writings, calculated to rouse the Nation to a sense of its rights' in the early 1790s, presumably in his capacity as newspaper editor.[1]

This final poignant letter speaks to an important facet of Goldsmith's life in London as a point of contact and introduction to London for many Irish migrants. William Hodson might be the most obvious example but Goldsmith's sense of responsibility to the newly arrived stretched well beyond his familial duties, as Robert Day reported to Prior.[2] Goldsmith was an important figure of inspiration for a new generation of Irish playwrights working in London, such as John O'Keeffe (1747–1833), Leonard MacNally (1752–1820), Dennis O'Bryen (1755–1832), and indeed Jackman, whose play *The Milesian* featured 'Charles Marlove' in homage to the character in *She Stoops to Conquer*.[3]

The copy-text is a photocopy of the manuscript in the British Library and has never been published. The location of the original is unknown. Our dating of the letter in March is speculative, though the year 1774 appears to have been marked on the original in another hand. It was likely written as Goldsmith was in his final illness, and as Jackman was attempting to establish himself in the theatre scene at the time by contacting the Irish author of *She Stoops to Conquer*.

Mr. Goldsmith presents his Compliments to Mr. Jackman, and begs his pardon for not being able to attend him this day, as he finds himself too ill to Stir abroad.

1 *Lloyd's Evening Post*, 19–21 November 1794.

2 'The Poet frequented much the Grecian Coffee-house, then the favourite resort of the Irish and Lancashire Templars; and delighted in collecting around him his friends, whom he entertained with a cordial and unostentatious hospitality' (*P*, II: 357). As Craig Bailey has shown, the Grecian was a key site of Irish networking for the newly arrived Irish, particularly law students: Craig Bailey, *Irish London: Middle-Class Migration in the Global Eighteenth Century* (Liverpool University Press, 2013). See also Goldsmith's reflections on Irish hospitality in 'A Description of the Manners and Customs of the Native Irish' (*CW*, III: 24–9).

3 David O'Shaughnessy, '"Rip'ning buds in freedom's field": Staging Irish Improvement in the 1780s', *Journal for Eighteenth-Century Studies* 38.4 (2015), 541–54.

BIBLIOGRAPHY

Primary Sources

Goldsmith Manuscripts by Location

Beinecke Rare Book and Manuscript Library, Yale University

Letter 4 to T. Contarine, GEN MSS 1429 33.904; Letters 20 and 21 to J. Bindley, GEN MSS MISC. 171. F-1; Letters 28 and 54 to James Boswell, GEN MSS 89 23.541; Letter 48 to D. Garrick, GEN MSS 69; Letter 56 to T. Percy, GEN MSS 1429 8.210.

Bibliotheca Bodmeriana, Cologny, Switzerland

Letter 49 to J. Cradock.

Bodleian Library, Oxford

Letter 60 to T. Cadell, Ms Montagu d.1 fol.227r.

British Library

Goldsmith-Percy Papers, vol. I. Add. MS 42515:

Letter 6 to T. Contarine; Letters 7 and 11 to D. Hodson; Letter 8 to E. Mills; Letter 12 to H. Goldsmith; Letter 26 to A. Percy; Letters 27 and 46 to T. Percy; Letter 34 to C. Mackenzie; Letter 37 to B. Langton; Letter 43 to J. Eyles; Letters 44 and 50 to the Duke of Northumberland.

Also: Percy's copy of Letter 3 to R. Bryanton.

Letter 29 to M. Goldsmith, Add MS 42181 fo. 20.

Letters 51 and 52 to W. Chambers, transcribed by Chambers, Add. MS 41134, fols. 21a, 21b; also: facsimile of Letter 66 to I. Jackman, RP 6992.

Edinburgh University Library, Centre for Research Collections

'A Tailor's Account' (1753), La.II.195.

Free Library of Philadelphia, Rare Book Department

William McIntire Elkins (1882–1947) Goldsmith Papers:

Letter 10 to J. Lawder; Letter 19 to J. Dodsley; Letter 33 to J. Reynolds.

William McIntire Elkins (1882–1947) Goldsmith–Newbery papers, 1761–7:

Letters 16 and 17 to J. Newbery.

Haverford College Pennsylvania, Quaker and Special Collections

Letter 42 to R. Penneck. Coll. No. 115.

Historical Society of Pennsylvania
Letter 57 to J. Nourse, Dreer Collection, II.230.15; Letter 41 to R. Penneck, Gratz Collection 10.39.50.

Houghton Library, Harvard University
Letter 14 to Mrs. Johnson, MS Hyde 77 (8.209); Letter 31 to D. Hodson, MS Eng 870 (60C); Letter 36 to D. Hodson, MS Eng 870 (60A); Letter 45 to T. Bond, MS Eng 870 (60D); Letter 62 to Garrick, MS Eng 870 (60B); Letter 63 to D. Garrick, MS Hyde 6 (6).

Huntington Library, San Marino, California
Letter 1 to D. Hodson, HM118; Letter 2 to T. Contarine (facsimile), FAC455.

Morgan Library, New York
Letter 64 to C. Bunbury, MA 1297.

New York Public Library
Letter 24 to D. Garrick, MSS Coll 4417.
Also: facsimile of Letter 55 to Hester Thrale.

Royal College of Surgeons of England
Letter 30 to W. Hunter, Hunter–Baillie Collection, vol. 1, no. 41.

Royal Irish Academy
Letter 9 to R. Bryanton, MS.3.D.8 (9).

Rosenbach of the Free Library Philadelphia
Letter 61 to T. Cadell.
Also: facsimiles of Letter 15 to Mrs. Johnson; Letter 39 to J. Cradock.

Rothschild, Loren R., Private collection, Los Angeles, California
Letter 22 to G. Baker; Letter 59 to C. Burney.

Society of Antiquaries London
Letter 35 to G. Selwyn, Cely–Trevilian Bequest (MS444) V, 164–5.

Somerville College Library, Oxford
Letter 40 to J. Lee, Amelia B. Edwards Archive 58.

Taylor Library at Princeton University Library, Rare Books and Special Collections
Letter 5 to D. Hodson; Letter 65 to J. Nourse, Taylor Collection, Box 7a, Folder 11.

Victoria and Albert Museum, London
Letter 13 to R. Griffiths, Forster Collection; Letter 23 to G. Colman.

Other Manuscripts

Bodleian Library, Oxford. MS Abinger c. 1.

British Library, Add. MS 42515, fols. 118, 119; Add. MS 43377C, fo. 6; Journal of Thomas Percy, Add. MS 32336; Covent Garden Ledgers, Egerton MS 2277, 2278.

John Mitford Collection, Yale University Library, Osborn FC76 1/38, 39; Trinity College Dublin, 1641 Depositions.

Folger Library, Washington DC. PN 2598. M2 C7.

Royal Academy of Arts Archives, Joshua Reynolds' Pocketbook, REY/1/15.

Printed

Periodicals

Critical Review; *Daily Advertiser* (Letter 53); *European Magazine and London Review*; *Gentleman's Magazine*; *Lloyd's Evening Post* (Letter 18); *London Chronicle*; *London Packet*; *Middlesex Journal: Or, Universal Evening-Post*; *Monthly Review*; *Morning Chroicle; Public Advertiser*; *St. James's Chronicle*; *Or, the British Evening-Post* (Letter 25); *Whitehall Evening Post.*

Books

Goldsmith, Oliver. *An History of the Earth, and Animated Nature*, 8 vols. London: Printed for John Nourse, 1774.

An History of England, in a Series of Letters from a Nobleman to his Son, 2 vols. London: Printed for J. Newbery, 1764.

A Survey of Experimental Philosophy, Considered in its Present State of Improvement, 2 vols. London: Printed for T. Carnan and F. Newbery jun., 1776.

New Essays, edited by Ronald S. Crane. University of Chicago Press, 1927.

(ed.). *Poems for Young Ladies. In Three Parts. Devotional, Moral, and Entertaining*. London: J. Payne, [1767]).

The Collected Letters, edited by Katharine C. Balderston. Cambridge University Press, 1928.

The Collected Works, edited by Arthur Friedman, 5 vols. Oxford: The Clarendon Press, 1966.

The Complete Poetical Works, edited by Austin Dobson. London: H. Frowde, 1906.

The Grecian History, from the Earliest State to the Death of Alexander the Great, 2 vols. London: Printed for J. and F. Rivington, T. Longman, G. Kearsley, W. Griffin, G. Robinson, R. Baldwin, W. Goldsmith, T. Cadell and T. Evans, 1774.

The Grumbler, edited by Alice Perry. Cambridge, MA: Harvard University Press, 1931.

The History of England, from the Earliest Times to the Death of George II, 4 vols. London: Printed for T. Davies, Becket and De Hondt, and T. Cadell, 1771.

The Miscellaneous Works, 4 vols. London: Printed for J. Johnson, G. and J. Robinson, W. J. and J. Richardson, W. Otridge and son, T. and C. Rivington, J. Matthews, J. Walker, W. Lowndes, J. Scatcherd, G. Wilkie, P. Mcqueen, Longman and Rees, Vernor and Hood, Cadell, Jun. and Davies, Murray and Highley, and E. Newbery, 1801.

The Miscellaneous Works, edited by James Prior, 4 vols. London: John Murray, 1837.

The Poetical Works. London: Printed for Suttaby, Evance and Company, 1811.

The Poetical Works. London: Aldine, 1835.

The Present State of the British Empire in Europe, America, Africa, and Asia. London: Printed for W. Griffin, J. Johnson, W. Nicoll, and Richardson and Urquhart, 1768.

The Roman History, from the Foundation of the City of Rome, to the Destruction of the Western Empire, 2 vols. London: Printed for S. Baker and G. Leigh, T. Davies, and L. Davis, 1769.

The Works, edited by J. W. M. Gibbs, 5 vols. London: G. Bell, 1884.

Secondary Sources

Pre-1800

Boswell, James. *Boswell in Search of a Wife 1766–1769*, edited by F. Brady and F. A. Pottle. London: William Heinemann, 1957.

The Correspondence of James Boswell with Certain Members of the Club, edited by Charles N. Fifer. London and New York: Heinemann and McGraw-Hill, 1976.

The Correspondence of James Boswell with David Garrick, Edmund Burke, and Edmond Malone, edited by Peter S. Baker, Thomas W. Copeland, George M. Kahrl, Rachel McClellan and James M. Osborn, with the assistance of Robert Makin and Mark Wolleager. London and New York: Heinemann and McGraw-Hill, 1987.

Life of Johnson, edited by G. B. Hill and L. F. Powell, 6 vols. 1791; Oxford: Clarendon Press, 1934–50.

London Journal 1762–1763, edited by F. A. Pottle. Edinburgh University Press, 1991.

Private Papers from Malahide Castle. In the Collection of Lt. Colonel Ralph Hayward Isham, edited by Geoffrey Scott and Frederick A. Pottle, 18 vols. Mount Vernon, NY: William Edwin Rudge, 1929–32.

Burke, Edmund. *The Correspondence*, edited by Thomas W. Copeland, Lucy S. Sutherland, George H. Guttridge, *et al.*, 10 vols. Cambridge University Press, 1960.

Burney, Frances. *Memoirs of Doctor Burney*, 3 vols. London: Edward Moxon: 1832.

The Early Journals and Letters, edited by Lars E. Troide, 3 vols. Oxford: Clarendon Press, 1988.

[Butler, Lady Harriot]. *Memoirs of Lady Harriot Butler: now first published from authentic papers, in the lady's own hand-writing*. London: printed for R. Freeman, [1761].

Campbell, Thomas. *A Philosophical Survey of the South of Ireland, in a Series of Letters to John Watkinson, M. D.* London: Printed for W. Strahan; and T. Cadell, 1777.

Chambers, William. *A Dissertation on Oriental Gardening; by Sr William Chambers, Comptroller-General of His Majesty's Works, &c. The Second Edition, with Additions. To which is Annexed, an Explanatory Discourse, by Tan Chet-qua, of Quang-chew-fu, Gent.* London: Printed for W. Griffin, T. Davies, J. Dodsley; Wilson and Nicoll; J. Walter, and P. Elmsley, 1772.

Cooke, William. 'Table Talk; or, Characters, Anecdotes, etc. of Illustrious British Characters, during the last Fifty Years: Dr. Goldsmith', *European Magazine* 24 (1793).

Cradock, Joseph. *Literary and Miscellaneous Memoirs*, 4 vols. London: Printed for the Author, 1826–8.

D'Argens, Jean Baptiste de Boyer, Marquis. *Chinese Letters, Being a Philosophical, Historical, and Critical Correspondence Between a Chinese Traveller at Paris, and his Countrymen in China, Muscovy, Persia and Japan*, no translator given. London: Printed for D. Browne and R. Hett, 1741.

Fothergill, John. *A Complete Collection of the Medical and Philosophical Works.* London: Printed for John Walker, 1781.

Glover, Richard. *The Life of Oliver Goldsmith: written from personal knowledge, authentic papers, and other indubitable authorities.* London: Printed for J. Swan, 1774.

Grose, Francis. *A Classical Dictionary of the Vulgar Tongue*, 3rd edition. London: Hooper and Co., 1796.

Hickey, William. *Memoirs of William Hickey*, edited by Alfred Spencer, 2 vols. London: Hurst & Blackett, 1913–25.

Holberg, Lewis. *A Journey to the World Underground. By Nicholas Klimius.* London: Printed for T. Astley and B. Collins, 1742.

Memoirs, no translator given. 1737; London: Hunt and Clarke, 1829.

Horace. *Satires, Epistles and Ars Poetica,* edited by H. Rushton Fairclough. London: William Heinemann; New York: G. P. Putnam, 1926.

Houstoun, James. *Dr. James Houstoun's Memoirs of his own Life-Time.* London: Printed for Liaston Gilliver, 1747.

Hume, David. *The History of England, from the invasion of Julius Cæsar to the revolution in 1688, a new edition*, 8 vols. London: for T. Cadell, 1778.

Johnson, Samuel. *The Letters*, edited by Bruce Redford, 5 vols. Princeton University Press, 1992–4.

Kenrick, William. '*On Dr.* Goldsmith'. In *A New Select Collection of Epitaphs*, edited by T. Webb, 2 vols. London: Printed for S. Bladon, 1775.

Poems; Ludicrous, Satirical and Moral. London: Printed for J. Fletcher, [1768].

Lettsom, John Coakley. *Some Account of the late John Fothergill, M.D.* London: Printed for C. Dilly, L. David, T. Cadell and J. Phillips, 1783.

Marana, Giovanni Paola. *The Eighte Volumes of Letters Writ by a Turkish Spy, who liv'd five and forty years, undiscover'd at Paris*, translated by William Bradshaw. 1684; London: Printed for H. Rhodes and S. Sare, 1702.

Mason, William. *An Heroic Epistle to Sir William Chambers, Knight, Comptroller General of his Majesty's Work and Author of a late Dissertation on Oriental Gardening.* London: Printed for J. Almon, 1773.

Montaigne, Michel de. *Les Essais. The Montaigne Project: Villey Edition of the Essais with Corresponding Digital Page Images from the Bordeaux Copy.* https://www.lib.uchicago.edu/efts/ARTFL/projects/montaigne.

Montesquieu, Charles-Louis de Secondat, Baron de. *Persian Letters*, translated by C. J. Betts. 1721; London: Penguin, 1993.

Nugent, Thomas. *The Grand Tour, Or, A Journey through the Netherlands, Germany, Italy, and France*, 4 vols. 1749; London: Printed for J. Rivington and Sons, B. Law, T. Caslon, G. Robinson, T. Cadell, W. Goldsmith, J. Bew, S. Hayes, W. Fox and T. Evans, 1778.

Percy, Thomas. *Reliques of Ancient English Poetry*, 3rd edition, 3 vols. London: Printed for J. Dodsley, 1775.

Percy, Thomas, and Edmond Malone. *The Correspondence of Thomas Percy & Edmond Malone*, edited by Arthur Tillotson. Baton Rouge: Louisiana State University Press, 1944.

Playstowe, Philip. *The Gentleman's Guide in his Tour Through France.* Bristol, [1766].

Pointon, Priscilla. *Poems on several occasions. By Miss Priscilla Pointon, of Lichfield.* Birmingham, 1770.

Pope, Alexander. *The Correspondence*, edited by George Sherburn, 5 vols. Oxford: Clarendon Press, 1956.

Reynolds, Joshua. *Portraits*, edited by Frederick W. Hilles. New York: McGraw-Hill, 1952.

[Rider, William]. *Historical and Critical Account of the Lives and Writings of the Living Authors of Great Britain.* London: Printed for the Author, 1762.

Sterne, Laurence. *A Sentimental Journey through France and Italy.* 1768; Oxford University Press, 1984.

Trusler, John. *The London Adviser and Guide: Containing every Instruction and Information useful and necessary to Persons living in London, and coming to reside there* ... London: printed for the author, 1786.

Walpole, Horace. *Anecdotes of Painting in England*, edited by Frederick W. Hilles and Philip B. Daghlian, 5 vols. New Haven: Yale University Press, 1937.

'Introduction' (1779). In William Mason, *Satirical Poems*, 31–3. Oxford: Clarendon Press, 1926.

Memoirs of King George II, edited by John Brooke, 3 vols. New Haven: Yale University Press, 1985.

'Notes to the Author's Preface' [To 'An Heroic Epistle to Sir William Chambers, Knight, &c. &c.']. In William Mason, *Satirical Poems*, 39–45. Oxford: Clarendon Press, 1926.

The Yale Edition of Horace Walpole's Correspondence, edited by W. S. Lewis, 48 vols. New Haven: Yale University Press, 1967.

Post-1800

A Catalogue of Autographs Letters, Original Documents Being Composed of James R. Osgood's Collection and Other Valuable and Desirable Specimens Recently Purchased, Forming in All One of the Finest Assortments Ever Offered for Sale in America March 4, 1886. New York: William Evarts Benjamin, 1886.

A Catalogue of the Harleian Manuscripts in the British Museum, 2 vols. London, 1808.

Anon. *Maxims, Morals, and Golden Rules*, 4th edition. London: James Madden & Co., 1844.

Bailey, Craig. *Irish London: Middle-class Migration in the Global Eighteenth Century.* Liverpool University Press, 2013.

Balderston, Katharine C. 'New Goldsmith Letters', *The Yale University Library Gazette* 39.2 (1964), 71–2.

The History and Sources of Percy's Memoir of Goldsmith. Cambridge University Press, 1926.

Barfoot, C. C. '"Envy, Fear, and Wonder": English Views of Holland and the Dutch 1673–1764'. In *The Great Emporium: The Low Countries as a Cultural Crossroads in the Renaissance and the Eighteenth Century*, edited by C. C. Barfoot and Richard Todd, 207–47. Amsterdam: Rodopi, 1992.

Barnouw, A. J. 'Goldsmith's Indebtedness to Justus Van Effen', *Modern Language Review* 8 (1913), 314–23.

Barry, Alda Milner. 'A Note on the Early Literary Relations of Oliver Goldsmith and Thomas Percy', *The Review of English Studies* 2 (1926), 51–61.

Bataille, Robert C. *The Writing Life of Hugh Kelly: Politics, Journalism, and Theater in Late-Eighteenth-Century London.* Carbondale: Southern Illinois University Press, 2000.

Bergin, John. 'Irish Catholics and their Networks in Eighteenth-Century London', *Eighteenth-Century Life* 39.1 (2015), 66–102.

Brooks, Christopher. 'Goldsmith's *Citizen of the World*: Knowledge and the Imposture of "Orientalism"', *Texas Studies in Literature and Language* 35 (1993), 124–44.

Brown, J. E. 'Goldsmith's Indebtedness to Voltaire and Justus van Effen', *Modern Philology* 23 (1926), 273–84.

Brown, Keith. 'A Kind of Comradeship: Goldsmith and the Late Famous Baron Holberg', *English Studies: A Journal of English Language and Literature* 61.1 (1980), 37–46.

Brown, Michael. *The Irish Enlightenment.* Cambridge, MA: Harvard University Press, 2016.

Bryant, Donald Cross. *Edmund Burke and his Literary Friends.* St. Louis: Washington University Press, 1939.

Budd, Declan, and Ross Hinds. *The Hist and Edmund Burke's Club: An Anthology of the College Historical Society, the Student Debating Society of Trinity College Dublin, from its Origins in Edmund Burke's Club 1747–1997.* Dublin: Lilliput Press, 1997.

Clarke, Norma. *Brothers of the Quill: Oliver Goldsmith in Grub Street.* Cambridge, MA: Harvard University Press, 2016.
Cole, Richard Cargill. *Irish Booksellers and English Writers, 1740–1800.* Atlantic Highlands, NJ: Mansell, 1986.
Conant, Martha Pike. *The Oriental Tale in England in the Eighteenth Century.* New York: Columbia University Press, 1908.
Cox, Michael F. 'The Country and Kindred of Oliver Goldsmith', *Journal of the National Literary Society* 1 (1901–3), 81–111.
Crane, R. S., and H. J. Smith. 'A French Influence on Goldsmith's *Citizen of the World*', *Modern Philology* 19.1 (1921), 83–92.
Crane, R. S., and J. H. Warner. 'Goldsmith and Voltaire's *Essai Sur Les Mœurs*', *Modern Language Notes* 38.2 (1923), 65–76.
Cunningham, Andrew. 'Medicine to Calm the Mind: Boerhaave's Medical System, and Why it was Adapted in Edinburgh'. In *The Medical Enlightenment of the Eighteenth Century*, edited by Cunningham and Roger French, 40–66. Cambridge University Press, 1990.
Dai, David Wei–Yang. 'A Comparative Study of D'Argens *Lettres Chinoises* and Goldsmith's *Citizen of the World*', *Tamkang Review* 10.2 (1979), 183–97.
Davidson, Levette Jay. 'Forerunners of Goldsmith's *The Citizen of the World*', *Modern Language Notes* 36.4 (1921), 215–20.
Davies, Thomas. *Memoirs of the Life of David Garrick*, 2 vols. Boston: Wells and Lilly, 1818.
Dircks, Richard J. 'The Genesis and Date of Goldsmith's *Retaliation*', *Modern Philology* 75.1 (1977), 48–53.
Dixon, Peter. *Oliver Goldsmith Revisited.* Boston: Twayne, 1991.
Dobson, Austin. *Life of Oliver Goldsmith.* London: Books for Libraries Press, 1888.
Fairbrother, E. H. 'Lieut. Henry Goldsmith: the Poet's Nephew', *Notes and Queries* 12.4 (July 1918): 177–8.
Fenton, Seamus. *It All Happened: Reminiscences.* Dublin: M. H. Gill, 1949.
Ferguson, Oliver W. 'The Materials of History: Goldsmith's *Life of Nash*', *PMLA* 80.4 (1965), 372–86.
Fitzmaurice, Lord Edmond. *Life of William, Earl of Shelburne, afterwards First Marquess of Landsdowne. With Extracts from his Papers and Correspondence*, 3 vols. London: Macmillan, 1875.
Forster, John. *The Life and Adventures of Oliver Goldsmith.* London: Chapman and Hall, 1848.
Freeman, Arthur. 'New Goldsmith?' *Times Literary Supplement* 5411 (15 December 2006), 15.
Freeman, Morton S. *A New Dictionary of Eponyms.* Oxford University Press, 1997.
Gaussen, Alice C. C. *Percy, Prelate and Poet.* London: Smith, Elder, & Co., 1908.
George, M. Dorothy, and Frederick Stevens (eds.). *A Catalogue of Political and Personal Satires Preserved in the Department of Prints and Drawings in the British Museum*, 12 vols. London: British Museum, 1870–1954.

Ginger, John. *The Notable Man: The Life and Times of Oliver Goldsmith*. London: Hamilton, 1977.

Goslings, W. R. O. 'Leiden and Edinburgh: The Seed, the Soil and the Climate'. In *The Early Years of the Edinburgh Medical School*, edited by R. G. W. Anderson and A. D. C. Simpson, 1–24. Edinburgh: The Royal Scottish Museum, 1976.

Griffin, Michael. *Enlightenment in Ruins: The Geographies of Oliver Goldsmith*. Lewisburg: Bucknell University Press, 2013.

Gwynn, Stephen. *Oliver Goldsmith*. London: Thornton Butterworth, 1935.

Hamilton, David. *The Healers: A History of Medicine in Scotland*. Edinburgh: Canongate, 1981.

Harp, Richard L. 'Introduction'. In Thomas Percy, *Life of Oliver Goldsmith*, edited by Richard L. Harp, viii–xxviii. 1801; Salzburg: Institüt für Englische Sprache und Literatur, 1976.

Harris, John. *Sir William Chambers: Knight of the Polar Star*. London: A. Zwemmer, 1970.

Harth, Phillip. 'Goldsmith and the Marquis D'Argens'. *Notes and Queries* 198 (1953), 529–30.

Hazlitt, William. *Conversations of James Northcote*. London: Henry Colborn and Richard Bentley, 1830.

Heuser, Wilhelm. *Die Kildare-Gedichte*. Bonn: P. Hanstein, 1904.

Hume, Robert. *The Rakish Stage: Studies in English Drama 1660–1800*. Carbondale: Southern Illinois University Press, 1983.

Irving, Washington. *Oliver Goldsmith: A Biography*. London: Henry G. Bohn, 1850.

Joyce, James. *The Critical Writings*. New York: Viking, 1959.

Kaufman, Matthew H. *Medical Teaching in Edinburgh during the Eighteenth and Nineteenth Centuries*. The Royal College of Surgeons of Edinburgh, 2003.

Kelly, J. J. 'The Early Haunts of Oliver Goldsmith', *The Irish Monthly* 7 (1879), 194–205.

Kelly, James. *Sport in Ireland, 1600–1840*. Dublin: Four Courts, 2014.

Loudon, Irvine. *Medical Care and the General Practitioner 1750–1850*. Oxford: Clarendon Press, 1986.

Lucas, Angela M. *Anglo-Irish Poems of the Middle Ages*. Dublin: Columbia Press, 1995.

MacNeice, Louis. *The Poetry of W. B. Yeats*. London: Oxford University Press, 1941.

Mason, William Shaw. *A Statistical Account, or Parochial Survey of Ireland*, 3 vols. Dublin: at the Faulkner Press, 1815–19.

McKillop, Alan D. 'Local Attachment and Cosmopolitanism: The Eighteenth-Century Pattern'. In *From Sensibility to Romanticism: Essays Presented to Frederick A. Pottle*, edited by Frederick W. Hilles and Harold Bloom, 191–218. New York: Oxford University Press, 1965.

Mitford, John. 'The Life of Oliver Goldsmith'. In Oliver Goldsmith, *The Poetical Works*, vii–cviii. London: Aldine, 1835.

Murray, Patrick. 'The Riddle of Goldsmith's Ancestry', *Studies* 63 (1974), 177–90.

Namier, Lewis, and John Brooke. *The History of Parliament: The House of Commons 1754–1790*, 3 vols. London: Secker & Warburg, 1985.
Nangle, Benjamin C. *The Monthly Review, First Series, 1749–1789: Indexes of Contributors and Articles*. Oxford: Clarendon Press, 1934.
Newell, R. H. 'Remarks, Attempting to Ascertain, Chiefly from Local Observation, the Actual Scene of The Deserted Village'. In Oliver Goldsmith, *The Poetical Works*, 57–81. London: Printed for Suttaby, Evance and Company, 1811.
Nichols, John. *Illustrations of the Literary History of the Eighteenth Century: Consisting of Authentic Memoirs and Original Letters of Eminent Persons*, 9 vols. London: for the Author, 1822.
O'Shaughnessy, David. '"Bit, by some mad whig": Charles Macklin and the Theater of Irish Enlightenment', *Huntington Library Quarterly* 80.4 (2017), 559–84.
'Making a Play for Patronage: Dennis O'Bryen's *A Friend in Need is a Friend Indeed* (1783)', *Eighteenth-Century Life* 39.1 (2015), 183–211.
'"Rip'ning buds in freedom's field": Staging Irish Improvement in the 1780s', *Journal for Eighteenth-Century Studies* 38.4 (2015), 541–54.
Percy, Thomas. 'The Life of Dr. Oliver Goldsmith'. In Oliver Goldsmith, *The Miscellaneous Works of Oliver Goldsmith, M.B.*, 4 vols. 1: 1–118. London: for J. Johnson *et al.*, 1801.
Pitman, James Hall. *Goldsmith's Animated Nature: A Study of Goldsmith*. 1924; Hamden: Archon, 1972.
Pollard, Mary. *A Dictionary of Members of the Dublin Book Trade 1550–1800*. London: Bibliographical Society, 2000.
Dublin's Trade in Books, 1550–1800. Oxford: Clarendon Press, 1989.
Powell, Martyn J. 'Shelburne and Ireland: Politician, Patriot, Absentee.' In *An Enlightenment Statesman in Whig Britain: Lord Shelburne in Context, 1737–1805*, edited by Nigel Aston and Clarissa Campbell Orr, 141–59. Woodbridge: The Boydell Press, 2011.
Prior, James. *Life of Oliver Goldsmith, M. B.*, 2 vols. London: John Murray, 1837.
Raithby, John (ed.). *The Statutes of the Realm*, 11 vols. London: Record Commission, 1810–25.
Ribeiro, Aileen. 'The King of Denmark's Masquerade', *History Today* 27.6 (1977), 385–9.
Rothschild, Loren R. *Verses in Reply to an Invitation to Dinner at Dr. George Baker's*. Los Angeles: Rasselas Press, 1994.
Rousseau, G. S. (ed.). *Goldsmith: The Critical Heritage*. London: Routledge, 1974.
Russell, Gillian. *Women, Sociability, and Theatre in Georgian London*. Cambridge University Press, 2007.
Seitz, R.W. 'Goldsmith and the "Annual Register"', *Modern Philology* 31.2 (1933), 183–94.
'Goldsmith and the *Present State of the British Empire*', *Modern Language Notes* 45 (1930), 434–8.
'Goldsmith to Sir William Chambers' (1773), *Times Literary Supplement* 1808 (Sept. 1936), 772.

Sells, A. Lytton. *Les Sources Françaises de Goldsmith*. Paris: Librairie Ancienne Edouard Champion, 1924.

Oliver Goldsmith: His Life and Works. London: George Allen & Unwin, 1974.

Sharpe, Kevin. 'Private conscience and Public Duty in the Writings of Charles I', *The Historical Journal* 40.3 (1997), 643–65.

Smith, Hamilton Jewett. *Oliver Goldsmith's* The Citizen of the World: *A Study*. New Haven: Yale University Press, 1926.

Spector, Robert Donald. *English Literary Periodicals and the Climate of Opinion During the Seven Years' War*. The Hague: Mouton, 1966.

Struthers, John. *Historical Sketch of the Edinburgh Medical School*. Edinburgh: Maclachlan and Stewart, 1867.

Taylor, Richard C. *Goldsmith as Journalist*. London: Associated University Presses, 1993.

Thomas, George, Earl of Albemarle. *Memoirs of the Marquis of Rockingham and his Contemporaries. With Original Letters and Documents Now First Published*, 2 vols. London: Samuel Bentley, 1852.

Ward, Robert E. 'A Letter from Ireland: A Little-Known Attack on David Hume's "History of England"', *Eighteenth-Century Ireland* 2 (1987), 196–7.

Wardle, Ralph. *Oliver Goldsmith*. Lawrence: University of Kansas Press, 1957.

Watt, James. 'Goldsmith's Cosmopolitanism', *Eighteenth-Century Life* 30.1 (2006), 56–75.

'"The Indigent Philosopher": Oliver Goldsmith'. In *The Blackwell Companion to Irish Literature*, edited by Julia M. Wright, 2 vols., I: 210–25. Oxford: Blackwell, 2010.

Werkmeister, Lucyle. *The London Daily Press 1772–1792*. Lincoln: University of Nebraska Press, 1963.

Wheatley, Henry B. *London Past and Present Its History, Associations, and Traditions*, 3 vols. London: John Murray, 1891.

Woods, Samuel H., Jr. 'Images of the Orient: Goldsmith and the Philosophes', *Studies in Eighteenth-Century Culture* 15 (1986), 257–70.

INDEX